The
Smoothbore Volley
That Doomed
the Confederacy

The Smoothbore Volley That Doomed the Confederacy

THE DEATH OF STONEWALL JACKSON AND OTHER CHAPTERS ON THE ARMY OF NORTHERN VIRGINIA

Robert K. Krick

Louisiana State University Press ✠ Baton Rouge

CLOTH

12   11   10   09   08   07   06   05   04   03
6   5   4   3   2

PAPER

13   12   11   10   09   08   07   06   05   04
5   4   3   2   1

DESIGNER: Barbara Neely Bourgoyne
TYPEFACE: ACaslon
TYPESETTER: Coghill Composition Co., Inc.
PRINTER AND BINDER: Thomson-Shore, Inc.

Library of Congress Cataloging-in-Publication Data
Krick, Robert K.
    The Smoothbore Volley that doomed the Confederacy : the death of Stonewall Jackson
and other chapters on the Army of Northern Virginia / Robert K. Krick.
        p.   cm.
    Includes index.
    ISBN 0-8071-2747-7 (cloth); ISBN 0-8071-2971-2 (pbk.)
    1. Confederate States of America. Army of Northern Virginia   History.   2. Confederate
States of America. Army of Northern Virginia—Biography.   3. Generals—Confederate
States of America—Biography.   4. United States—History—Civil War, 1861–1865—
Regimental histories.   5. United States—History—Civil War, 1861–1865—Campaigns.
I. Title.

E470.2.K75   2002
973.7'455—dc21

                                                                    2001038830

The paper in this book meets the guidelines for permanence and durability of the Committee
on Production Guidelines for Book Longevity of the Council on Library Resources. ∞

Contents

Illustrations

Preface

No military formation in all the annals of American military history exceeds in reputation the Army of Northern Virginia. Some modern scholarship insists that the focus of attention on the army is unbalanced and unwarranted. No judgment about that subjective matter can obscure the salient fact that the story of the army of R. E. Lee and Stonewall Jackson always has riveted the interest of Americans—and not a few foreigners too—for more than a century. The army's leaders have intrigued successive generations of readers and surely will continue to do so.

The essays in this book examine pieces of the army's history across a broad and diverse spectrum. Two deal with Lee's most famous subordinate, Thomas J. Jackson, one of them concerning a notable court-martial. Two others deal with Lee's most controversial subordinate, James Longstreet—again, one concerning a famous court-martial. General Robert E. Rodes appears as a superbly competent division commander; General Maxcy Gregg as a prototype of the successful politician-general; Colonel R. W. Carter as a failure, cashiered for cowardice; and the Shenandoah Valley irregular cavalry as a study in indiscipline. The penultimate chapter discusses books about the army—good and bad—as the means by which we observe the story after the passage of so many years. The final chapter examines the rich olio of sources (many of them newly available) that provide access to the lives and records of Confederate soldiers.

Seven of these ten essays have appeared in print before in some form. Several contained no documentation in their first appearances. All have been substantially revised and expanded with new material, in some instances to double their original size. "The Smoothbore Volley . . . ," for instance, has been augmented by material from a newly discovered cache of manuscripts that surely must be the most significant untapped resource on the Battle of Chancellorsville. New material from that collection added to the story of Stonewall Jackson's mortal wounding without changing the outlines to any notable degree. The sites where each chapter originally appeared are described in the first note of the respective chapters, with an expression of appreciation for the rights to republish. The original publishers granted those rights in every instance without hesitation or caveat.

Abbreviations

AU   Auburn University, Auburn, Alabama

CSR   Compiled Service Records, housed at the National Archives

FSNMP   Fredericksburg and Spotsylvania National Military Park, Fredericksburg, Virginia

MOC   Museum of the Confederacy, Richmond, Virginia

LC   Library of Congress, Washington, D.C.

NA   National Archives, Washington, D.C.

NCDAH   North Carolina Department of Archives and History, Raleigh

OR   U.S. War Department, *The War of the Rebellion: The Official Records of the Union and Confederate Armies*, 127 vols., index, and atlas (Washington, D.C.: Government Printing Office, 1880–1901)

PLD   Perkins Library, Duke University, Durham, North Carolina

SHC   Southern Historical Collection, Wilson Library, University of North Carolina, Chapel Hill

SHSP   *Southern Historical Society Papers*, 52 vols. (Richmond, 1876–1959)

USAMHI   U.S. Army Military History Institute, Carlisle Barracks, Pennsylvania

VHS   Virginia Historical Society, Richmond

VMI   Virginia Military Institute, Lexington

WVU   West Virginia University, Morgantown, West Virginia

The
Smoothbore Volley
That Doomed
the Confederacy

1

The Smoothbore Volley That Doomed the Confederacy

Nineteen men in two distinct groups rode forward from the coalescing Confederate lines west of Chancellorsville at about 9:00 P.M. on May 2, 1863. Only seven of the nineteen came back untouched, man or horse. Although one of those nearest the offending musket muzzles, Major General A. P. Hill escaped among the unscathed handful. Lieutenant General Thomas J. "Stonewall" Jackson, among those farthest from the flash point, was one of the five men killed or mortally wounded. The capricious paths of a few dozen one-ounce lead balls caroming off the dense shrubbery of Spotsylvania's Wilderness that night had much to do with the course of the Civil War.

From every imaginable perspective, the afternoon of May 2 had been a stunning Confederate success of unprecedented magnitude. Lee and Jackson had crafted between them a dazzling tactical initiative that sent Stonewall covertly all the way across the front of a Federal army that outnumbered the southerners by more than two to one. The redoubtable corps commander managed the remarkable march without serious interruption, arrayed his first two divisions in a wide line, and descended upon the Federals like a thunderbolt. Those northerners who rallied bravely against the tide faced an inexorable outflanking by the outriders of Jackson's line, who stretched far beyond the center of the attack in both directions. In this fashion Jackson routed one Union corps, trapped another out of the line, and left the others shaky, uncertain, and vulnerable to be stampeded.

This chapter originally appeared in *Chancellorsville: The Battle and Its Aftermath*, edited by Gary W. Gallagher. Copyright © 1996 by the University of North Carolina Press. Reprinted by permission of the publisher. This version includes a few revisions and some new material.

Southern soldiers enjoying the chance to steamroller their enemy observed their legendary leader throughout his victorious advance. Darkness and confusion would lead to disastrous results, causing some southerners to fire mistakenly at Jackson, but during the early evening, everyone knew where he was. The adjutant of a Georgia regiment in the attack's front rank recalled that after the fighting had died down, the ground appeared "to tremble as if shaken by an earthquake, the cheering is so tremendous, caused by Gen. Jackson riding along the line." Members of the 18th North Carolina of James H. Lane's brigade, which within an hour would inadvertently fire on Jackson, saw their hero pass "about twilight." The Tar Heels cheered him and were gratified when Stonewall "took off his hat in recognition of their salutation." [1]

The divisions of Robert E. Rodes and Raleigh E. Colston had carried Jackson's attack forward. Most of A. P. Hill's division, last in the long column during the flanking march, had not maneuvered out of column and into line of battle. As darkness closed in on the victorious but exhausted Confederates, the need to advance fresh and better-organized troops to the front rank became obvious. Lane's five regiments drew the assignment. A. P. Hill ordered Lane to push them forward and then spread them to the right and the left, perpendicular to the Orange Plank Road, in preparation for a novel night attack. The North Carolinians hesitated in the road, uncertain how to form line because "on each side the shrubbery was so dense as to render it impossible to march."[2]

Jackson's plan to attack despite the steadily thickening darkness foundered first on a whimsical exchange of artillery fire. Southern guns in a small roadside clearing near a country schoolhouse and shop to the west of Lane's regiments opened a ranging fire into the woods toward Chancellorsville. The dreadful idea to begin this firing probably originated with an artillery captain eager to make noise. Northern guns responded in far greater numbers, wreaking havoc on the unfortunate North Carolina infantrymen standing in the road in ranks, having arranged themselves as a conveniently enfiladed target. The shot and shell came "as thick as hail." Major W. G. Morris of the 37th

1. Richard W. Freeman, "Stonewall Jackson's Death," (*Atlanta*) *Sunny South*, December 19, 1896; Van Valentine Richardson, "The Death of Stonewall Jackson," *Fayetteville (N.C.) Observer*, February 20, 1884. Freeman was a sergeant in the 44th Georgia. Captain Richardson commanded Company C of the 18th North Carolina.

2. W. G. Morris (major and later lieutenant colonel of the 37th North Carolina) to James H. Lane, January 3, 1895, folder 113, and James H. Lane to A. C. Hamlin, [1892], James H. Lane Papers, AU; *OR* 25(1):916 (all references are to series 1). Of Hill's six brigades, only those of Henry

Last meeting of Generals Lee and Jackson, morning of May 2, 1863. From an early engraving.

North Carolina swore that he had "never experi[e]nced such a shelling." General Lane shouted to his men to lie down in the road; most had probably tumbled into the thickets before their general could summon the yell. A lieutenant in the 37th recalled that the troops "buried our faces as close to the ground as possible and I expect some of us rubbed the skin off our noses trying to get under it."[3]

A. P. Hill and Stonewall Jackson ignored the intense fire as they conversed with each other on horseback, so "deeply absorbed" that enemy shells burst "all around[,] . . . plowing up the ground" under their horses' feet, "without either of them taking the slightest notice." Major William H. Palmer, Hill's bright and capable chief of staff, managed to locate General Lane in the scrubby underbrush, and the two men quickly agreed that the fire must be halted before the troops could make any further movement. Palmer rode back

Heth and Dorsey Pender initially formed into line. The road was a highway of early 1850s vintage, the Orange Plank Road, on the same right-of-way here as the century-old Orange Turnpike.

3. W. G. Morris to James H. Lane, January 3, 1895, and James H. Lane to A. C. Hamlin, [1892], Lane Papers, AU; Octavius A. Wiggins speech on Chancellorsville, 1895, box 75, folder 1, Military Collection, NCDAH.

to the schoolhouse and shut down the Confederate artillery, and the enemy stopped firing as well soon after the provocation ended. The shelling had lasted about fifteen minutes.[4]

As soon as the firestorm ceased, Lane moved his five North Carolina regiments into position as ordered. The 28th faced east on his far left, with the 18th just to its right. The right of the 18th anchored on the Orange Plank Road. The 37th continued the front south of the road, with the 7th on its— and the brigade's—right. In accordance with the tactical dogma of the era, Lane provided a healthy screen of skirmishers well to the front in the form of the entire 33rd North Carolina. All of this infantry deployment transpired without the firing of a gun. Crude Federal works of earth and logs paralleled the brigade front, but Lane did not position his men behind that shelter; their mission was to attack, not defend. The 28th and 18th pushed a bit farther to the front on Lane's instructions, poised for the advance that Jackson had ordered. Lane then went to his right to bring the 37th and 7th into the same alignment. Once this was accomplished, the attack could begin.[5]

Three Confederate artillery pieces stood in the road near the middle of Lane's infantry array, each from a horse artillery battery. This mobile arm had served as Jackson's support from the outset of his attack. Four guns of the Lynchburg Beauregard Rifles, under Captain Marcellus N. Moorman, had stood in the road two miles to the west when Jackson launched his assault. Moorman was at the front at dark with one of those guns, which was commanded by Lieutenant Robert P. Burwell. The other two belonged to McGregor's Battery and Breathed's Battery (under Lieutenant Philip P. Johnston). Major Robert F. Beckham was the ranking horse-artillery officer present. Jackson's artillery chief, Colonel Stapleton Crutchfield, directed the horse-artillery pieces to prepare to move to the rear to allow his more conventional batteries to take over.[6]

4. James H. Lane, "The Death of Stonewall Jackson," *Fayetteville (N.C.) Observer*, January 23, 1884; William Fitzhugh Randolph, *With Stonewall Jackson at Chancellorsville* (N.p., n.d.), 7–8; Mary Anna Jackson, *Memoirs of Stonewall Jackson by His Widow, Mary Anna Jackson* (Louisville, Ky.: Prentice, 1895), 545–46; James H. Lane to A. C. Hamlin, [1892], Lane Papers, AU. Randolph was a captain in the 39th Virginia Cavalry Battalion and played a role in the deadly drama about to unfold. His turn-of-the-century pamphlet is full of anomalies and even outright errors, but some of the color warrants its use.

5. Walter Clark, ed., *Histories of the Several Regiments and Battalions from North Carolina in the Great War, 1861–'65*, 5 vols. (Raleigh: E. M. Uzzell, 1901), 1:376, 2:659; *OR* 25(1):916, 920.

6. William H. Palmer, "Another Account of It," *Confederate Veteran* 13 (May 1905): 232–33; John J. Shoemaker, *Shoemaker's Battery, Stuart Horse Artillery, Pelham's Battalion, Afterwards Commanded by Col. R. P. Chew, Army of Northern Virginia* (Memphis, Tenn.: S. C. Toof, 1908), 34;

The most important job in the unfolding Confederate line belonged to the men of the 33rd North Carolina, far out front on the skirmish line. The regiment entered action 480 strong, about 20 percent above the average number of troops in a Confederate regiment at the time. The men of the 33rd recognized that they held "the post of danger, but it was also the post of honor." It became conventional, in the aftermath of the battle, to accuse Lane erroneously of causing Jackson's impending mishap by not sending out skirmishers. Captain R. E. Wilbourn, whose account of riding alongside Jackson is the most important of the many sources on the event, set the tone: "This lamentable affair was caused by not having any skirmishers or pickets in front of our lines—a piece of negligence unexcusable." In truth, Wilbourn and Jackson never quite reached the well-established, well-situated, and well-instructed line of skirmishers. The 33rd's three field-grade officers spread out to control their unit—the colonel on the road and his two subordinates at the far flanks, all "within short range of the enemy's skirmishers." As the historian of the 7th, on the right of the main line, declared: "Everyone knew they were [there]." The historian of the 37th noted accurately that the 33rd fanned out across "the entire front of the brigade." Lane's line could not have been drawn better.[7]

The setting in which Lane built his line while Stonewall Jackson waited impatiently contrasted starkly with the violence of the afternoon. The front edge of the fluid battle zone was almost eerily calm. "The firing had ceased," Wilbourn wrote, "and all was quiet,—the enemy having in the darkness . . . disappeared entirely from our sight." In the stillness, Yankee voices shouting commands echoed faintly through the woods from several hundred yards away, making "a great hum of human voices generally." An unsettling exception to the silence was "the mournful cry of the whippoorwill," General Lane

---

Marcellus N. Moorman, "Narrative of Events and Observations Connected with the Wounding of General T. J. (Stonewall) Jackson," in *SHSP*, 30:111–13. Shoemaker called the officer commanding the piece "Lt. Birl," which after some deciphering in official records was identified as "Burwell" rendered with a Virginian accent. Moorman's intermittently useful account is marred by his egocentric view, which assumes that all three pieces belonged to his battery and ignores the presence of his superior, Major Beckham. Moorman's pretensions are thoroughly debunked in a letter that also provides much other positive detail about the occasion, R. F. Beckham to R. P. Chew, October 28, 1908, copy in the author's possession.

7. Clark, ed., *Histories of the Several Regiments and Battalions from North Carolina*, 1:376, 2:559, 659; R. E. Wilbourn to R. L. Dabney, December 12, 1863, Charles William Dabney Papers, SHC; *OR* 25(1):922. Lane wrote that his skirmishers were deployed "at least 400 yds" to the front, James H. Lane to A. C. Hamlin, June 19, 1895, Augustus C. Hamlin Papers, Houghton Library, Harvard University, Cambridge, Mass. (collection cited hereafter as ACH Papers/Harvard).

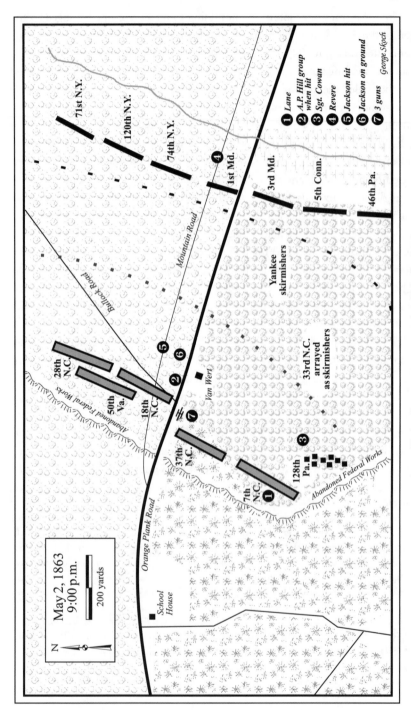

Area of Jackson's reconnaissance, night of May 2, 1863

recalled, "ringing in my ears from every direction." (The species still fills the Chancellorsville woods with its ominous calls today.) The sun had set at 6:49 P.M., but the moon would be full on May 3, so its brightness was near the peak. Even so, the dense undergrowth produced a darkness in which Lane could not read his watch.[8]

Stonewall Jackson rode restlessly in the rear of the forming brigade, impressing upon every ranking officer he met the importance of exploiting the advantage they had won. Near the schoolhouse he encountered General Rodes, who spiritedly asserted, "My Division behaved splendidly this evening." Jackson agreed and promised to say so in his official report. A bit closer to the front, Stonewall met A. P. Hill, to whom he spoke emphatically: "Press them, Gen. Hill; press them, and cut them off from the United States Ford." Jackson then encountered General Lane, who was calling for Hill in the darkness. Stonewall made clear to the brigadier that he wanted the night attack to go forward: "Push right ahead, Lane, right ahead!" Lane knew better than to solicit further details from his old Virginia Military Institute professor, so he continued to make preparations for the attack. In these encounters, Jackson used a "peculiar wave of the hand" to emphasize his intentions. Wilbourn described this ardent gesticulation as "characteristic of his determination and energy,—throwing forward his body and extending his hand beyond his horse's head, with as much force and earnestness as if he was trying to push forward the column with his hand." The lunge beyond his horse's head, a gesture enthusiastic enough to verge on the acrobatic, clearly conveyed to subordinate observers the general's customary intensity.[9]

8. R. E. Wilbourn to R. L. Dabney, December 12, 1863, Dabney Papers, SHC; *OR* 25(1):1010; Lane, "Death of Stonewall Jackson"; Randolph, *With Stonewall Jackson*, 7; James H. Lane to A. C. Hamlin, [1892], Lane Papers, AU; James Power Smith, "Stonewall Jackson's Last Battle," in *Battles and Leaders of the Civil War*, ed. Robert Underwood Johnson and Clarence Clough Buel, 4 vols. (New York: Century, 1887–88), 3:209; "Who Fired the Bullet That Killed Gen. Stonewall Jackson?," *Rockbridge County News*, January 12, 1951 (quoting 1901 Memphis paper); *Richardson's Virginia & North Carolina Almanac* (Richmond: J. W. Randolph, [1862]).

9. David J. Kyle, "Jackson's Guide When Shot," *Confederate Veteran* 4 (September 1896): 308–9; R. E. Wilbourn to R. L. Dabney, December 12, 1863, Dabney Papers, SHC; Palmer, "Another Account," 232; Murray Forbes Taylor, "Stonewall Jackson's Death," *Confederate Veteran* 12 (October 1904): 493; William H. Palmer to A. C. Hamlin, April 19, 1895, ACH Papers/Harvard; Jackson, *Memoirs*, 547; Lane, "Death of Stonewall Jackson"; James H. Lane to A. C. Hamlin, [1892], Lane Papers, AU; "Stonewall Jackson!," *Richmond Dispatch*, October 26, 1875. The latter source includes accounts by several officers, including one of many by Dr. H. H. McGuire. The most important is a detailed narrative by an anonymous staffer under A. P. Hill. The M. F. Taylor account also appeared in substantially the same form in the *Fredericksburg Journal*, October 22,

Traditional reconstructions of Jackson's ride in front of his forming lines depict his party as accompanied by A. P. Hill, with their staff members intermixed. Both generals did ride to the front, surrounded by aides and couriers. The two men and their accompanying cavalcades were quite widely separated, however, and out of touch with each other. The confusion probably originated in the incontrovertible fact that Captain James Keith Boswell, Stonewall's topographic engineer, rode next to Hill. This came about at the last minute when Jackson detailed Boswell to help Hill understand the ground. The corps commander had asked Hill how well he knew the road toward the United States Ford (Bullock Road). Even though he was a native of nearby Culpeper, Hill had been away for years on army duty and admitted, "I am entirely unacquainted with the topography of this country." Jackson "instantly replied: 'Capt. Boswell, report to Gen. Hill.'" To his division commander, Stonewall added the admonition: "Allow nothing to stop you; press on to the United States ford." Jackson then moved forward, leaving Boswell behind with Hill.[10]

Hill's gathering entourage, tagging well behind Jackson and his group, eventually numbered ten men. Hill rode on the Plank Road in the center of a three-man cluster, with Captain Boswell on his right and Major William H. Palmer on his left. Grouped slightly behind them were seven mounted men:

> Captain Conway Robinson Howard, engineer officer
> Lieutenant Murray Forbes Taylor, aide-de-camp
> Captain Benjamin Watkins Leigh, aide-de-camp
> James Fitzgerald Forbes, temporary volunteer aide
> Sergeant George W. Tucker, chief courier
> Private Richard J. Muse, courier
> Private Eugene L. Saunders, courier

Hill's party did not follow Jackson's precise route, nor did it depart at once when Jackson disappeared into the shadowed woods astride his famous mount, Little Sorrel.[11]

1904. The original typescript of Taylor's account, in the author's possession, includes some material excluded from the published versions.

10. Palmer, "Another Account," 232; Taylor, "Stonewall Jackson's Death," 493; anonymous Hill staff member, in "Stonewall Jackson!," *Richmond Dispatch*, October 26, 1875. In R. E. Wilbourn to Jubal A. Early, March 3, 1873, vol. 6, Jubal A. Early Papers, LC, Wilbourn also specified a gap of "fifty or sixty yds." between Hill and Jackson.

11. R. E. Wilbourn to R. L. Dabney, December 12, 1863, Dabney Papers, SHC; Palmer, "Another Account," 232; James H. Lane to A. C. Hamlin, [1892], Lane Papers, AU; Robert K. Krick, *9th Virginia Cavalry* (Lynchburg: H. E. Howard, 1988), 72; Richard O'Sullivan, *55th Virginia Infantry* (Lynchburg: H. E. Howard, 1989), 142, 149; Jackson, *Memoirs*, 427. A sketch drawn by

Jackson's escort included almost precisely the same number of men as Hill's. The general's brother-in-law Joseph G. Morrison described the party as numbering "eight in all." A lieutenant in the 18th North Carolina confirmed the count when he estimated that the Jackson and Hill groups between them totaled "perhaps 20 horsemen"; the two lists given here total nineteen. If Morrison meant eight riders in addition to Jackson, the estimate matches precisely the known participants—all but one of them identified by some other member of the party rather than merely in an autobiographical account:

Captain Richard Eggleston Wilbourn, signal corps
Captain William Fitzhugh Randolph, 39th Virginia Cavalry Battalion, which
    supplied couriers
Lieutenant Joseph G. Morrison, aide-de-camp
William E. Cunliffe, signal corps enlisted man
W. T. Wynn, signal corps enlisted man
Private David Joseph Kyle, 9th Virginia Cavalry
Private Joshua O. Johns, 39th Virginia Cavalry
Private Lloyd T. Smith, 39th Virginia Cavalry

Wilbourn rode at Jackson's left side, with Cunliffe and Wynn immediately behind them. The couriers formed into "columns of two" to extend the cavalcade.[12]

William H. Palmer (in ACH Papers/Harvard), uncovered since the first publication of this essay, conforms to the listing of Hill's party precisely but adds a courier named Kirkpatrick, who was killed.

12. J. G. Morrison to Jubal A. Early, February 20, 1879, vol. 10, Early Papers, LC; Alfred H. H. Tolar, "Stonewall Jackson," *Wilmington (N.C.) Daily Review*, December 15, 1883; R. E. Wilbourn to R. L. Dabney, December 12, 1863, Dabney Papers, SHC; Randolph, *With Stonewall Jackson*, 8; R. E. Wilbourn to Jubal A. Early, February 12, 1873, in Jubal A. Early, *Lieutenant General Jubal Anderson Early, C.S.A.: Autobiographical Sketch and Narrative of the War Between the States* (Philadelphia: J. B. Lippincott, 1912), 214. The only person claiming to have been in the cavalcade not identified by someone else was Lloyd T. Smith, a seventeen-year-old member of the 39th Virginia Cavalry Battalion. Smith's claim is in Philip A. Bruce, ed., *History of Virginia*, 6 vols. (Chicago: American Historical Society, 1924), 5:286. Smith's story seems to be valid. He made no extravagant claims of positioning at center stage, and his unit unquestionably supplied the couriers. An important anonymous account in *Land We Love* 1 (July 1866): 179–82 has previously been attributed to Joe Morrison because internal evidence suggests his authorship and the journal was edited by his brother-in-law D. H. Hill. Morrison in his letter to Early, February 20, 1879, vol. 10, Early Papers, LC, however, states: "I have never written anything connected with [Jackson's wounding] for the press or contributed my testimony to the establishment of truth." This declaration by Morrison, thirteen years after the *Land We Love* article appeared, seems to abolish earlier assumptions. Morrison remains a possible author of the 1866 article, however, if his 1879 pro-

The most important member of Jackson's party for historical purposes was the man with the least standing at the time—nineteen-year-old Private David Kyle of the 9th Virginia Cavalry. In his admirable *Lee's Lieutenants*, Douglas Southall Freeman attributes special merit to Kyle's account because the veteran had, Freeman learned from a friend, hunted in the area and bought cattle nearby during the 1890s, making Kyle, after the fact, "entirely familiar with the terrain." What Freeman did not know was that David Kyle literally was serving as a scout and guide in his own backyard. He had lived before the war on the Bullock farm that gave the adjacent road its name. But for the dense thickets hugging the ground, Kyle could have seen his own back porch from the route of Jackson's cavalcade. In the smoke-streaked, flaming, chaotic Wilderness that night, David Kyle knew precisely where he was. No one else could have been certain of much. Kyle, furthermore, reinforced his understanding of events by walking over the ground again on May 4, 1863.[13]

Private Kyle found himself guiding the legendary Stonewall Jackson around his home-cum-battlefield by a quirky circumstance. At about 3:00 P.M. Brigadier General William Henry Fitzhugh "Rooney" Lee, R. E. Lee's son and former commander of the 9th Virginia Cavalry, sent Kyle to deliver a dispatch to Major General J. E. B. Stuart. Lee warned the courier that the main roads might be infested with Yankees, so Kyle detoured across country toward Parker's Store, then carefully wound his way northward. He passed Jackson's troops on the Brock Road, then struck out again on byways past Lacy's Mill to Ely's Ford. Kyle found Stuart near the gate to the Ely yard and delivered the dispatch. The general asked about Kyle's leisurely pace, and the young cavalryman explained about the necessarily circuitous route. Stuart asked how well Kyle knew the country. Thomas Frazer Chancellor, another

nouncement is viewed as having a central caveat about "for the press." The article wrongly identifies Boswell as with the group but mentions Wilbourn, Morrison, and "five or six couriers," further validating the eight-man register of participants listed in the text.

13. Krick, *9th Virginia Cavalry*, 84, 123; Douglas Southall Freeman, *Lee's Lieutenants: A Study in Command*, 3 vols. (New York: Charles Scribner's Sons, 1942–44), 2:563n; U.S. Eighth Census, 1860, Schedule 1, "Free Inhabitants, Spotsylvania County, Virginia," p. 72, M653, NA. The 1860 census showed Kyle as a native of Maryland, age sixteen (December 17, 1843–February 1, 1900). His sister, Catharine Kyle Bullock, age eighteen, and Oscar Bullock, age thirty-five, had two children. David had been living with his sister and family since 1857. For two years before that he resided with the Dowdall family on what would become the Chancellorsville battlefield. Family information from William Arthur Robertson, Jr., to R. K. Krick, November 1, 1997. Kyle's account of his review of the terrain two days later is from an important letter that he wrote to the historian Augustus C. Hamlin, November 8, 1894, ACH Papers/Harvard.

local boy, happened to be standing nearby and piped up, "He knows every hog-path." With that reassurance, Stuart sent Kyle out at 6:30 P.M. with a message for Jackson enclosed in a large sealed envelope.

Kyle circled southwest, then southeast, to reach the intersection of the Orange Plank Road and the Orange Turnpike opposite Wilderness Church. Confused officers there told him he might find Jackson westward on the Plank Road. Within a half-mile, better-informed sources prompted the courier to retrace his steps. Kyle happened upon Rev. Melzi Chancellor, "a man whome I had known for some time and had confidence in." Chancellor lived at the southeast corner of the intersection and had just returned from guiding Jackson himself, having left the general "on the right hand side near Powells old field . . . the spot which I knew so well," Kyle recalled; he might have said the same about his familiarity with the rest of the scene toward which he now headed.

Just as Kyle neared the field, he saw several horsemen ride into the road and turn toward the front. He hurried to catch up and asked the hindmost where Jackson was. "There he is to the right in front," the aide answered. Kyle spurred forward, saluted the general, and handed over the large envelope. Jackson pulled up Little Sorrel, turned the horse's head to the right road edge, and read what Stuart had sent. As Kyle glanced around the familiar scenes of his youth, he noticed the nearby road to Hazel Grove and the schoolhouse farther to the front; he also saw an unfamiliar sight—piles of dead horses in and around the road, the debris from a recent charge by the 8th Pennsylvania Cavalry. When Jackson finished reading, he tersely asked Kyle, "Do you know all of this country?" When the youngster answered positively, Jackson said simply, "Keep along with me," then rode eastward again.[14]

Jackson went forward, impelled by a hunger for information, as his conversations with subordinates make clear. He was, a Stonewall Brigade veteran commented, "always a great hand to wander about. . . . He had to see for himself." Hill followed fifty or more yards behind as a matter of military eti-

14. The preceding account is based entirely on Kyle's own recollection of the afternoon and evening. Kyle's invaluable narrative in *Confederate Veteran* ("Jackson's Guide") includes some of these details but not as many as the ten-page penciled original, which runs fully one-third longer than the edited (and somewhat revised) published version. A typescript is at the FSNMP library. The published version will be cited whenever possible because it is more readily available to students, and the account at FSNMP will be cited only when it offers elaboration or (less often) variant language or details. In at least two places, the editorial pen at *Confederate Veteran* obscured as it attempted to smooth.

quette. He had been in the middle of the road, surrounded by mounted staff, when Jackson's group headed out. "As soon as . . . Hill saw Jackson ride in front of his lines," one of the former's aides wrote, "he felt it his duty, as a subordinate, to join him, and accordingly he also rode forward."[15]

Both of the regular staff members accompanying Jackson thought, almost certainly erroneously, that their chief was looking for the advanced Confederate skirmish line. They also presumed, undoubtedly in error, that the skirmish line was missing or misaligned. Under a narrow construction, it might be asserted that David Kyle was responsible for the death of Stonewall Jackson because it was Kyle's well-informed and skillful guidance that led the general on what would be a fatal route. Had the local boy not been present, Jackson almost surely would have reconnoitered carefully down the main road. Both Morrison and Wilbourn held this view. In fact, however, Kyle steered Jackson onto the (apparently) far more appropriate corridor of the Mountain Road and pointed him eastward on that dark tunnel through the brush.[16]

Kyle rode quietly with the Jackson cavalcade beyond the schoolhouse he knew so well and around the curve in the road just east of that point. He noticed reserve infantry in ragged alignment, most of it facing away from the front. After a pause during which Jackson conversed with other officers (evidently the encounters with Lane and Hill), the group moved ahead to another forward infantry line. The men of this thin force responded to a query from Kyle by identifying themselves as members of the 55th Virginia and the 22nd Virginia Battalion, both of Brigadier General Henry Heth's brigade. Jackson veered to the left of the main road and halted, the junctions of the Bullock and Mountain Roads with the Plank Road visible on either side. Kyle informed the general that one road went to the Bullock house (his home) and the other "ran sorter parallel with the plank road and came out on it about a half a mile below." Probably suspicious of the strange guide's credentials, Jackson curtly ordered Kyle to lead the way. The boy did so for about two hundred yards; at that point the general, satisfied at last, caught up and kept abreast of him.[17]

15. James C. Bosserman, "Bullets Didn't Kill 'Stonewall' Jackson," *Richmond Times-Dispatch*, October 12, 1930; anonymous Hill staff member, in "Stonewall Jackson!," *Richmond Dispatch*, October 26, 1875; Taylor, "Stonewall Jackson's Death," 493; R. E. Wilbourn to Jubal A. Early, March 3, 1873, vol. 6, Early Papers, LC.

16. R. E. Wilbourn to R. L. Dabney, December 12, 1863, Dabney Papers, SHC; *Land We Love* 1 (July 1866): 181; J. G. Morrison to R. L. Dabney, October 29, 1863, Dabney Papers, SHC.

17. Kyle, "Jackson's Guide," 308; Kyle manuscript account, FSNMP.

There can be little doubt that Stonewall Jackson made his eastward ride on the Mountain Road and that he was shot near that corridor and not the main (Orange Plank) road. Whether he took the Mountain Road all the way from the main road, however, or instead went north on the southernmost leg of Bullock Road to reach the Mountain Road is less certain. Kyle's own account may be interpreted either way, but it is more logical if taken to mean that Jackson took the Mountain Road entirely. Major Palmer's version refers to the Hazel Grove road as being part of the intersection Jackson used, which means that the Mountain Road, being appreciably farther west, must have been his initial route.[18]

The nineteenth-century historian Augustus C. Hamlin, though ardently polemical in northern outlook and primarily concerned with the Federal Eleventh Corps, devoted more careful attention to Jackson's foray than any other early student. Hamlin noted cogently that the cannon fire from Fairview that had recently swept the main road made it an undesirable avenue for reconnaissance. The slightly more northerly road missed that beaten zone and also took Jackson a bit closer to the sensitive enemy sector that interested him. Hamlin sensibly accepted Kyle's account as the best extant and also adduced testimony from two (unidentified) 18th North Carolina officers who "declared that Jackson did not pass by them but turned off to the left of their rear and passed out of view in the forest." Most of the road complex remained distinctly visible ("although long out of use") when Hamlin examined the scene in the 1890s. The Mountain Road maintained a parallel course, "sixty to eighty yards distant" from the Plank Road in the vicinity of Jackson's wounding. Its westernmost leg had disappeared, however, and for that incorrect reason Hamlin concluded (perhaps correctly) that Jackson rode up the beginning of the Bullock Road to reach the Mountain Road.[19]

Jackson and his eight companions continued east on the Mountain Road until nearly to the 33rd North Carolina skirmish line. There is no indication that the skirmishers saw Jackson or that his party saw them, but it seems likely that each was aware of the other's presence. From their advanced vantage point, the southerners listened intently to the sounds of enemy preparations. Ringing axes told of Federal pioneers frantically throwing obstacles in the way

18. Palmer, "Another Account," 232.

19. A. C. Hamlin, in Jackson, *Memoirs*, 549–51; Augustus Choate Hamlin, *The Battle of Chancellorsville: The Attack of Stonewall Jackson and His Army upon the Right Flank of the Army of the Potomac at Chancellorsville, Virginia, on Saturday Afternoon, May 2, 1863* (Bangor, Maine: Author, 1896), 108.

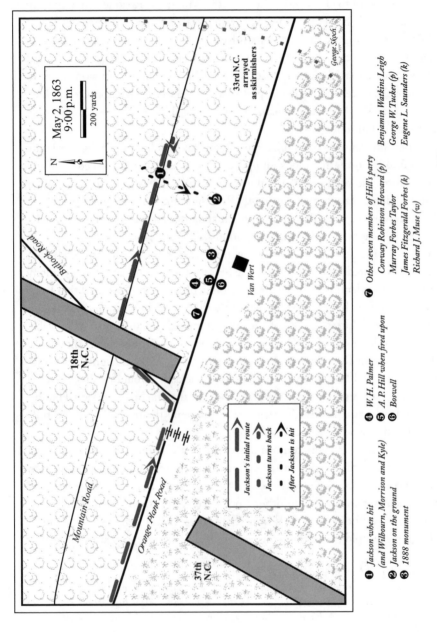

May 2, 1863
9:00 p.m.

N

200 yards

Bullock Road

18th N.C.

Mountain Road

Orange Plank Road

37th N.C.

Van Wert

33rd N.C. arrayed as skirmishers

George Skoch

Jackson's initial route

Jackson turns back

After Jackson is hit

1 *Jackson when hit (and Wilbourn, Morrison and Kyle)*
2 *Jackson on the ground*
3 *1888 monument*

4 *W. H. Palmer*
5 *A. P. Hill when fired upon*
6 *Boswell*

7 *Other seven members of Hill's party*
Conway Robinson Howard (p)
Murray Forbes Taylor
James Fitzgerald Forbes (k)
Richard J. Muse (w)

Benjamin Watkins Leigh
George W. Tucker (p)
Eugene L. Saunders (k)

Jackson's movements on the Orange Plank Road and Mountain Road, night of May 2, 1863

Stonewall Jackson rode forward of his line through the dense thickets. An 1880s engraving.

of a Confederate advance. Commands echoed distinctly through the woods. After questioning eyewitnesses and cross-checking accounts, Jackson's aide James Power Smith later concluded that Jackson actually "passed the swampy depression and began the ascent of the hill toward Chancellorsville"; an advance that far, however, is hardly credible. Kyle, who was present at the time and far more accurate than Smith, thought the enemy was two to three hundred yards distant; he could hear them best from the vicinity of the Fairview clearing south of the main road. "It seemed that the officers were trying to form their men in line," Kyle recalled. In retrospect, the courier estimated that the quiet pause at the apogee of the advance lasted "from two to four minutes." Then Jackson reined Little Sorrel around and started to retrace his steps.[20]

Meanwhile, the tactical situation west of the general, and especially southwest beyond the Plank Road, had shifted dangerously. Immediately after Jackson left him, General James H. Lane hurried toward the right of his brigade to prepare it for the mandated advance. The chaos and uncertainty he encountered deflected him from that purpose. A swarm of Federals had by accident curled up between the outer skirmish line, manned by the 33rd North Carolina, and the 7th North Carolina, the regiment farthest to the right in Lane's main line. Most of the disoriented northerners belonged to the 128th Pennsylvania. That unit's lieutenant colonel, Levi H. Smith, tried to unsnarl the confusion by waving a white handkerchief and asking troops in each direction whose cause they favored. The 7th North Carolina promptly corralled Smith, who naively claimed the immunity of a white flag—as though front-line reconnaissances could be executed without risk. "The simpleton imagined Gen. Lane would allow him to return," one Tar Heel chortled. Lieutenant James W. Emack of the 7th, with help from four subordinates, raked in at least two hundred of Smith's regiment as prisoners. Carolinians gleefully harvesting trophy swords and muskets by the armful filled the woods on Lane's right. General Lane was himself near the right of his brigade, so he knew nothing at all of what happened to Jackson; but he was not directly involved in the 7th's encounter with the Yankees.[21]

The confusion incumbent on the capture of so many enemy soldiers in unexpected proximity contributed to the events that followed. At this critical

20. Jedediah Hotchkiss, *Virginia*, vol. 3 of *Confederate Military History*, ed. Clement A. Evans, 12 vols. (Atlanta: Confederate Publishing Company, 1899), 386; Smith, "Stonewall Jackson's Last Battle," 211; Kyle, "Jackson's Guide," 308; Kyle manuscript account, FSNMP; A. C. Hamlin, in Jackson, *Memoirs*, 551–52.

21. Moorman, "Narrative of Events," 113; James H. Lane to A. C. Hamlin, [1892], Lane Papers, AU; James H. Lane, "How Stonewall Jackson Met His Death," in *SHSP*, 8:494 (also published in *Our Living and Our Dead* 3 [July 1875]: 33–36); Clark, ed., *Histories of the Several Regiments and Battalions from North Carolina*, 1:377, 2:559; James S. Harris, *Historical Sketches of the Seventh Regiment North Carolina Troops* (Mooresville, N.C.: Mooresville Printing Company, [1893]), 28–29; *OR* 25(l):184, 916; James H. Lane to A. C. Hamlin, November 17, 1892, ACH Papers/Harvard.

juncture, a Federal officer rode toward the far right of the 33rd's skirmishers, behind whom the Pennsylvanians' capture had just unfolded. The Federal probably was Brigadier General Joseph F. Knipe, until recently colonel of the 46th Pennsylvania. Knipe had approached his old regiment, rejected its intelligence about rebels nearby in front, "raved . . . in language more forcible than polite," and then dashed forward alone. "He did not go far, or stay long when he got there," the 46th's historian gloated, noting that Knipe lost his hat in his undignified scramble to escape.[22]

During his brief foray, Knipe, or a fellow officer in the vicinity, called out loudly for "General Williams," referring to Alpheus S. Williams of the Federal Twelfth Corps. Captain Joseph H. Saunders, whose Company A of the 33rd North Carolina held down the far right of the skirmish line, meanwhile had gone with Lieutenant Colonel Robert V. Cowan toward the Plank Road to check for further orders. Nineteen-year-old Sergeant Thomas A. Cowan was therefore left in charge opposite the inquisitive Yankee. Young Cowan challenged the Federal, who responded that he and his party were "friends." "To which side?" "To the Union." Cowan stepped back to his company and ordered it to fire toward the sounds. Men across an arc of hundreds of yards distinctly heard a single shot ring out, quickly picked up by the rest of Company A and then the remaining skirmishers in the area. The musketry became sharper and rolled northward in ever-heavier volume from both the picket line and the startled Confederates in the main line (who, of course, were firing toward the rear of their own skirmishers!). The colonel of the 7th described the sequence and the portentous single shot: "The enemy manifested impatience, and a shot was fired towards our right which caused the Seventh to fire a Volley."[23]

Stonewall Jackson had not ridden far on his return trip toward the lines of the 18th North Carolina when Sergeant Cowan's encounter triggered fire hundreds of yards away to the southwest. The deadly volleys scything through

22. Alexander W. Selfridge, "Who Shot Stonewall Jackson?" in *Camp-Fire Sketches and Battle-Field Echoes*, comp. W. C. King and W. P. Berry (Springfield, Mass.: W. C. King, 1889), 377–79.

23. Joseph H. Saunders, "Stonewall Jackson—His Wounds, &c.," *Fayetteville (N.C.) Observer*, February 6, 1884; A. C. Hamlin, in Jackson, *Memoirs*, 548; James H. Lane to A. C. Hamlin, [1892], Lane Papers, AU; J. S. Harris to A. C. Hamlin, December 8, 1894, ACH Papers/Harvard. J. G. Morrison to Jubal A. Early, February 20, 1879, vol. 10, Early Papers, LC, never heretofore published or used, confirms the evidence that the opening rounds came from the skirmish line, not the main line: "My recollection is that it was in advance of where our line was supposed to [have] been."

the Wilderness brush had nothing to do with Jackson, having been initiated far away in an unrelated episode. Despite the conventional wisdom about Jackson's wounding, no Confederate initially opened fire directly on the general's party by mistake. Cowan and his men were shooting at a real threat in a reasonable manner. The other Carolinians who volleyed into the darkness far to Cowan's north were firing at absolutely nothing at first. Then, when Jackson and Hill and their escorts stumbled noisily into the confused tableau, the Confederate line continued its fire toward the frightening specter of what seemed like approaching enemy troops.

Captain Wilbourn's memory of those frantic moments sifted through the complexities and focused on the simple facts. He recalled that the general had ridden eastward and that fire had suddenly burst from the Confederate line. Wilbourn remembered that Jackson turned toward the rear to avoid the fire that started far off near the 7th North Carolina. According to Wilbourn's account, Stonewall swerved north away from the initial firing at about the same time that he spun back toward the east. Two other contemporary witnesses not far from the scene echoed this simplistic construction of events.[24]

As the only man on the reconnaissance who knew where he was, David Kyle was able to track Jackson's movements with considerable precision. When the general had his fill of listening to Federal noise and started back whence he had come, Kyle rode directly behind him. Within about seventy-five yards, however, four or five mounted men filtered into the gap between Kyle and Jackson, and the youngster "sorter reigned my horse in a little" and kept pace about ten yards behind. As the party came opposite the Van Wert house, Stonewall turned Little Sorrel's head to the left and started to leave the Mountain Road, changing his direction from west to south. "Just as his horse[']s front feet had cleared the edge of the road whilste his hind feet was still on the edge of the bank," Kyle wrote, the widely heard single shot rang out far to the south. "In an instant it was taken up, and nearer there were five or six shots . . . and then suddenly a large volley, as if from a Regiment."[25] Sergeant Tom Cowan's shot at the inquisitive Yankee had unleashed a rolling

24. R. E. Wilbourn to R. L. Dabney, December 12, 1863, Dabney Papers, SHC; R. E. Wilbourn to Jubal A. Early, February 12, 1873, in Early, *Autobiographical Sketch and Narrative*, 214; Jedediah Hotchkiss to his wife, May 19, 1863, Hotchkiss Papers, LC (microfilm roll 4, frames 515–16); *Land We Love* 1 (July 1866): 181. Neither Wilbourn nor whoever wrote the *Land We Love* article ever did figure out that the 33rd North Carolina was picketing to their front. Hotchkiss implies the same misconception.

25. Kyle manuscript account, FSNMP; Kyle, "Jackson's Guide," 308.

barrage that inexorably spread toward Jackson's vicinity and quickly struck him down.

Stonewall Jackson's location vis-à-vis A. P. Hill's party is instructive in determining precisely where the general suffered his deadly wounds. Major Palmer estimated that he and Hill and Boswell were about sixty yards in front of the 18th North Carolina. Jackson was about sixty yards beyond Hill. Because Hill was at the edge of the Plank Road and Jackson was deeper in the woods on the Mountain Road, the sixty-yard gap between the two generals ran diagonally northeast rather than due east down the main road. Jackson's distance eastward from the 18th North Carolina, therefore, was a bit less than one hundred yards. The next morning Murray Forbes Taylor drove A. P. Hill to the scene in an ambulance. The two men saw a cluster of familiar horses, dead in heaps where Hill's party had been struck the night before. Hill directed Taylor to proceed about seventy-five to one hundred yards farther east, then stopped the ambulance and pointed out the place where he had found Jackson after he was wounded. This location was not, of course, the exact site where Stonewall had been hit, but it helps to confirm the considerable distance eastward from Hill's party to Jackson's.[26]

The monument erected in 1888 to commemorate Jackson's wounding was designed to mark the spot where he was tended, not where the volley struck him. Even for that event, the monument is located a bit too far west. Surgeon Benjamin P. Wright of the 55th Virginia went forward to aid Jackson when beckoned by A. P. Hill. He recalled going past "Van Worts Shop" for "about twenty steps further" before reaching the knot of worried Confederates "on the left of the road." Van Wert's house stood directly across the road from the 1888 monument, however.[27]

James Power Smith reached his chief just before the wounded general began the difficult trek rearward. Smith later participated in the erection of the crude 1887 marker and the final, adjacent 1888 monument and concluded that Jackson actually was succored "a few rods . . . farther to the front than where the . . . monument now stand[s]." This view conforms precisely with Wright's recollection. At the time of the 1880s commemoration, dispute arose

26. Palmer, "Another Account," 232–33; Taylor, "Stonewall Jackson's Death," 494; R. E. Wilbourn to Jubal A. Early, March 3, 1873, vol. 6, Early Papers, LC.

27. Benjamin P. Wright, "Recollections of the Battle of Chancellorsville and the Wounding of General Jackson," typescript, bound vol. 176, FSNMP. The foundation of the Van Wert house was destroyed, incredibly, in 1972 by the Virginia Department of Highways despite being situated on property of the National Park Service.

about whether the wounding site was along Plank Road or Mountain Road. One of the Talleys who farmed just west of Chancellorsville had marked a stump on the Mountain Road as the location, but that identification had vanished long ago without permanent record. At the dedication of the large 1888 monument, Smith and other contemporaries made it abundantly clear that they were marking the spot where aides gathered around the stricken Stonewall, *not* an estimate of the wounding location.[28]

David Kyle's account makes the Mountain Road the almost inarguable site of Jackson's wounding. A. C. Hamlin concluded aptly that the general's position when hit "was about 60 or 70 paces north of the plank road [from] where the monument now stands." If Hamlin had factored in a few more yards of easterly distance, he would have been exactly right. Kyle himself wrote to Hamlin, "Gen Jackson was not wounded on the Plank or Pike Road but was wounded on that old mountain road." The Mountain Road trace that Hamlin examined in the 1890s survived into the 1920s, when a government survey team drew the trace about sixty yards north of the main road. During an 1890s visit to the site William H. Palmer of Hill's staff measured the distance between the two roads as "53 paces" and declared that "Jackson was on the mountain road when shot." Longtime battlefield resident James M. Talley measured the distance as sixty-five yards. The Mountain Road can no longer be discerned in the vicinity with any clarity because the National Park Service thoroughly destroyed the area by constructing a modern building and a parking lot in 1963 and a series of water and sewage treatment facilities in the 1970s. The location of the 1963 building, however, somehow ended up missing the best estimate of where Jackson was hit by a tiny margin; the site lies a

---

28. James Power Smith to George H. Stuart, April 27, 1905, FSNMP. A rod—also called a pole or a perch—measures 16.5 feet. A newspaper account of the monument's dedication declared that Jackson actually was struck "about 150 yards further down in the woods" but that the monument had been sited to ensure visibility from the road ("Monument to 'Stonewall' Jackson," *[Atlanta] Sunny South*, July 7, 1888). John W. Thomason's account of the placement of the first, unmarked stone in 1887 is garbled (*Jeb Stuart* [New York: Charles Scribner's Sons, 1934], 389). The best report of the earlier stone is in Sallie M. Lacy, "Jackson Marker Placing Recalled," *Fredericksburg Free Lance–Star*, May 16, 1938. Sallie was the daughter and sister-in-law of the two men who put up the first stone. In a letter to Jed Hotchkiss, July 10, 1888 (Hotchkiss Papers, VHS), Smith supplied the useful information that he had paced the distance from the 1888 monument to the "shop" or schoolhouse and found it to be 1,546 feet. A reporter at the dedication who talked with Smith and Vespasian Chancellor and others concluded that Jackson had been shot as much as "a quarter of a mile" into the woods ("Stonewall Jackson: His Death and Monument Dedication," *National Tribune*, August 2, 1888). That estimate is too great, although easily understandable given the denseness of the thickets, but it is an important bit of evidence.

Stonewall Jackson and his staff, several of whom clustered
around him as he lay wounded.

few yards off its southeast corner and just below the southwest corner of the
parking lot.[29]

Within moments after the fatal bullets sped through the Wilderness, men
began to speculate on their origins with a mixture of guilt, concern, and abject
curiosity. Lane's North Carolinians unquestionably fired most—and probably

29. A. C. Hamlin, in Jackson, *Memoirs*, 549, 552; D. J. Kyle to A. C. Hamlin, November 8,
1894, ACH Papers/Harvard; James M. Talley to A. C. Hamlin, June 1, 1892, ACH Papers/Har-
vard; War Department survey transit books, book 2, [1927?] (no later than 1933), FSNMP. The

all—of the deadly rounds that decimated Hill's and Jackson's parties. The 18th North Carolina stood opposite both impact zones and received the most blame, no doubt correctly. The two bullets that shattered Stonewall Jackson's left arm disappeared after they accomplished their deadly harm, probably passing through the limb after impact or else falling out of the sleeve that was ripped open to tend the wounds. A third ball, however, remained in the general's right hand. When surgeon Hunter Holmes McGuire removed it, he found it to be "the round ball, (such as is used for the smooth-bore)."[30]

By May 1863, the well-supplied Federal armies had virtually eliminated the use of obsolete smoothbore muskets. Ordnance-poor Confederates did not enjoy that luxury. The dichotomy is useful for historical purposes—a round ball means Confederate origin. Ordnance returns taken not long before Chancellorsville, however, show that the 18th had only one-third as many smoothbores as the 28th to its left (in Jackson's general direction). The 37th North Carolina, just beyond the Plank Road, carried four times as many smoothbores as the 18th. A single muzzle delivered the single round ball that hit Jackson's right palm, of course, but the statistics raise the possibility that oblique fire from either side of the 18th must be considered. The colonel of the 28th was so little affected by the incident, however, that his lengthy official report does not even mention the night of May 2. One North Carolina source placed the 50th Virginia Infantry to the left of the 18th North Carolina, but the 50th must have been a bit to the rear as well, judging from Lane's failure to mention it as he shook out his line.[31]

---

westbound lanes of the modern highway that bisects the battlefield follow the original route of the Orange Plank Road. The distance is ninety-five yards from the road to the edge of the parking lot and ninety-five yards from the east edge of Bullock Road to the 1888 monument. A comparison of the Van Wert site, the 1888 monument, the two roads, and the documentary evidence places Jackson's wounding two-thirds of the way from the modern road to the parking lot and forty yards east of the longitude of the 1888 monument. When Frederic Bancroft and two Confederate artillerists visited the site in 1903, they could not find the trace (Bancroft to A. C. Hamlin, October 25, 1903, ACH Papers/Harvard). E. P. Alexander had been skeptical of the Mountain Road location, but in a letter dated November 12, 1903, he admitted to Hamlin, "I am equally sure it was on the Mountain road & just as you describe it" (ACH Papers/Harvard). Palmer's notes and sketch, in ACH Papers/Harvard, are undated but drawn on hotel stationery with the printed date 189–. Palmer's other quote in the text is from his letter of September 15, 1894, to Hamlin.

30. Hunter Holmes McGuire, *The Confederate Cause and Conduct in the War Between the States* (Richmond: L. H. Jenkins, 1907), 222. McGuire's several other accounts of treating Jackson confirm the ordnance identity.

31. The ordnance returns, for which I thank Bill McDaid, historian of Lane's brigade, were recorded by James A. W. Bryan on April 3 and 4, 1863, and are in vol. 59, Bryan Family Papers,

The view from the deadly end of the muzzles, as seen by Hill's detachment at very short range from the 18th, was unequivocal. Every survivor of the group attributed the fire to Lane's brigade and the 18th regiment. In Lane's words, "Gen. Hill always told me that he thought . . . the 18th regiment" had hit Jackson. As Murray Forbes Taylor lay trapped under his horse, he heard Hill shouting at the 18th, "You have shot your friends. You have destroyed my staff." The general often discussed with Lieutenant Taylor what had happened: "He saw the troops fire; saw his staff destroyed," and the fire came from the 18th. Some of the troops also saw Hill under startling circumstances. A captain in the regiment recalled Hill's familiar figure dashing toward them, so close that it was illuminated by the flickering muzzle blasts.[32]

Jackson and his escort could see less well, having much more brush between them and the Carolinians, but they too harbored no doubts about the source of the gunfire. The general himself said, as if in bewilderment, "All my wounds are by my own men." When Wilbourn remarked that "they certainly must be our troops," he saw Jackson "nod assent" and look toward his lines "with apparent astonishment . . . as if at a loss to understand." Wilbourn noticed that the fire came from near ground level and presumed that the Tar Heels had been "stooping down or on their knees." Lieutenant Morrison, who soon dashed in among the troops, found them "all lying down . . . owing to the thick underbrush & the habit of the men to shelter themselves." No one with Jackson doubted that the fire came from the 18th North Carolina. Wilbourn even insisted, inaccurately, that "not a gun was fired by the enemy" during the uproar.[33]

SHC. The actual numbers of .69 and higher caliber (thus smoothbore) shoulder arms in the brigade were 64 in the 7th, 67 in the 18th, 184 in the 28th, 86 in the 33rd, and 271 in the 37th. The report of the 28th is in *OR* 25(1):921. The historian of the 18th in Clark, ed., *Histories of the Several Regiments and Battalions from North Carolina*, 2:72–73, is the sole source mentioning the 50th Virginia (for which no known ordnance returns survive).

32. Palmer, "Another Account," 233; anonymous Hill staff member, in "Stonewall Jackson!," *Richmond Dispatch*, October 26, 1875; Lane, "Death of Stonewall Jackson"; typescript of Murray Forbes Taylor account, in the author's possession; Richardson, "Death of Stonewall Jackson." Richardson reported that Hill cornered Colonel Purdie and "had a conversation" with him that must have been heated. Tolar in "Stonewall Jackson" wrote that Hill gave Purdie "a severe reprimand, then and there" but subsequently retracted the comments once the circumstances became clear.

33. *Richmond Enquirer*, May 13, 1863; *Land We Love* 1 (July 1866): 181; J. G. Morrison to Jubal A. Early, February 20, 1879, vol. 10, Early Papers, LC; J. G. Morrison to R. L. Dabney, October 29, 1863, and R. E. Wilbourn to Dabney, December 12, 1863, Dabney Papers, SHC; Wilbourn to [John Esten Cooke], May 1863, Charles J. Faulkner Papers, VHS; Wilbourn to Early, February 12, 1873, in Early, *Autobiographical Sketch and Narrative*, 214–15; *Shepherdstown Register*,

The North Carolinians behind the guilty muskets also knew at once what they had done. Major John Decatur Barry confessed to General Lane as soon as the two men met that he had ordered his men to fire the deadly volley. An officer in the 18th wrote, "Our regiment was fully aware of the terrible mistake . . . within 10 minutes after it happened." The first shots from the 18th erupted inexorably as the fire swept up the line from the south. The troops continued to fire, however, because they were uncertain who was thrashing about on horseback just to the regiment's front. That perceived threat came from Hill and his friends, not the more distant and probably invisible Jackson. Lieutenant Colonel Forney George of the 18th summarized the matter succinctly: "General A. P. Hill and staff . . . rushed upon our line . . . when our men, thinking it was a cavalry charge from the enemy, fired several rounds at them." The effect of Hill's party was magnified when the 18th's own commander, Colonel Thomas J. Purdie, dashed back on the Plank Road toward his regiment from a foray out front, shouting to the 18th to fix bayonets (which only 63 percent of the regiment had).[34]

The cavalry charge motif runs deep through most Carolinian accounts and understandably so, even if the original flurry of fire came as an instinctive extension of the volleys south of the Plank Road. The horsemen in the thick brush to the front could hardly be Confederate skirmishers since those friends were afoot. Hill's cavalcade's "appearance in the gloom . . . was well calculated to create the impression that the enemy's cavalry were advancing." "The rattle as if a squadron of horsemen was bearing down . . . at a rapid speed," an intelligent officer remembered, left as "the only reasonable conclusion . . . that it was a cavalry charge." Major Barry, whose direct orders to fire made him most responsible, told General Lane that he heard the skirmish fire and then horsemen and presumed that enemy riders had penetrated the 33rd North Carolina's screen. Dozens of men cried "cavalry charge!" The recent surprising—to both sides—eruption of the 8th Pennsylvania Cavalry into the midst of Jackson's corps nearby probably contributed to the mind-set.[35]

May 5, 1883. The less reliable Randolph reported that Jackson said to him, " 'Wild fire, that, sir; wild fire' . . . in his usual rapid way" (*With Stonewall Jackson*, 10).

34. James H. Lane to A. C. Hamlin, December 9, 1894, ACH Papers/Harvard; Tolar, "Stonewall Jackson"; *OR* 25(1):920; A. C. Hamlin, in Jackson, *Memoirs*, 553. The percentage of bayonets on hand is from the ordnance returns in vol. 59, Bryan Family Papers, SHC.

35. Clark, ed., *Histories of the Several Regiments and Battalions from North Carolina*, 2:72–73; Lane, "How Stonewall Jackson Met His Death," 494; Tolar, "Stonewall Jackson"; James H. Lane to Charles E. Jones, October 26, 1898, Lane Papers, AU; Lane, "Death of Stonewall Jackson"; *Richmond Enquirer*, May 13, 1863; Randolph Barton, aide to General Paxton, in John Bigelow, Jr.,

Honest but confused Carolinians had to confess uncertainty about the circumstances in the smoking woods. One soldier admitted, "I do not know
whether I fired or not so great was the excitement." None could say with even
remote certainty where his missiles went. Some veterans refused for years to
talk about the event, eventually confessing late in life, even on their deathbeds,
that they had harbored guilty worries. Members of the 33rd, far to the front
and between two fires, faced the most difficult situation. The fire into their
backs from Lane's main line forced them forward into the Yankees, who, of
course, fired on them as well. The regiment lost a number of men who became
Federal prisoners in the melee, and its lieutenant colonel fell hard hit.[36]

Some grieving Confederates inevitably placed the blame for Stonewall's
loss on the 18th North Carolina and the aggressive Major Barry. One Second
Corps staff officer stated bluntly in an official report written the day before
Jackson's death: "General Lane got scared, fired into our own men, and
achieved the unenviable reputation of wounding severely . . . Jackson." A Virginia artillery captain whose guns were threatened by the ill-conceived fire also
derided Barry's behavior and reasoning. Near the turn of the century, a historian wrote that Lane's "whole brigade has been blended in the severe denunci-
ations hurled upon them in this unfortunate affair." General Lane wrote with
pride of A. P. Hill's reaction: "In all my intercourse with [Hill] I never heard
him . . . censure the 18th." Lane defended Barry as "one of those fearless,
dashing officers who was especially cool under fire."[37]

James H. Lane remained a brigadier general for the rest of the war, despite
apparently successful performances in all of the army's major battles. Even
when casualties and other exigencies thrust untried youngsters into brigade
command and Lee faced a desperate shortage of leadership, Lane stayed in his
1862 rank as one of the senior brigadiers in Confederate service. It is impossible to attribute his stagnation to stigmata accumulated on May 2, 1863; but it
is equally impossible to ignore the possibility. No one could blame Lane in
person for what happened, but the odor of the catastrophe lingered in southern nostrils as events made Jackson's absence loom ever more dire.

The Campaign of Chancellorsville: A Strategic and Tactical Study (New Haven: Yale University Press,
1910), 317n.

36. Richard M. V. B. Reeves memoir, Confederate Veteran Papers, Perkins Library, Duke
University, Durham; George W. Corbett manuscript account, FSNMP; *OR* 25(1):922. A relatively
unknown account of Jackson's wounding is in *Salem (N.C.) People's Press*, May 22, 1863.

37. *OR* 25(1):1010; Moorman, "Narrative of Events," 113–14; James H. Lane to A. C. Hamlin, [1892], Lane Papers, AU; James H. Lane to A. C. Hamlin, n.d., in Jackson, *Memoirs*, 557.

Major Barry certainly suffered no retardation of advancement, moving upward through three ranks to brigadier general in just more than a year after Chancellorsville. Even so, family lore holds that Barry carried Jackson's fate on his soul and ended the war a heartbroken man. That tradition suggests that Barry succumbed to melancholia when he died in 1867 at the age of twenty-seven, less than two years after the war's end.[38]

Given Stonewall Jackson's immense fame, it is hardly surprising that a wide range of Federals sought credit for having fired the fatal bullets. Some of them are ingenuous and credible, though errant; others are palpable hoaxes of varying caliber. One of many apt rejections of the notion of Federal responsibility came from a Confederate surgeon close to the front who saw the muzzle flashes of the fatal volleys. "Our men jumped up and seized their arms," he recalled, but the regimental commander steadied them by saying logically: "Those are our men firing, you did not hear any bullets pass our way." Among the reasonably modulated, but mistaken, Federal claims are those from the 46th Pennsylvania, 124th New York, 20th Massachusetts, and 1st Massachusetts.[39]

The most widely repeated Federal claim is also the most ludicrous. General Joseph W. Revere, a grandson of the 1775 lantern-watching horseman, concocted soon after the war a fantastic fable worthy of Baron von Munchhausen. Revere insisted that in the spring of 1852 he had met Major Thomas J. Jackson on a Mississippi riverboat. The major, suddenly both irreligious and garrulous for the only time in his adult life, forced upon Revere his notions of

38. Conversation of the author with E. M. "Tiny" Hutton, aide to U.S. congressman Thomas N. Downing of Virginia, in 1975. Hutton, who died in 1979, had familial connections with the Barry clan and had always heard the story told in this fashion.

39. Wright, "Recollections"; Selfridge, "Who Shot Stonewall Jackson?" (for 46th Pennsylvania claims); Charles H. Weygant, *History of the One Hundred and Twenty-fourth Regiment, N.Y.S.V.* (Newburgh, N.Y.: Journal Printing House, 1877), 110–13; John L. Parker, *History of the Twenty-second Massachusetts Infantry* (Boston: Press of Rand Avery Company, 1887), 301 (for 20th Massachusetts claims); J. H. Stine, *History of the Army of the Potomac* (Philadelphia: J. B. Rodgers, 1892), 358–61; Nicholas Murray Butler, *A Little Fifer's War Diary* (Syracuse, N.Y.: C. W. Bardeen, 1910), 190. Selfridge's account is the most believable of the Federal claims. Henry Kyd Douglas, a quondam member of Jackson's staff but not a paragon of reliability, wrote years later, "I heard then & believe the shot in the right hand was from the enemy" (Douglas marginalia on his copy of G. F. R. Henderson, *Stonewall Jackson and the American Civil War*, 2:555, Antietam National Battlefield, Sharpsburg, Md.). The right hand wound was the one most unequivocally demonstrable as of Confederate origin. Another flurry of "Who Killed Jackson?" articles appeared in the *National Tribune*, September 23, October 14, November 4, November 18, and December 9, 1926. Correspondence between H. McGuire and Jed Hotchkiss, ridiculing tales of Federal origins for the fatal shots, dated May 16 to June 22, 1896, is in the Hotchkiss Papers, Alderman Library, University of Virginia, Charlottesville.

astrology. Sometime later, Jackson the star gazer forwarded an elaborate chart showing that Saturn, Mars, and Jupiter would be aligned in a manner "quite dangerous and malign" in the first days of (mirabile dictu) May 1863. "It is clear to me," Jackson supposedly told Revere, "that we shall both be exposed to a common danger at the time indicated."

The northern general was positioned opposite the Second Corps on the night of May 2. He claimed to have ridden upon a knot of shadowy figures tending a wounded officer—Stonewall Jackson, of course. Most of Revere's fable is susceptible to thorough debunking from available documents. The notion of a mysterious "dark rider" observing through the bushes, however, got a boost from an early Jackson biography that recorded such an event with eager relish. The "silent personage," his identity "left to conjecture" by the biographer—reminiscent of der grau Fremde of Mozart's last days—appealed to mid-nineteenth-century tastes. In consequence, Revere's chimerical nonsense received wide play. Revere's own Chancellorsville experience, Jackson fantasies aside, put him under a cloud. A court-martial found him guilty of misbehavior before the enemy. Perhaps dabbling creatively with the riveting story of Jackson's wounding seemed like a useful diversion to the besieged Revere.[40]

More than a few Confederates also launched whoppers about Jackson's death, some of them genuinely convinced in their dotage that fading memories placed them in the spotlight. Others employed uncomplicated, garden-variety lies. A longtime colleague of evangelist Dwight L. Moody announced in 1914 that he had shot Stonewall by accident (then supported the wounded hero's head on an overcoat from his pack—"the same one that Gen McPherson had died on at Atlanta"). A member of the distant 1st Louisiana admitted late in life that he really fired the shot. A Virginia officer announced that he drove Jackson's ambulance to the rear—well before sundown on May 2! A kinswoman of the general's widow spun a delicious tale, tongue firmly in cheek, about Jackson's escape and reappearance at his wife's door in 1888 (she

40. Joseph W. Revere, *Keel and Saddle: A Retrospect of Forty Years of Military and Naval Service* (Boston: James R. Osgood, 1872), 254–57, 276–77; John Esten Cooke, *Stonewall Jackson: A Military Biography* (New York: D. Appleton, 1866), 422. Revere's imaginary construction is thoroughly demolished in Jubal A. Early, "Stonewall Jackson—The Story of His Being an Astrologer Refuted—An Eye-witness Describes How He Was Wounded," in *SHSP*, 6:261–82 (published earlier in *Southern Magazine* 12 [1873]: 537–55). The proceedings of the court that found Revere guilty of misbehavior at Chancellorsville are in Record Group 153, Records of the Judge Advocate General's Office (Army), Entry 15, Court Martial Cases, File #mm118, NA. I have the diligent and knowledgeable Thos. and Bev Lowry of the Index Project to thank for a synopsis of Revere's trial.

sequestered the prodigal in a closet and supplied him with Gideon Bibles and lemons). The most outlandish of the fables depicts Jackson changing places with a Yankee, going west to become prominent as the scout "California Joe," and dying under the guns of Swiss assassins hired by a thorough and vengeful U. S. Grant in 1876.[41]

Another spectacularly ludicrous account of Jackson's wounding appeared in a glossy magazine in 1999. It insists that a disgruntled member of the 10th Virginia Infantry named Preston Layman managed to fire a fatal shot somehow, despite his regiment's location far from the scene and despite a dozen other starkly contradictory facts. No one ever went broke underestimating the taste of the American public, as a sage has well said: such blague reflects poorly on authors and publishers in the long run but sells tabloids in the short term.[42]

None of these digressions from the truth has any intrinsic historical significance. Taken together, however, they and many others like them illustrate anew the tremendous stature of Jackson. Such figures, grown immeasurably larger than life, always attract quaintly American nonsense. The Jackson of legend looms as large on the nation's historical landscape as any figure of any era and therefore inevitably receives his share of the foolishness.

Three balls hit Jackson, even though he was among the farthest from the offending muskets of any of the nineteen Confederates in the two scouting

41. J. S. F. Saul account, 1914, in E. M. Douglas to Librarian of Congress, May 20, 1941, Ms. AC65077, LC; "Who Fired the Bullet That Killed Stonewall Jackson?," *Rockbridge County News*, January 12, 1951; James H. Lane to A. C. Hamlin, [1892], Lane Papers, AU; Augusta Eugenia Barringer, "A Definitive Account of the 'Wounding' and Death of Thos. J. ('Stonewall') Jackson," typescript, in the author's possession; John Murphy accounts, in letters of Roy A. Wykoff to Fredericksburg-area newspapers, October 10, 27, 1958, FSNMP. Three earnest but unreliable claims are in *Blackwood's Magazine*, October 1930; A. C. Atkins manuscript account, NCDAH; and Randolph, *With Stonewall Jackson*. The Barringer burlesque on the subject is very cleverly done but was rejected by conservative editors early in this century.

42. Jame E. T. Lange and Katherine DeWitt, Jr., "Was Stonewall Jackson Fragged," *North & South* 2 (February 1999): 10–15. A skilled rejoinder by Stephen W. Sears appeared in the same organ, 2 (September 1999): 5, together with a really fatuous counter by the authors. The editor of that journal had solicited my opinion of a draft that, amazingly, called the general Thomas Jefferson Jackson, had the 10th Virginia in the Stonewall Brigade, and otherwise displayed the trappings of stunning historical confusion, fairy tales aside. The editor ignored my response, which suggested that, although "the booboisie has a limitless appetite for foolish tales, especially if they involve conspiracy and improbable nonsense," the magazine should reject the article "in the interest of dignity and prudence." The original of the familiar "underestimating" quote in full was: "No one in this world, so far as I know—and I have searched the record for years, and employed agents to help me—has ever lost money by underestimating the intelligence of the great masses of the plain people" (H. L. Mencken, "Notes on Journalism," *Chicago Tribune*, September 19, 1926).

parties. A. P. Hill's detachment, much closer and less screened by woods, suffered dreadfully. The general himself, unlike his nine companions, responded to an instinctive voice and "lay down on his face in the road" rather than dashing into the woods. That reaction saved him. Just to his right, Captain Boswell instantly fell dead, two bullets (rifled, not smoothbore) through his heart. Two men in Jackson's party saw Boswell's famous black stallion dash toward the enemy, loose chain halter rattling furiously, and rightly feared the worst for their comrade.[43]

Major Palmer's horse was killed and his shoulder was broken in the melee: "My right arm was torn from the socket," he recalled, "and for some time I lay insensible." Captain Conway R. Howard's horse took a bullet, panicked, and carried his helpless rider through most of the Federal army to the Chancellorsville clearing; along the way, fire that was poured at him cut away the reins and the stirrups but left Howard untouched, albeit a prisoner. Sergeant George W. Tucker underwent an almost identical ordeal and found himself being interrogated by General Joseph Hooker's staff at Chancellorsville Inn. Bullets killed courier Eugene L. Saunders, hit courier Richard J. Muse in the face twice (he survived), and killed Muse's horse. James F. Forbes was mortally wounded and died during the night at Melzi Chancellor's house. The only two staff members not killed, injured, or captured were Benjamin Watkins Leigh and Murray Forbes Taylor, each of whose horses was killed. Only A. P. Hill among his ten-man party escaped unscathed together with his mount. Hill was trying to pry the helpless Lieutenant Taylor out from under his horse, dead from five bullet wounds, when word came that Jackson lay wounded to the front. "Help yourself," Hill muttered to Taylor, "I must go to Gen. Jackson."[44]

43. Palmer, "Another Account," 233; Randolph, *With Stonewall Jackson*, 9; R. E. Wilbourn to Jubal A. Early, March 3, 1873, vol. 6, Early Papers, LC; Hotchkiss to his wife, May 19, 1863, Hotchkiss Papers, LC. A sketchbook that was in Boswell's shirt pocket survives at the Museum of the Confederacy, Richmond, Virginia, showing the clear imprint of a rifled minié ball that passed through it.

44. Account by William H. Palmer in his papers, VHS; Taylor, "Stonewall Jackson's Death," 493–94; James H. Lane to A. C. Hamlin, [1892], Lane Papers, AU; Palmer, "Another Account," 233; anonymous Hill staff member, in "Stonewall Jackson!," *Richmond Dispatch*, October 26, 1875; R. E. Wilbourn to R. L. Dabney, December 12, 1863, Dabney Papers, SHC; typescript of Murray Forbes Taylor account, in the author's possession; Lane, "Death of Stonewall Jackson"; B. W. Leigh, "The Wounding of Stonewall Jackson," *SHSP*, 6:232; O'Sullivan, *55th Virginia Infantry*, 142, 149; Eugene L. Saunders and Richard J. Muse Compiled Service Records, M324, rolls 967, 969, NA. Tucker survived to be the sole companion of A. P. Hill under similar melancholy circumstances in April 1865. Leigh shared Hill's instinct to dismount and lie down, but his horse "was

Jackson's party suffered less drastically than Hill's, at least in quantity, as would be expected because of its distance from the flash point. Bullets killed signal corps courier William E. Cunliffe "[with]in a few feet of Gen. J" and wounded courier Joshua O. Johns. The latter's horse carried him into enemy hands to join Tucker and Howard. Morrison's and courier Lloyd T. Smith's horses were killed, but seven animals escaped harm. Jackson's other four companions—Wilbourn, Randolph, Wynn, and Kyle—remained untouched, man and horse. Wilbourn correctly attributed the escape of most of the party to "the thickness of the woods [which] afforded some shield." To that physical factor Wilbourn insistently appended his conviction that "nothing but the gracious interposition of divine Providence saved any of us . . . [or] none of the party would have survived to give an account of this melancholy event." A less relentlessly devout mind would have wondered whether Providence cared—or whether it had perhaps rejected Thomas Jackson as a ward. Six of the nine men in the group were untouched by bullets. Since five bullets found their mark in the nine-man cavalcade, Jackson's odds of being hit at all were only one in two. For three of the five bullets to hit one man—the devout and invaluable Jackson—defied the odds by a staggering ratio and surely must have prompted even hardened pietistic zealots to reconsider some dearly held tenets.[45]

By the time A. P. Hill reached Stonewall, aides had lifted their stricken chief from his horse and begun initial treatment of his wounds. The general suffered from four injuries—three bullet wounds and a scratched face. The scratches, ugly but inconsequential in the struggle for life that lay ahead, came from a post oak on the southern side of the Mountain Road with a limb that extended northward to the road's edge. Little Sorrel had wheeled violently away from the muzzle blasts along the 18th North Carolina's line and passed under the limb, which had "come near pulling" the wounded rider out of the saddle. Wilbourn's horse followed with like results. Both men lost their hats but managed to stay mounted. Jackson somehow caught the bridle in his right hand, which was mangled by a bullet, and by agonizing exertion turned the animal back toward the Confederate line. He was unable to stop Little Sorrel

---

rearing and plunging so violently that I could not do so." Then a bullet hit the animal, which made a "frantic leap—and whether he threw me or I managed to get off myself, I am unable to say," Leigh admitted.

45. R. E. Wilbourn to [John Esten Cooke], May 1863, Charles J. Faulkner Papers, VHS; J. G. Morrison to R. L. Dabney, October 29, 1863, and Wilbourn to Dabney, December 12, 1863, Dabney Papers, SHC; Bruce, *History of Virginia*, 5:286.

General Hill binding the wounds of General "Stonewall" Jackson

completely. Jackson's "terribly" lacerated face would be repaired hours later with isinglass.[46]

One of the three bullets that hit Jackson tore through the inside of his right palm, that arm having been raised either to shield his face from the brush, in instinctive reaction to the fire, or in a typical gesture of prayerful supplication. A soldier in William Dorsey Pender's brigade found Jackson's gloves the next day (with "T. J. JACKSON, Virginia . . . printed neatly on the wrist of each") and eventually sent them to the general's widow. Mary Anna Jackson kept them as "a harrowing relic indeed, but . . . I could not bear that *anyone else* should have them." The right gauntlet showed an entry wound "just above the base of the thumb." The missile broke two fingers and caused enough damage

46. Kyle manuscript account, FSNMP; R. E. Wilbourn to R. L. Dabney, December 12, 1863, Dabney Papers, SHC; Kyle, "Jackson's Guide," 308; anonymous Hill staff member, in "Stonewall Jackson!," *Richmond Dispatch*, October 26, 1875. A soldier later found Jackson's cap and gave it to General Pender (Wm. D. H. Covington [38th North Carolina] to Mary Anna Jackson, June 26, 1863, WVU; two unidentified newspaper clippings on the same topic accompany the original letter).

to fill the glove with blood by the time A. P. Hill gently pulled it from Jackson's hand. The projectile, a round ball and therefore surely Confederate ammunition, lodged just under the skin on the back of the general's hand. Mary Anna Jackson retained the round ball as another terrible memento. "It almost breaks my heart to look at it," she told a friend that July.[47]

The other two bullets did far more damage. Both hit Jackson's left arm. Each caused enough destruction to warrant amputation of the arm according to the current surgical practices. The forearm wound, however, actually escaped attention for hours because a more serious wound near the shoulder made the lower extremity numb. Surgeon McGuire, who performed the amputation, described the lower ball as "having entered the outside of the forearm, an inch below the elbow [and] came out upon the opposite side, just above the wrist." In an earlier account, McGuire placed the exit wound "through the palm of the hand," but the hole in the left glove was "on the wrist, near the top." The rain slicker that was Jackson's outer garment survives and shows a bullet hole low on the forearm, apparently the lower entry point. No visible exit hole for the wound exists high on the left arm, but there are ample alternative explanations for that fact.[48]

Jackson suffered most from the bullet that shattered his upper left arm. It struck, McGuire wrote, "about three inches below the shoulder-joint, the ball

47. McGuire, *Confederate Cause and Conduct*, 222; Wm. D. H. Covington to Mary Anna Jackson, June 26, 1863 (and newspaper clippings), WVU; R. E. Wilbourn to R. L. Dabney, December 12, 1863, Dabney Papers, SHC; Mary Anna Jackson to Mrs. Brown, July 9, 1863, Wimberley Library, Florida Atlantic University, Boca Raton. A claim to possession of another of the deadly rounds is in "It Killed Stonewall Jackson," *Fredericksburg Free Lance*, January 23, 1897. More evidence on the recovered gloves and caps is in S. J. Greene to A. C. Hamlin, March 17, 1894, ACH Papers/Harvard.

48. R. E. Wilbourn to R. L. Dabney, December 12, 1863, Dabney Papers, SHC, says of the wound in Jackson's lower left arm that "no one knew of it till the surgeon got ready to amputate" (and Wilbourn provided initial first aid). The same evidence is in "Lt. [James Power] Smith's Narrative," Dabney Papers, SHC. McGuire's more formal account is in *Confederate Cause and Conduct*, 222; a sketchier early version obviously by him is in the *Richmond Enquirer*, May 13, 1863. The physical evidence from the glove is in news clippings accompanying Wm. D. H. Covington to Mary Anna Jackson, June 26, 1863, WVU. The slicker is at the Virginia Military Institute, Lexington. Evidence from the gauntlet (no doubt pulled very high up the wrist) and rain slicker may show an exit point for the lower wound, with entry through a now-repaired segment of the coat. McGuire's evidence on the entry point seems immutable. I am grateful to the efficient and cordial Colonel Keith E. Gibson of VMI for measuring and drawing both the raincoat and Jackson's handkerchief (see n. 52).

dividing the main artery, and fracturing the bone." The bullet-torn slicker bears a hole precisely three inches down the sleeve, and Jackson's arm certainly was fractured. McGuire may have been mistaken in his presumption that the ball severed the main artery, however, in light of evidence explained below.[49]

Captain Wilbourn and General Hill performed most of the first aid that Jackson received while still beyond the Confederate front line. Getting Jackson dismounted had been difficult for both the general and Wilbourn, one of whose arms was essentially useless because of an old wound not yet fully healed. Fortunately, Jackson had fallen against his aide's good side as he collapsed off of Little Sorrel's back. Soon thereafter, A. P. Hill had arrived. Hill's expressions of sorrow have often been represented as a sort of deathbed rapprochement with Jackson, the generals having been starkly at odds for many months theretofore. In fact, recently uncovered evidence shows that the two men had somehow worked their way to good terms by the eve of the Chancellorsville campaign.[50]

Between them, Hill and Wilbourn ripped open the layers of sleeves concealing Jackson's damaged arm, pulled off his blood-filled gauntlets, and applied primitive bandages. An arriving staff officer found Hill with Jackson's "head on his breast." They tied handkerchiefs above and below the upper-arm

49. McGuire, *Confederate Cause and Conduct*, 222; *Richmond Enquirer*, May 13, 1863. For the remarkable career of Jackson's rain slicker, which traveled around the world, sometimes in anonymity, see David F. Riggs, "Stonewall Jackson's Raincoat," *Civil War Times Illustrated* 16 (July 1977): 36–41. (See also "Sold for a Gallon of Meal," *Fredericksburg Free Lance*, July 28, 1891, and "The Coat Worn by Gen. Jackson When Killed," *Fredericksburg Free Lance*, June 12, 1888.) Other relics of the event included Jackson's field glass and haversack (which contained papers, envelopes, and two religious tracts), picked up by Wilbourn (R. E. Wilbourn to R. L. Dabney, December 12, 1863, Dabney Papers, SHC); a book of Napoleon's maxims that had been a gift from J. E. B. Stuart (Douglas Southall Freeman, *A Calendar of Confederate Papers* [Richmond: Confederate Museum, 1908], 519n); and a medicine case ("Has Relic of 'Stonewall,'" *Fredericksburg Free Lance*, December 8, 1914).

50. "Statement of James P. Smith, A.D.C. of the circumstances connected with the wounding of Lt. Gen. Jackson and his removal from the field," Jedediah Hotchkiss Papers, New York Historical Society, New York; R. E. Wilbourn to R. L. Dabney, December 12, 1863, Dabney Papers, SHC. The evidence of an accommodation between the generals is in an account by Conway R. Howard to Jed Hotchkiss recorded in Hotchkiss's notes on blank pages of an 1857 Mossy Creek Academy catalog under the title "Incidents Relating to the Life of Gen. Jackson Compiled by Jed. Hotchkiss Capt. & Top. Engr. 2nd Corps A.N.Va.," University of Virginia. Howard's matter-of-fact, detailed account rings true and seems reliable. I thank Steve Ritchie of Indiana for the discovery of this rich, untapped source of Jackson material.

General "Stonewall" Thomas J. Jackson Raincoat

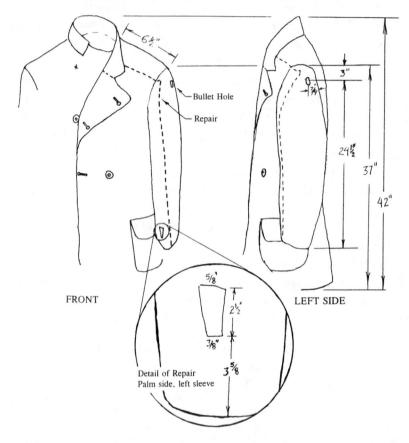

Diagram indicating location of bullet holes in the rain slicker Jackson wore on the night of May 2, 1863. The garment is in the Virginia Military Institute Collection. Sketch by Colonel Keith E. Gibson.

wound and fashioned a third handkerchief into a sling. Although Jackson had of course bled considerably from his torn and broken arm, it seems likely that the artery had not yet ruptured. Wilbourn wrote not long after the event that the wound "had apparently ceased bleeding and we indulged the hope that the artery was not cut." When surgeon Benjamin P. Wright of the 55th Virginia reached the general and examined the arm, he found that the ersatz bandaging had already been done and noted that "the hemorrhage had been slight." A tourniquet soon arrived and Hill suggested that Wright put it on Jackson, but the lack of bleeding seemed to make the appliance superfluous.[51]

Surviving physical evidence supports the notion that Stonewall Jackson's bleeding had been controlled and was therefore presumably only venous. The general's daughter gave one of the handkerchiefs that had bound the wound to the Virginia Military Institute after the war. Too small to have been the sling, it must have been used to bandage the wound, yet the linen material is blood-spotted rather than drenched or heavily stained. No more than 10 percent of the material is affected.[52]

More than a dozen officers and men tended Stonewall Jackson as his aides moved him in agonizing stages toward the rear. The journey proceeded by mixed means, all of them interdicted by savage artillery fire. He first was carried awkwardly by three aides, who took laborious steps while supporting him, and then transported in three or four spells on a litter. Most of the men who took part in this phase of what would become the Confederacy's Passion Play left accounts of their involvement—some confused or exaggerated but most reasonably reliable. That halting hegira, leading inexorably toward an amputation table, lies beyond the scope of this essay about the fatal volley. Two painful falls along the route, however, must be examined in order to weigh the impact of the volley.

Jackson fell from the litter a first time when an enlisted man bearing the front left corner was shot down with serious wounds to both arms. Private John James Johnson, Company H, 22nd Virginia Battalion, lost his right arm at the shoulder socket, and his left arm was "so completely paralysed as to be useless." The same fire wounded at least one other of the stretcher men at the same time. A contemporary source reported that the litter bearers had been carrying Jackson at shoulder height, and Joe Morrison estimated that "the General fell about 3 feet." With jagged bone ends adjacent to the delicate

51. R. E. Wilbourn to Jubal A. Early, February 12, 1873, in Early, *Autobiographical Sketch*, 215–16; R. E. Wilbourn to R. L. Dabney, December 12, 1863, Dabney Papers, SHC; "Lt. [James Power] Smith's Narrative" in same collection; Wright, "Recollections."

52. Information and a measured drawing of the handkerchief from VMI. The linen bears Jackson's name and came directly from his daughter Julia. It measures 40.5 by 50.5 centimeters and is therefore far too small to have supported an arm as a sling. The deadly hemorrhaging that occurred after Jackson's two falls from the litter presumably flowed away (down the arm) from this handkerchief; but the initial frantic treatment—in pitch darkness—of a shattered arm with a severed artery would hardly have left the modest stains this linen piece bears.

This 1876 engraving depicts Jackson (third from left) walking with assistance soon after his wounding.

surface of the artery, a consequence of the fall must have been tearing of the vessel and resultant profuse bleeding. The party at the time had been cutting "obliquely across the . . . Plank road for the road that led to stoney ford . . . which is about two hundred yards from where he was put on the litter."[53]

Everyone agreed that this first fall caused Jackson incredible suffering. His brother-in-law Joe Morrison marveled that the general "did not even groan," but others heard Jackson moan "frequently and piteously." One account, late and with hearsay ancestry, declared that the general's left arm landed squarely on a roadside stump.[54] Since Jackson apparently fell from near shoulder height, and certainly must have been lying face-up on the litter, the sudden collapse of the left front corner of the litter would have put his right shoulder at immediate risk. From that height, however, and considering the credible reports of the damage and suffering inflicted on the battered arm, it is evident that the fall spun Jackson in an arc that landed his excruciatingly painful left side on the ground.

A second fall from the litter ensured the final destruction of Jackson's left arm. Three enlisted men and one officer carried the general through dense woods just south of the Plank Road, the officer supporting the front right corner. One of the soldiers "got his foot entangled in a grape vine and fell," Major Benjamin Watkins Leigh recalled, "letting General Jackson fall on his broken arm. . . . He must have suffered agonies." Leigh reported that this fall elicited the first audible indication of suffering from Jackson, but Morrison considered it "very light" in contrast with the first fall. Private Durant W. Busick of the 22nd North Carolina, who was one of the men helping with the

53. Kyle, "Jackson's Guide," 308–9; *Richmond Enquirer*, May 13, 1863; R. E. Wilbourn to R. L. Dabney, December 12, 1863, Dabney Papers, SHC; "Stonewall Jackson's Death," in *SHSP*, 10:143; J. G. Morrison to Jubal A. Early, February 20, 1879, vol. 10, Early Papers, LC; Kyle manuscript account, FSNMP. The good people of Fluvanna County raised money to buy Johnson "a little place and house, where he can be comfortably situated," although he was so badly hurt that he could not even feed himself. Johnson was living there in 1882, a solid but "very poor" citizen. He died October 26, 1899 ("Death of a Soldier Who Was Wounded When Carrying Stonewall Jackson from the Field," *Fredericksburg Free Lance*, November 9, 1899). The obituary, quoting Johnson, says two bearers were hit. A contemporary account ("Stonewall Jackson," *Winston (N.C.) Western Sentinel*, May 15, 1863), reported that all four bearers went down.

54. J. G. Morrison to R. L. Dabney, October 29, 1863, Dabney Papers, SHC; R. E. Wilbourn to Jubal A. Early, February 12, 1873, in Early, *Autobiographical Sketch*, 217; Wilbourn to Dabney, December 12, 1863, Dabney Papers, SHC; H. H. McGuire, "Jackson's Death," *Fredericksburg Star*, March 24, 1886; W. L. Goldsmith, in *Tales of the Civil War*, ed. C. R. Graham (Boston: Perry Mason, 1896), 519–20. The account of landing on a stump is from Bosserman, "Bullets Didn't Kill 'Stonewall' Jackson," whose late-life rambling deserves little credence.

Jackson arriving at McGuire's ambulance, in an 1888 engraving.

litter, attributed the stumble to tripping over one of the bodies of Confederates strewn thickly throughout the woods. Whatever the obstacle that caused the second drop, the consequences of the two incidents were damaging and perhaps fatal.[55]

The solid evidence from multiple sources that Jackson's arm was not bleeding at all when his trip to the rear began suggests that the artery remained intact at that point. When the general reached McGuire after the two falls, however, he had "lost a large amount of blood . . . and would have bled to death, but a tourniquet was immediately applied. For two hours he was nearly

55. Kyle manuscript account, FSNMP; Leigh, "Wounding of Stonewall Jackson," 233–34; J. G. Morrison to Jubal A. Early, February 20, 1879, vol. 10, Early Papers, LC; "Stonewall Jackson's Death," 143; "Who Killed Stonewall Jackson," *Shepherdstown Register*, November 26, 1881.

pulseless." Jackson calmly informed McGuire, "I fear I am dying." In sharp contrast to his normal habits, the suffering man asked repeatedly and urgently for spirits. McGuire found his patient's "skin clammy, his face pale, and his lips compressed and bloodless . . . and the thin lips so tightly compressed that the impression of his teeth could be seen through them."[56]

Pneumonia killed Stonewall Jackson on May 10. The fatal malady's etiology likely lay in an upper-respiratory infection that predated the wounds. Jackson's severe hurts, of course, impaired his body's ability to fight its battle against pneumonia, which almost certainly would not have developed, or at least not proved fatal, without the injuries. Was the trauma from the bullets' impact or the nearly fatal loss of blood from the subsequent litter accidents the decisive blow? Although the answer to this question can only be speculated, it is difficult to avoid the conclusion that the arterial bleeding constituted the greatest problem; the two falls therefore must be considered the fatal events. Jackson felt certain that he was dying at the time. Ten days after his death, a Virginia newspaper wrote that Jackson "himself attributed [the pneumonia] to the fall from the litter." The word throughout the army was that McGuire felt similarly, having commented "that the Genl's death was caused by the fall which he got when being carried off of the field . . . injuring the Gen's side so severely that he caught cold in it, and consequently could not get over so many diseases."[57]

The effect of Jackson's demise is incalculable, falling as it does into the realm of hypothesis. That it would affect Confederate morale immediately and harshly was so evident to all concerned that they made strenuous—but unavailing—efforts to conceal the fact of the wounding. As more than one contemporary noted, "in a very short time everybody knew it." Major W. G. Morris of the 37th North Carolina had rolled into a roadside ditch to nurse a wounded foot when Jackson's litter party halted within a few feet of him.

56. *Richmond Enquirer*, May 13, 1863; H. H. McGuire, in Jackson, *Memoirs*, 433; R. E. Wilbourn to R. L. Dabney, December 12, 1863, Dabney Papers, SHC; H. H. McGuire, in "Stonewall Jackson!," *Richmond Dispatch*, October 26, 1875. An interesting account of Jackson in the ambulance is William R. Whitehead, "Life and Experiences of an American Surgeon," manuscript narrative at the Denver Medical Library, Denver, Colo. Whitehead was surgeon of the 44th Virginia Infantry.

57. *Lexington (Va.) Gazette*, May 20, 1863; "The Civil War Diary of Peter W. Hairston," *North Carolina Historical Review* 67 (January 1990): 77; Daniel Perrin Bestor to "Dear Sister," June 1, 1863, Lida B. Robertson Papers, Alabama Department of Archives and History, Montgomery, Ala.

Morris until then had been "feeling cheerfull and comparatively happy" despite his pain. "You cant imagine what a change the thought of . . . Jackson being wounded made in my feelings," he wrote years later.[58]

Confederates yearned in vain for Stonewall's recovery, sensing the impact his absence would have. Not a few northerners greeted the general's death with mixed feelings. General Gouverneur K. Warren, soon to be a great northern hero at Gettysburg, wrote: "I rejoice at Stonewall Jackson's death as a gain to our cause, and yet in my soldier's heart I cannot but see him the best soldier of all this war, and grieve at his untimely end." An observant Englishman admitted that the dead leader "was not a great strategist" but marveled at Jackson's capacity for "triumphing over difficulties which stood in his way with a facility unknown to any other General." Because Jackson was the most famous American in Europe, his death made stunning headline news there.[59]

Southern patriots of pious bent filled their letters during May and June 1863 with resigned declarations about God's will and his obvious intention to raise up another Jackson to defend the cause. Such eager expectations constituted a classic case of whistling in the cemetery—the Lexington Cemetery, in this instance. Less naive soldiers, facing combat that now seemed more dangerous and less likely to succeed in the absence of their indomitable leader, sadly accepted the probability that their side had lost an irreplaceable asset. A member of the 26th Georgia wrote dolefully on May 15 that "all hopes of Peace and Independence had forever vanished." Two members of Lane's brigade reacted in a similar vein. Wesley Lewis Battle of the 37th North Carolina declared, "I don't think his place can ever be filled." Ross Marcius Gaston of the 28th North Carolina, in a postwar reminiscence, reflected: "We never got over Jackson's death, for all the men lost all hopes of success after he was gone." Joshua Howell of the 47th Alabama minced no words in describing the prospects to his wife in a letter dated May 14: "Stonewall Jackson was kild. . . . I think this will have a gradeal to due with this war. I think the north will whip us soon."[60] And so it came to pass, perhaps in some degree as the result

58. Goldsmith in Graham, *Tales of the Civil War*, 519–20; W. G. Morris to James H. Lane, January 3, 1895, folder 113, Lane Papers, AU (copy also in the ACH Papers/Harvard).

59. Emerson G. Taylor, *Gouverneur Kemble Warren: The Life and Letters of an American Soldier* (Boston: Houghton Mifflin, 1932), 112; "The Memory of Stonewall Jackson in England," *Columbia (S.C.) Daily Southern Guardian*, June 23, 1863; London *Times*, June 17, 1863; Anna J. P. Shaff[n]er, *Stonewall Jackson* (Washington, D.C.: N.p., 1936), 3.

60. Joseph Hilton to "Dear Cousin," May 15, 1863, Joseph Hilton Papers, Georgia Historical Society, Savannah; Wesley Lewis Battle to his father, May 16, 1863, Battle Family Papers, SHC;

of self-fulfilling prophecies like Howell's but primarily because Stonewall Jackson was no more.

A tangled skein of tactical developments led a teenaged sergeant to order a shot against a lost Yankee in the woods near Chancellorsville that dark night of May 2, 1863. The spark inevitably flared into fire from nearby lines. The firing spread northward, instinctive and unreasoning. It eventually resulted in the discharge of several hundred musket balls and rifled bullets eastward from the front of the 18th North Carolina toward the backs of friendly skirmishers—and through A. P. Hill's and Thomas J. Jackson's parties in the intervening ground. Most of the several dozen projectiles spinning toward Stonewall's precise location buried themselves in, or were deflected by, the dense growth that crowded the fire zone. The five that tore human flesh in Jackson's group were fiendishly effective. Six of Jackson's eight escorts escaped untouched. The relatively immense target that the general bestrode, Little Sorrel, remained unhit. As though vectored specially toward Jackson, three bullets missed every impediment and every other target, dodged precipitous laws of averages, and mortally wounded Lee's right arm. Nothing could have done more harm to the Army of Northern Virginia and to the nascent nation for which that army was the sturdiest underpinning.

Ross Marcius Gaston reminiscence, box 70, folder 52, Military Collection, NCDAH; Joshua Howell to his wife, typescript, May 14, 1863, FSNMP.

2

The Army of Northern Virginia's Most Notorious
Court-Martial: Jackson vs. Garnett

In March 1862, Thomas Jonathan Jackson stood on the brink of a campaign that would catapult him to immediate international fame. Eight months earlier he had won his nom de guerre at Manassas as a brigade commander. For four of the intervening months, "Stonewall" Jackson had commanded a small and somewhat raw Confederate force in Virginia's beautiful—and strategically crucial—Shenandoah Valley.

The four months in the Valley from November 1861 to early March 1862 had been more productive of frustration and discord than of substantial achievement. A winter campaign west and north from Winchester had been marginally successful, despite savage weather, until the campaign had fallen apart as the result of interference by the woefully inept War Department in Richmond. The buffoonery at the national capital actually prompted Jackson to resign. That remarkable denouement was deflected only as a result of hard work by interested Virginia politicians.

When General Jackson assumed command of the Shenandoah Valley, he needed a brigadier general to take over the leadership of his old brigade, the famous Stonewall Brigade, which shared Jackson's name and fame. He requested A. P. Hill (soon to become a strident adversary), and if he could not have Hill he wanted Robert E. Rodes. Instead, the authorities in Richmond sent out Richard Brooke Garnett, who had just won the wreath of a brigadier general, effective November 14, 1861.[1]

This chapter first appeared, without footnotes, in *Blue & Gray Magazine* 3 (July 1986): 27–32. It is reprinted here, with substantial revisions and additions, by permission.

1. T. J. Jackson to Maj. T. E. Rhett, Hd Qrs. Dept of N. Va., November 11, 1861, in posses-

When he moved to the Valley to take command of the Stonewall Brigade, Garnett left a role subordinate to the arrogant and querulous Colonel Thomas R. R. Cobb. The freshly minted general must have welcomed the chance to operate on a new stage away from Cobb's carping (though in fact Cobb had rather liked Garnett). It cannot have taken long for Garnett to discover that his new superior, though neither arrogant nor carping, was virtually impossible to please. As early as the second week in January, Jackson was writing to the secretary of war to declare that "General G. is not qualified to command a Brigade." He declared that he did not "feel safe in bringing [the brigade] into action under the present commander, as he has satisfied me that he is not able to meet emergencies even in the proper management . . . in camp and on the march."[2] Dick Garnett obviously approached his first battle under a tactical microscope.

Jackson had been in Confederate service for nearly a year by mid-March but had not commanded troops in an independent action of any size. His small army's bitter, bloody baptism at Kernstown on March 23, 1862, changed all of that and inaugurated a campaign that is among the most famous in the history of American arms. Jackson's first battle, however, can hardly be styled the early work of a master.

Jackson fought Kernstown on the basis of two premises that he entertained. The strategic imperative was to hold the interest of Federal forces in the Valley firmly enough to keep them from moving eastward toward Richmond by way of Fredericksburg. This paramount consideration was Jackson's lodestar, conveyed to him as orders, and also obvious to him personally as the essence of his mission. The tactical framework within which Jackson made the attack that brought on Kernstown, however, was based on faulty intelligence. The bad information came from Turner Ashby, who commanded a gaggle of poorly organized but extremely active cavalry under Jackson.

The tactical disasters at Kernstown that led to the court-martial of General Richard B. Garnett were a direct consequence of Ashby's reconnaissance before the battle. Normally nothing was more certain than intelligence gathered by Turner Ashby, but when Jackson moved Garnett and the rest of the army down the Valley toward Winchester on March 22 and 23, he operated under

sion of Jack Milne, Orlando, Fla.; Garnett's official CSR in M331, "Compiled Service Records of Confederate General and Staff Officers, and Non-Regimental Enlisted Men," NA.

2. Jackson to Judah P. Benjamin, January 10, 1862, Mississippi Department of Archives and History, Jackson.

a misapprehension. Ashby had reported that the sizable enemy force at Winchester was moving eastward across the mountains, doing precisely what Jackson was charged with preventing. The small (by Ashby's estimate) remaining
Federal strength in and around Winchester apparently offered precisely what
Jackson needed: a bite-sized detachment susceptible to a Confederate on-
slaught. Overwhelming the rear guard would oblige the departing Federals to
come back to the Valley, thus fulfilling Stonewall's strategic imperative.[3]

Jackson had not intended to fight on March 23—a Sunday, and therefore
sacred to him. Once the Federals had seen his force and been alerted to the
threat the Confederates posed, the general had no real choice but to pitch
into his foe. Artillery dueled along the Valley Turnpike, the Unionist gunners
holding an advantage based on both weaponry and ground. Jackson flung the
main body of his troops toward the left, in an early and awkward version of
the flanking maneuvers that soon would make him famous. Northern units
countered and musketry roared in daunting volume. Many more Yankees
proved to be in Winchester's environs than Ashby had imagined, and they
soon made it apparent that they were ready to fight. When an aide reconnoitering on high ground estimated the enemy force at ten thousand, Jackson
muttered, "say nothing about it, we are in for it."[4] The circumstances generated by extracting the "in-for-it" army from its predicament led to the Jack-
son-Garnett quarrel.

As the battle reached its crescendo and Garnett approached his personal
crisis, the infantry combat swirled in confusion around a famed stone wall
running about east to west across a ridge that dominated the battle's tactical
heart. Ashby feinted skillfully on the pike, and artillery fired nearby, but the
infantry climax came on the ridge and along the wall, well west of the pike.
There were too many Federals to be held in check, and the Confederate line
fell apart by stages. Garnett stood in the thick of the fray and had to face the
terrible responsibility of acknowledging that the line could not be held and

---

3. For an excellent summary of the Battle of Kernstown, illustrated by first-rate maps and color
photographs, see the special issue of *Blue & Gray Magazine* cited above, in which this chapter first
appeared. By far the best detailed account of Kernstown is the book-length study by Gary L. Ecel-
barger, *"We are in for it!": The First Battle of Kernstown* (Shippensburg, Pa.: White Mane, 1997).
The present chapter's examination of the Garnett-Jackson trial resulting from Kernstown necessarily avoids any extensive discussion of the battle proper.

4. Alexander S. Pendleton to his mother, April 3, 1862, as printed in William G. Bean, ed.,
"The Valley Campaign of 1862 as Revealed in Letters of Sandie Pendleton," *Virginia Magazine of
History and Biography* 78 (1970): 342.

The famous stone wall on Kernstown Battlefield, engraved from an 1885 photograph.

that retreat was necessary to save the army. In the absence of Jackson, Garnett ordered the retreat. There is no indication that he ever regretted his decision, nor is it reasonable to insist, or even easy to estimate, that he made the wrong choice. Stonewall Jackson, it would develop, did not agree.

Jackson's satisfaction with the results of Kernstown—he had achieved his primary strategic obligation by holding Federals in the Valley—did not extend to Richard B. Garnett's behavior. Eight days after the battle, Jackson sent his aide, Lieutenant Alexander S. "Sandie" Pendleton, to Garnett's headquarters with orders to arrest the brigadier general and relieve him of his command. The unfortunate brigadier had not had the faintest inkling that anything of the sort was coming. The men of the Stonewall Brigade flew into a rage about what they perceived as the mistreatment of their current commander by his predecessor. For Dick Garnett, the unexpected arrest unleashed a torrent of woes against which he struggled during the remaining fifteen months of his life.[5]

More than four months passed between Jackson's arrest of Garnett and the convening of a court-martial to try the charges. During that time, Jackson's incredibly strong will and his equally inflexible mind subtly worked on his memory of the desperate hours at Kernstown. When he finally sorted out all of Garnett's misdeeds to his own satisfaction, Jackson reduced them to seven specific charges under the general heading of "Neglect of duty."[6] Some of them are repetitious, some of them are confused, and most of them seem to be based on misunderstandings or even outright factual mistakes by Jackson:

1. That Garnett "did, after advancing with four regiments for some distance, leave three of them in rear and continued to advance with only one," and that he later proposed moving that one advanced regiment back to join the others, leaving the 37th Virginia, under Colonel Samuel V. Fulkerson, unsupported.

2. That Garnett "did so separate himself from his command that he could not be found by Maj. F[rancis] B[uckner] Jones, who was directed to deliver him an order."

3. That Garnett "did neglect to be with his leading regiment when it went into battle." Jackson apparently had formed this notion during the battle, reject-

5. Pendleton's description of the arrest, his own evaluation of Garnett, and the brigade's dis-gruntlement is in his letter to his mother, March 29, 1862, printed in Bean, ed., "The Valley Campaign of 1862," 343–45.

6. "Charges & specifications preferred by Maj Genl T. J. Jackson P.A.C.S. against Brig Genl. R. B. Garnett P.A.C.S.," Richard B. Garnett Papers, MOC.

ing at the time as "impossible" the assertion by one of his own aides that Garnett had accompanied the leading regiment.[7]

4. That Garnett "neglected to have a regiment in supporting distance of his leading one when it went into action."

5. That Garnett "did so neglect to post his regiments properly . . . that they became mixed together, when they should have been kept separate."

6. That Garnett "did . . . give the order to fall back, when he should have encouraged his command to hold its position."

7. That Garnett ordered the reserve regiment, the 5th Virginia, "to retreat, notwithstanding [the] regiment had not yet been brought into action, and should have continued to advance on the enemy, as it was doing at the time, in obedience to orders from Maj. Genl. T. J. Jackson."

The first five of the specifications contain very little actual substance. Number 4 simply rephrases Number 1. Number 2 is insignificant, if not downright silly—for in the midst of combat, Major Jones might well be expected to bear the onus of finding a hard-pressed brigade commander rather than the reverse. Number 3 seems to contradict Number 1, at least in general terms. Number 5 overlooks the exigencies of a desperate, losing infantry fight.

The heart of the case, of course, rests in the specifications numbered 6 and 7. Did Garnett leave before he should have left? Therein lurked the real question.

Garnett carefully explicated his position in a painfully drawn letter to Adjutant and Inspector General Samuel Cooper, dated from Staunton, Virginia, on June 20, 1862.[8] Garnett had been trying earnestly to have his case brought to trial, but the viscous bureaucracy was grinding paper without result. That left Garnett to plead his case in writing, in a closely reasoned essay of sixteen handwritten pages. He expended five pages on the first specification alone, but perhaps the Garnett positions can be summarized succinctly, with a few interlineations from other witnesses:

1. The advance of the leading regiment (the 33rd Virginia) was by Jackson's orders. Its failure to conform to Fulkerson's needs was simply the inevitable result of Jackson's habitual failure to let anyone know what was happening.

7. Summary of evidence accumulated by Garnett before mid-June 1862, Colonel James W. Allen still being alive, Garnett Papers, MOC.

8. Garnett Papers, MOC. The substance of Garnett's position, enumerated in the seven points that follow, is taken from the June 20 letter. The direct quotes in that same span also come from the June 20 letter except where individual notes supply other sources.

"Though *second in command*," Garnett complained, "Jackson did not communicate to me any *plan of battle*, if he had decided on one. I was consequently entirely ignorant of his schemes and intentions." Garnett was "confident all cause of complaint . . . would have been avoided" if Jackson had told him what was going on—an unthinkable alternative for the tight-lipped army commander. [All emphases in these quotes are from the original.]

2. Garnett's two absences from his leading regiment were both for the purpose of positioning batteries to his front, for perhaps five minutes each. The colonel of the 33rd in his official report happened to mention that his regiment "was almost the whole day under the eye" of Garnett. "This remark must have been overlooked or disregarded by Gen'l. Jackson," Garnett suggested. Five field officers supported the accused's contentions in this matter, including Jackson's special pet, E. Frank Paxton. Lieutenant Elliott Johnston, a Garnett aide, wrote that his general had been absent from the infantry "only once," for "a few moments," for the eminently apt purpose of positioning the Rockbridge Artillery.[9]

3. There seemed to Garnett to be no military rule that "would oblige me" to do what Jackson suggested as necessary in the third charge, but the allegation was not true anyway. He had made careful arrangements for the use of the regiments farther back in the column, following up when the first aide sent back for that purpose had been captured. Garnett presumed that this specification actually was "a covert insinuation" about being dishonorably away from the front, as specified in Number 2.

4. The colonel of the regiment providing the first support declared that the time of Garnett's absence was "less than 10 minutes," and his lieutenant colonel "says very confidently, that it was not over 5 minutes." All five regimental commanders asserted "that they *were* in supporting distance," none farther than three hundred yards from the front.[10]

5. Garnett pointed out that overlapping of regiments was made necessary by the enemy's movements, by the "wooded and broken country," and by the limited degree of cover available to the brigade. He also noted that every battle in the war to date had been fought in similar fashion. "All the field officers testify that there was not room to post two of our Regts in line . . . on the crest of the hill."[11]

6. Jackson formed his opinion in this regard "without *personal observation*, and [the opinion] is opposed, I am fully assured, to that of all the field officers of my brigade" as well as by everyone else present. "Indeed," Garnett declared, "it has been said, by some officers of high rank, that the order to fall back had

9. Statement of Elliott Johnston, July 25, 1862, Garnett Papers, MOC.
10. Summary of evidence accumulated by Garnett before mid-June, Garnett Papers, MOC.
11. Summary of evidence accumulated by Garnett before mid-June, Garnett Papers, MOC.

not been given soon enough." Among the salient reasons for the withdrawal was the alarming fact that ammunition was entirely gone in the 27th Virginia and nearly so in the other regiments.[12]

7. Garnett denied categorically the allegation that his regiments were posted improperly and mentioned that it too was "contradicted by Colonels of my brigade, in their *submitted* official reports." Jackson's ignorance of the facts in those reports, Garnett suggested, "argues either great malice or great carelessness on the part of my accuser."

In summarizing his position, Garnett cited his accuser's own correspondence with General Joseph E. Johnston, Jackson's superior, in which Jackson admitted having been deceived about Federal strength and then forced to retire because he was greatly outnumbered. Garnett also had come into possession of a copy of a letter in which Jackson "volunteered the opinion that 'Genl. Garnett is incompetent to command a brigade, and if he was given charge of a good brigade, it would become a bad one.' " That Jackson had made such judgment behind his back and without offering any evidence or specifications offended Garnett's sense of honor. Jackson's actual language had been close to what Garnett had heard. In forwarding the charges to Richmond, Stonewall wrote: "I have no desire to see the case pressed any further, but . . . I regard Gen. Garnett as so incompetent a Brigade Commander, that instead of building up a Brigade, a good one, if turned over to him, would actually deteriorate under the command."[13]

The most telling argument against Jackson, however, was the one which Garnett repeated in closing his plea to Samuel Cooper: "I was kept in as *profound ignorance* of his plans, instructions, and intentions, as the humblest private in his army." Garnett was admitting to his greatest shortcoming, an inability to guess what the mysterious Stonewall had in mind. The defect, universal in the army, hardly warranted dismissal.[14]

The field officers of the Stonewall Brigade eagerly sought to sustain Garnett. Colonel Arthur C. Cummings of the 33rd Virginia wrote three times offering encouragement, suggesting that his testimony would be more impressive if given in person and promising to return hurriedly from sick leave for

12. Statement of Elliott Johnston, July 25, 1862, Garnett Papers, MOC.

13. Garnett to A&IG Samuel Cooper, June 20, 1862, Garnett Papers, MOC; Jackson to Cooper, April 29, 1862, entry 218 in Jackson letterbook as transcribed at Roll 49, Frame 320, Jedediah Hotchkiss Papers, LC.

14. Garnett to Samuel Cooper, June 20, 1862, Garnett Papers, MOC.

"Stonewall" Jackson on the Field

that purpose. Colonel Andrew Jackson Grigsby of the 27th Virginia, noting that he had been closest of the field officers to Garnett, wrote that he would support the general "most cheerfully," not only in writing, but also "I hope the day may soon be where I can do the same before a court."[15]

Grigsby, who had attended West Point, was a fighter of wide reputation for bravery and for undaunted cursing, "a bluff soldier much given to swearing." The latter tendency, contemporary observers concluded, was what prompted Jackson to block Grigsby's promotion to brigadier general. A here-

15. To his chagrin, Cummings did not learn of the date of the trial in time to participate. He wrote on August 9 that he was leaving promptly by train and hoped to arrive in time to testify (Cummings to F. W. M. Holliday, August 9, 1862, Holliday Papers, PLD). On the fifth and the seventh, Cummings had sent encouraging notes directly to Garnett (Garnett Papers, MOC), promising to hurry north to testify despite suffering a debilitating abscess in one arm. Even had he been present, Cummings probably would not have had an opportunity to bear witness during the abbreviated trial. A. J. Grigsby to William Garnett, July 12, 1862, Garnett Papers, MOC. Grigsby also announced his intention to write directly to the secretary of war, but that correspondence has not been found.

tofore unpublished anecdote concerning Grigsby and the Garnett affair lends credence to that theory. After the war, Thomas H. Williamson of Jackson's staff reported that in May 1862, "I was sitting with Genl. T. J. Jackson & Col. Jack Grigsby. Genl. Jackson asked Col. Grigsby if the Stonewall Brigade could not have stood five minutes longer at Kernstown. Grigsby replied, 'No Sir, they could not have stood a damned second longer.'" Neither the substance nor the form of Grigsby's response can have endeared him to the general.[16]

Confederate senator R. M. T. Hunter of Virginia rallied to Garnett's defense in the political arena. In a letter on April 10, the senator offered whatever aid was in his power. Garnett's reply to Hunter focused on the need for help in getting a trial scheduled and in securing copies of pertinent documents. The general especially hoped to find a copy of Jackson's animadversions against him back in January, of which he had just heard. "I must confess this covert attack surprises me," Garnett told Hunter, "as I thought him incapable of such malicious and under hand dealings." Even at this early date, Garnett had garnered so much support from his regimental commanders that he was certain that Jackson's charges "can be *completely overthrown* [underlining in original]." To his credit, however, Garnett manfully rejected any notion of fighting the controversy in the popular press to the detriment of the army.[17]

To a considerable degree, the fate of Garnett in the forum of public opinion was sealed neither at Kernstown, the opening, losing, battle of the Valley Campaign, nor in the newspapers. Rather, it was sealed with the successes that followed at McDowell, Front Royal, Winchester, Cross Keys, and Port Republic. Stonewall Jackson carved his way into the hearts of the South and into the annals of military history in his remarkable 1862 campaign. The strong sympathy for Garnett in the army and in his brigade (the men of which had audibly hissed his replacement, General Charles S. Winder) was at first reflected throughout the country. Some who knew Garnett would have shared the opinion of him expressed by Eppa Hunton: "While he was not a man of much mental force, he was one of the noblest and bravest men I ever knew." Jackson's surgeon, Hunter Holmes McGuire, expressed similar sentiments, calling Garnett "a gallant man but a sort of red tape soldier." McGuire did not believe that Jackson had treated Garnett unjustly.[18]

16. McHenry Howard, *Recollections of a Maryland Confederate Soldier and Staff Officer Under Johnston, Jackson and Lee* (Baltimore: Williams & Wilkins, 1914), 83; unaddressed note by Williamson, April 14, 1881, Garnett Papers, MOC.

17. Garnett to R. M. T. Hunter, April [no day] 1862, Garnett Papers, MOC.

18. Eppa Hunton, *Autobiography of Eppa Hunton* (Richmond: Privately printed, 1933), 84;

The studied opinion that gradually took hold of the contemporary public, and perhaps of posterity as well, was nicely captured in a postwar article written by Henry Kyd Douglas of Jackson's staff. While he privately "disapprove[d] of Jackson's treatment of Garnett at Kernstown," the opinionated aide recognized what Stonewall had accomplished. In an account published eighteen years after the battle, Douglas wrote of Jackson's purposes: "If he erred in his condemnation and removal of Gen'l Garnett—a severe and cruel punishment for doing what every other officer in that little army except Jackson would have done—it was an error that the future operations and success of that army excused, perhaps justified. It taught Jackson's subordinates what he expected of them."[19]

Even so sturdy a supporter of Stonewall Jackson as the Confederate historian Douglas Southall Freeman marveled at the army commander's stern, relentless pursuit of his subordinate: "I never could understand why he persecuted such men as [Colonel William Gilham] and General Dick Garnett. Many people said, at the time, that the persecution of Garnett was without any excuse whatever except that General Jackson wanted to find a scapegoat."[20] There is no evidence, and little reason, to accuse Jackson of motives that craven, but the fact that Freeman entertained the notion is an interesting commentary on the merits of the case.

Whatever its causes and consequences, Garnett's travail continued into July 1862. He had been pleading for a trial for months, waiving considerations of rank in the composition of the court and otherwise seeking to expedite the process. The Adjutant and Inspector General's Office suspended Garnett's arrest on June 25, but Jackson evidently renewed the charges and rearrested the target of his wrath. The long-sought court was ordered to convene on July 16—and on that very day Jackson's portion of the army began a rapid movement away from Richmond toward Gordonsville. That delayed the trial, of course. On July 28, General R. E. Lee specified the composition of the court and the date it was to convene. Generals Richard S. Ewell, Jubal A. Early, Isaac R. Trimble, and James J. Archer were to sit in judgment of Garnett. When the court finally met on August 6, at Ewell's headquarters near Orange

---

McGuire to Jedediah Hotchkiss, May 22, 1894, Hotchkiss Papers, Alderman Library, University of Virginia, Charlottesville.

19. Manuscript marginalia by Douglas in his copy of Henderson's biography of Jackson, 2:454, in collections of Antietam National Battlefield Park, Sharpsburg, Md.; Douglas in *Hagerstown (Md.) Mail*, November 5, 1880.

20. D. S. Freeman to Mrs. Delia Page Marshall, July 12, 1943, VMI.

Court House, the climax seemed at last to be at hand. As the affair developed, further anticlimax intervened.[21]

One man took the stand on August 6: Thomas J. Jackson, known as "Stonewall." Garnett personally grilled his former superior, with no holds barred. Garnett's questions were predictable and pointed: "Did you communicate this plan to me. . . ?" (of course not). "Could you . . . judge well of the strength of the positions of the enemy before the battle commenced?" "When Col. Fulkerson first moved off . . . did you or not direct me to send one regiment to support him?" ("I did not," Jackson retorted.) "What was the nearest you were to the [infantry] when it was first engaged with the enemy?" "Did you not write to . . . Johnston . . . that you had been deceived with regard to the number of the enemy?" And so it went throughout the day.

Dick Garnett's copy of the transcript survives in Richmond, together with other important manuscript material on the case. In the margin of his transcript, Garnett noted with some frequency next to Jackson's responses: "Lie." He also drew a little oblong device, with a slash through the middle, next to what he thought to be dishonest answers by the enthusiastically religious Stonewall. The marks festoon the margins with considerable regularity.[22]

On the second day, August 7, Sandie Pendleton took the stand.[23] Young Pendleton had expressed frank doubt that his chief would win the case, although he supported him firmly. The night before, Sandie had written home that "the case will most probably go by default in favor of Garnett." Pendleton based his judgment about the case in part on the death of Major Francis B. Jones during the battles around Richmond. Jones's testimony would have been central to proof of some of Jackson's allegations, Sandie thought. Major Jones had written in his own diary on April 2, however, that, although Jackson had interviewed him extensively about Garnett and Kernstown, Garnett's arrest "fell like a thunderbolt," and Jones expressed "astonishment & sorrow to lose so valuable & so gallant an officer." Garnett also had lost the testimony of witnesses favorable to him, who had been killed around Richmond. An im-

---

21. Special Orders No. 146, Adjutant & Inspector General's Office, June 25, 1862; General Orders No. 89, Army of Northern Virginia, July 28, 1862. Several of Garnett's pleas for a trial are in the Garnett Papers, MOC, beginning on May 6 and running through July.

22. Garnett's copy of the transcript (Garnett Papers, MOC) includes the written word "lie" eight times and many more of the skeptical marks.

23. The volume of Pendleton's testimony (Garnett Papers, MOC) is just about precisely one-half the length of Jackson's, which suggests that the August 7 proceedings continued until about noon.

portant member of Jackson's staff, Lieutenant George G. Junkin, had been captured at Kernstown and remained a prisoner of war.[24]

In fact, the case went to no victor and Sandie never finished testifying because on August 7 Jackson ordered his army to lunge across the Rapidan and go after John Pope's Federal force. Hypothesis is by definition an impossibly inexact undertaking. It is hard, though, to avoid wondering whether Mighty Stonewall was not encouraged, at least subconsciously, to move into action as an alternative to suffering further probing by a court-martial that was not working out at all well.

Jackson's move, whatever its genesis, led to the Battle of Cedar Mountain, where Garnett's successor in command of the Stonewall Brigade, Charles Winder, was killed. The disrupted court never reconvened. Within less than a month, R. E. Lee released Garnett from arrest and assigned him to General James Longstreet's portion of the Army of Northern Virginia. Garnett took command of the Virginia brigade in General George E. Pickett's division that had been Pickett's own and led it during the fighting in Maryland in September 1862.[25]

Garnett was still leading the brigade when he died on July 3, 1863, at the forefront of Pickett's division in its ill-starred attack at Gettysburg. A few weeks before his death, incredibly enough, Garnett had served as an honorary pallbearer at the funeral of his nemesis, Stonewall Jackson, saying of the dead southern hero: "I believe he did me great injustice, but I believe also he acted from the purest motives. He is dead. Who can fill his place!"[26]

As befits the unhappy defendant in so famous a military case, Garnett's death included mystery. There even remains considerable uncertainty about what the man looked like. That Garnett was killed on July 3, 1863, is not

24. A. S. Pendleton to mother, August 5, 1862, William N. Pendleton Papers, SHC; Francis Buckner Jones diary, April 2, 1862, Winchester-Frederick County Historical Society, Handley-Page Library, Winchester, Va. In a letter to William Garnett, July 12, 1862 (Garnett Papers, MOC), A. J. Grigsby bewailed the loss of Colonel James W. Allen of the 2nd Virginia in that regard. Colonel John Echols, in a letter dated July 30, 1862 (Garnett Papers, MOC), pointed out that Jackson had dealt directly with the 27th Virginia through the agency of the absent Junkin.

25. Many months after Garnett's trial was interrupted, it remained in legal limbo. General Lee was typically determined to smooth over the problem rather than nurture it. Ewell, the ranking officer of the court, told another officer nine months later (letter to Colonel F. W. M. Holliday, March 26, 1863, Holliday Papers, PLD) that he had instructions "not to reconvene without further orders—Please let it be known if anyone asks you."

26. Henry Kyd Douglas, *I Rode with Stonewall* (Chapel Hill: University of North Carolina Press, 1940), 38.

questioned; but his body never was found, and his sword turned up years later in a Baltimore pawnshop.[27] In 1986, the question of Garnett's appearance was the subject of a remarkable court case in Essex County, Virginia. For many decades, Richard Brooke Garnett has been identified with a familiar photograph of a dark-haired, clear-eyed, black-bearded man in the high-collared uniform of a Confederate general. His cousin Robert Selden Garnett (1819–61), also of Essex County, also in the United States Military Academy class of 1841, was the first Confederate general killed in the war. Robert has been represented by another photograph, apparently correctly identified, showing him with a thin mustache, clean-shaven chin, and long sideburns.[28]

General Robert Selden Garnett, CSA, first cousin of Richard B. Garnett.

There is strong—virtually incontrovertible—evidence that Richard had "light hair and blue eyes, and he wore no full beard," and in fact that no picture of him exists. The photograph long identified as being of Richard probably depicts Robert. Whether the black-bearded fellow really is Robert seems uncertain, and it is hardly likely that a modern court could certify the facts with authority, to say nothing of changing them. The legal hearing took place on April 18, 1986, perhaps because March 23—the anniversary of Richard's Kernstown crisis—fell on Sunday that year, making impossible an otherwise appealing scheduling gesture.[29]

Thomas J. Jackson continues to grow larger than life as the passing years push his era further into the past. While Jackson's memory is hymned in a bad new biography every few months, and by worthwhile new scholarship every few years, Rich-

27. A nice, detailed study of this mystery is Stephen Davis, "The Death and Burials of General Richard Brooke Garnett," *Gettysburg Magazine* 5 (July 1991): 107–16.

28. For a summary of Garnett's life, including the question of the photographic variants, see Robert K. Krick, "The Parallel Lives of Two Virginia Soldiers, Armistead and Garnett," in Gary W. Gallagher, ed., *The Third Day at Gettysburg and Beyond* (Chapel Hill: University of North Carolina Press, 1994), 93–131. A joint biography of the two Generals Garnett is Matthew W. Burton, *The River of Blood and the Valley of Death* (Dayton, Ohio: General's Books, 1998).

29. G[arnett] B. Waggener to "Dear Miss Harrison," August 4, 1908 (two letters of that date), MOC, and the author's discussions with the late (and incomparable) Eleanor Brockenbrough of that institution. See also Krick, "Parallel Lives," 95–96, 124–25, which provides citation for four newspaper articles about the 1986 court case.

This image has been repeatedly published as a likeness of General Richard Brooke Garnett, but there is convincing family evidence that he looked nothing like this. The picture may actually be another of Robert S. Garnett, from a different angle and at a different time (and with a different hairstyle) than the other. There is no reliably identified image of Richard B. Garnett extant.

ard Brooke Garnett slips steadily into oblivion, except for attention to his role as the great man's foil in the most notorious court-martial in the history of the Army of Northern Virginia. There really is nothing in the record that would warrant any other result, and yet the circumstances of the whole business leave us longing for more details about Garnett, more details about his fateful decision to retreat at Kernstown, more material with which to understand and evaluate the whole affair. Even if such new light becomes available, it will not likely alter the total on the balance sheet. The Garnett affair "taught Jackson's subordinates what he expected of them," as Kyd Douglas pointed out with keen hindsight. What he expected was nothing more nor less than unquestioning, rote, mindless obedience to orders, without any hope of understanding their context or their intent.

3

"If Longstreet . . . Says So, It Is Most Likely Not True": James Longstreet and the Second Day at Gettysburg

When General James Longstreet died in 1904, he had long since passed his optimal life span for Confederate image building. Had the bullet that maimed the general in the Wilderness on May 6, 1864, killed him instead, there can be little doubt that a bronze equestrian Longstreet would stand on Richmond's Monument Avenue today. Through four postwar decades, however, the contentious Longstreet launched a steady flood of attacks against his former Confederate colleagues, often straying from the demonstrable truth and regularly contradicting his *own* accounts from one article to the next. When a Petersburg newspaper called Longstreet's poison-pen ventures the "vaporings of senility and pique," it echoed the views of millions of southerners.[1] The general's modern supporters insist that in analyzing his war record, we must ignore his late-life posturing, and in fact that is both appropriate and readily achievable in weighing his style during the 1860s. Although the senility doubtless was something new, however, the pique was not a sudden anomaly, sprung whole from the postwar ground.

The change in southern attitudes toward James Longstreet after the war came in large part not simply in response to his postwar political maneuvering

This chapter first appeared in Gary W. Gallagher, ed., *The Second Day at Gettysburg* (Kent, Ohio: Kent State University Press, 1993), 57–86, 182–84. It is republished here, edited and with additions, by kind permission of Kent State.

1. *Petersburg Index-Appeal* of undetermined date cited in a clipping in Reel 59, Frame 91, Jedediah Hotchkiss Papers. One of many similar comments came from an artillery field officer of Longstreet's own corps, who called the general's writings "a tissue of nonsense" (Frank Huger to Fizhugh Lee, April 24, 1896, copy in the author's possession).

but because he survived to reveal glimpses of his soul that left observers repulsed. The record shows that Longstreet operated at times during the war with an unwholesome and unlovely attitude. He had a tendency to be small-minded and mean-spirited, and he behaved in that fashion to the detriment of his army on a number of occasions, including during the second day at Gettysburg.

By December 1861, James Longstreet had experienced a meteoric rise in rank. A few months earlier he had been a major and paymaster in the U.S. Army; now he was a major general of infantry. No one in the army had fared better and most had done far less well. No observers had thought of heaping calumny on Longstreet's head for any reason—justified or not. He was in no way controversial. He was, nevertheless, a confirmed sulker—apparently entirely of his own volition, without having been forced to it by a hostile public opinion, because none such existed. A young Texan on his staff, who was friendly with Longstreet and remained so into old age early in the twentieth century, described Longstreet's tendency to pout in a letter written to his mother that month: "On some days [Longstreet is] very sociable and agreeable, then again for a few days he will confine himself mostly to his room, or tent, without having much to say to anyone, and is as grim as you please." The general behaved that way when he was unwell, as might be expected, but he also acted in that fashion when "something has not gone to suit him. When anything has gone wrong, he does not say much, but merely looks grim." The staff had learned to expect this behavior and did not "talk much to him" before finding out if he was in "a talkative mood."[2] It would be hard for a Longstreet detractor, convinced of the general's tendency to sulk, to fabricate a more telling description of his demeanor when "something [had] not gone to suit him."

A member of J. E. B. Stuart's staff described Longstreet's personal style at about the same period. W. W. Blackford and Stuart boarded for a time at the same house in Fairfax Court House with Longstreet. Blackford wrote: "Longstreet . . . impressed me then as a man of limited capacity who acquired reputation for wisdom by never saying anything—the old story of the owl. I do not remember ever hearing him say half a dozen words, beyond 'yes' and 'no,' in a consecutive sentence, though often in company with his old companions of the old army." A civilian woman who had dinner with Longstreet the following year described his gruff performance as being "shy and embarrassed in manner."[3]

2. Thomas Jewett Goree to his mother, December 14, 1861, in Langston James Goree, ed., *The Thomas Jewett Goree Letters* (Bryan, Tex.: Family History Foundation, 1981), 111.
3. W. W. Blackford, *War Years with Jeb Stuart* (New York: Charles Scribner's Sons, 1945), 47;

General James Longstreet

Longstreet's stolid persona often produced in observers the certainty that he must surely be a bulwark in a storm. The general did perform in just that manner for the Army of Northern Virginia on several crucial occasions. His style, however, may also have been mixed with more than a tincture of the dullard. Was Longstreet a quiet genius or just quietly slow? A bulwark or a dullard? He probably combined elements of both. At West Point, where one of his roommates was the notorious John Pope, Longstreet displayed no hint of mental agility. He finished fifty-fourth among fifty-six graduates in the class of 1842. His worst mark was fifty-fifth in Ethics, behind even the spectacularly unethical Earl Van Dorn.[4]

The phenomenon of dullard as bulwark is a familiar one in military history.

diary of Matilda Hamilton of "Prospect Hill," near Fredericksburg, December 28, 1862, typescript in the author's possession.

4. A. P. Stewart in "Soldiers Note Book," *Atlanta Journal*, November 13, 1890; *Official Register of the . . . U.S. Military Academy . . . June, 1842* (New York: J. P. Wright, 1842), 8.

In a wonderfully droll eighteenth-century book of satirical advice to army of-ficers, a British veteran commented on the syndrome: "Ignorance of your pro-fession is . . . best concealed by solemnity and silence, which pass for profound knowledge upon the generality of mankind." Longstreet's own dear friend both before and after the war, Ulysses S. Grant, is among the prominent Americans most often discussed in that vein. An English diplomat com-mented that Grant, during his attempts to cope with the duties of president, could not "deliver himself of even the simplest sentence." During the midst of the Belknap scandal, Grant appeared so indifferent to the mess and its resul-tant turmoil that James A. Garfield wrote in his diary: "His imperturbability is amazing. I am in doubt whether to call it greatness or stupidity."[5] Opinions vary, and always will, about the characteristics of long-dead historical figures. If there was something of the dullard in James Longstreet's mix, it probably served him well on some occasions, just as the misanthropic tunnel vision of Longstreet's bête noir, Stonewall Jackson, proved to be an asset in that offi-cer's aggressive military behavior. The sullen side of Longstreet's dull person-ality, however, also contributed to his military failures.

A popular and appropriate query posed by Longstreet supporters runs something like this: If the general was given to sulking, and was otherwise deficient in dedication and deportment, why were he and Lee on such good terms? To quote Gary W. Gallagher, Longstreet was a man "whose friendship he [Lee] valued." Lee's calm, poised style included an ingenuous element that accepted individuals at face value. He also recognized that the raw material at hand was the best to be had in his country. Lee concluded a May 1864 review of the performance of a brigadier general by posing the query, "Besides, whom would you put in his place?"[6] In any event, there is ample evidence that Lee was genuinely fond of Longstreet, and of course he valued his subordinate's high services to the army. It is interesting to speculate how Lee would have reacted had he known the extent of Longstreet's disloyalty, or whether he in fact was aware of the situation. Because Lee declared that he did not believe Longstreet would say such things—precisely the things Longstreet said re-peatedly for thirty years after Lee's death—when he heard rumors of them, he probably remained unaware of Longstreet's distaste for him.

5. [Francis Grose], *Advice to the Officers of the British Army* (London: W. Richardson, 1783), 8; Sir Edward Thornton and James A. Garfield as quoted in William S. McFeely, *Grant: A Biography* (New York: Norton, 1981), 383, 434.

6. Gallagher, ed., *Second Day at Gettysburg*, 22; Douglas Southall Freeman, *R. E. Lee: A Biogra-phy*, 4 vols. (New York: Charles Scribner's Sons, 1934–36), 3:331.

The true nature of the corps commander's feelings for Lee stands out beyond any shadow of doubt in a letter written by Longstreet to Joseph E. Johnston on October 5, 1862. Just four months earlier, Lee had taken over Johnston's army as it crouched beneath the gates of Richmond, having just been beaten at Seven Pines—a battle in which, not coincidentally, Longstreet had conspired with Johnston to transfer blame dishonestly to an innocent colleague. Now Lee had completely remade the face of the war, having driven the enemy army from the verge of his own capital and pursued it across the Potomac. Longstreet clearly wanted his pliant collaborator back and professed to know that the army preferred to be rid of Lee (an idea either patently dishonest or else breathtakingly out of touch with the ranks): "I feel that you have their hearts more decidedly than any other leader can ever have. The men would now go wild at the sight of their old favorite." Speaking for himself, Longstreet quailed at the prospect of being stuck longer with Lee: "I cant become reconciled at the idea of your going west." Could Johnston find some means to return to the army even in a subordinate role, Longstreet had "no doubt but the command of the entire Army" would fall to him "before Spring." Having been thus blunt, the disgruntled general implied that he would love to say more: "Cant always write what we would like to say." While laboring under Lee's misrule, Longstreet and his staff had used captured champagne to drink to Johnston "whenever we opened a bottle" but thought of Johnston "more seriously at other times."[7] Had Lee seen this missive or learned of its contents indirectly (as he may have done), it probably would have made not one whit of difference in his calm, pragmatic dealings with Longstreet.

There can of course be no grounds for denying Longstreet the right to dislike Lee or to prefer Joseph E. Johnston. His distaste for Lee does put him in the rather select, if not exclusive, company of Roswell S. Ripley, apparently the only other general officer who actively disliked the army commander after he began active operations in June 1862. Longstreet's anti-Lee posture wins for him the approval of his modern soulmates, historians eager to debunk Lee's wartime status in the South. More important for present purposes is the degree to which the subordinate disdained the superior, as an element in considering Longstreet's response to those instances when he did not get his way.

A traditional folk saying summarizes how alarmingly easy it is to fool your-

---

7. James Longstreet to Joseph E. Johnston, October 5, 1862, Longstreet Papers, PLD.

self, how readily you may fool a superior, but how impossible it is to fool subordinates over the long term. Stonewall Jackson's worldview left him unpopular with virtually every immediate subordinate; basking in his reflected glory was far more comfortable among officers and men a layer or more away from his difficult presence. None of Jackson's bruised officers ever expressed much doubt, however, about their general's wholehearted commitment to the tasks at hand—which single-mindedness was, in fact, the cause of much of the abrasion in the first place.

A great many of James Longstreet's subordinates liked and admired him, including such clever and thoughtful fellows as E. P. Alexander and G. Moxley Sorrel. Those two men also provide some pointed critique of his attitude at Gettysburg. Longstreet's own favorites included generals such as Robert Toombs, who deserves consideration as at least a finalist for designation as worst general officer in the entire history of the Army of Northern Virginia. According to one of his staff, Longstreet "had a high opinion of Toombs, and I heard him say that if Toombs had been educated at West Point . . . he would have been as distinguished as a soldier as he was as a civilian." Longstreet also "was exceedingly fond" of George E. Pickett, perhaps because the younger man was one of the few antebellum graduates of West Point with a worse scholastic record than his own. Sorrel recalled how "taking Longstreet's orders in emergencies, I could always see how he looked after Pickett, and made us give him things very fully; indeed, sometimes stay with him to make sure he did not get astray." A third favorite was General Louis T. Wigfall (to whom Longstreet was, in his own words, "strongly attached"), a military failure as pronounced as any in the army, excepting, always, Toombs.[8]

Others of Longstreet's subordinates displayed considerable discomfort with the corps commander's attitude. Cadmus Marcellus Wilcox served long and faithfully as a brigade commander for the first half of the war and then as a major general at the head of a division during the rest of the conflict. In November 1862 he was anxiously seeking a means to leave Longstreet's corps, presumably because of discontent with its commander. The details are not clear because Lee typically destroyed his half of the correspondence with Wilcox and then gently persuaded the disgruntled general to look beyond local issues to the good of the army and the country. Wilcox's attitude toward

8. Raphael J. Moses, "Autobiography," 54, SHC; G. Moxley Sorrel, *Recollections of a Confederate Staff Officer* (New York: Neale, 1905), 54; Longstreet to Joseph E. Johnston, October 5, 1862, Longstreet Papers, PLD.

Longstreet is anything but indistinct in two letters he wrote soon after the war, which apparently never have been published. Writing to a fellow First Corps general, the usually reticent Wilcox declared emphatically, "I never had any respect for Longstreet's ability for I always knew he had but a small amount." Furthermore, Wilcox had "always regarded him as selfish & cold h[e]arted, caring for but little save his own self." General Wilcox insisted that at Frayser's Farm and Williamsburg, the brigade commanders suffered because of Longstreet's absence from the front "& we brigadiers talked of it." To Wilcox's chagrin, Longstreet "is spoken of as the hard & stubborn fighter, his troops did fight well, but not from any inspiration drawn from him & he of course gets the credit of it."[9]

As Longstreet fell into steadily greater disfavor after the war, he adopted the expedient of blaming his difficulties on individuals hostile to him because of political considerations and his other unpopular postwar traits. His modern supporters believe that whole-souled admiration for the general faded after the war for irrelevant reasons and under the prompting of consciously dishonest Lost Cause mythmakers. Longstreet might be viewed as a man far ahead of his times, with his very 1990s-like stance of insisting that, having outraged much of the community by one set of actions, he was immune to criticism for anything else: obviously everyone hated him and therefore must be ignored as prejudiced; citing a recidivist's chronic misdeeds is unfair, we are told. The innocence-through-unpopularity motif might in fact obtain in some instances. Longstreet really did a thorough job of making himself unlovable, and he prompted some outraged hyperbole in the process. Cadmus Wilcox, however, was anything but a controversialist. He was about the quietest man of his rank in the matter of postwar speaking and writing and quarreling. Wilcox's private letters to a friend of Longstreet's—not to some fiendish Lost Cause journal—scarcely can be impeached as polemics. Right or wrong, General Wilcox simply and privately thought little of Longstreet's ability and appreciated even less his "selfish & cold h[e]arted" attitude.

Major General Lafayette McLaws of Georgia was among the most pointed detractors Longstreet ever earned. His position is the more remarkable because for a long time the corps commander viewed McLaws as a special pro-

9. Douglas Southall Freeman, *Lee's Lieutenants*, 3 vols. (New York: Charles Scribner's Sons, 1942–44), 2:620 n.60 (where the year is misdated by typographical error); Cadmus M. Wilcox to E. P. Alexander, March 10, February 6, 1869, Alexander Papers, SHC; Cadmus M. Wilcox to D. H. Hill, Hill Papers, NCDAH.

tégé. McLaws provides key testimony about his chief at Gettysburg and Knoxville, cited below, but this generic commentary on Longstreet's "contemptible mode of procedure" summarizes his notions: "You can follow Longstreet's career, from the First battle of Manassas to the close of the war, and you will see that the first act, in any engagement, was to call for reinforcements; not that any reinforcements were needed, but that was his policy." McLaws knew from close experience that Longstreet's reports "will lay the blame of failure . . . upon some one else, and in case of real fiasco he will undertake to do something where success is impossible and find faults and lay the blame of the failure in his last venture upon some one else he has a spite against. All this is to draw attention away from his own mismanagement of the real issue."[10]

The best example of the blame-shifting technique cited by McLaws was Seven Pines. In a fantastic display of poor planning, miscommunication, and arrant ineptitude, James Longstreet left the presence of Joseph E. Johnston with instructions to march northeastward up the Nine Mile Road to implement the army commander's sloppy and casual battle plan; but somehow he contrived in befuddlement to head more than ninety degrees away from his intended goal. No major battle in Virginia includes any more bizarre confusion. In the process Longstreet blocked for long hours the route of troops under General Benjamin Huger who were earmarked for triggering the attack. Some have suggested that Longstreet consciously scrambled the plan in order to reach an area where distinction might be found, but that seems unlikely. McLaws noted that Longstreet "disobeyed his orders (supposed to be from stupidity)." The general's sometime apologist, Porter Alexander, wrote of his "great blunder & non performance at Seven Pines." Far more significant than the peculiar events was Longstreet's apparently instinctive reaction to blame it all on a convenient bystander. With Johnston's connivance, he succeeded in blaming Huger—who had been most directly wronged—as the author of the confusion! As Douglas Southall Freeman has noted, "Longstreet, whose conduct at Seven Pines was most subject to question, emerged not only without blame but also with prestige increased."[11] Huger proved to be a fortuitous

10. Lafayette McLaws to Charles Arnall, February 2, 1897, Roll 34, Hotchkiss Papers, LC.

11. McLaws to Arnall, as cited in note 10; E. P. Alexander to August C. Hamlin, November 22, 1903, Hamlin Papers, Houghton Library, Harvard University, Cambridge, Mass.; Freeman, *Lee's Lieutenants* 1:259–60. An important early summary of the Seven Pines fiasco is an endorsement on his report by G. W. Smith dated June 1865, in the Schoff Collection, Clements Library, University of Michigan, Ann Arbor.

choice as scapegoat, since he soon demonstrated a genuine tendency toward sluggishness.

Later that summer Longstreet had occasion to refine his technique. When his friend and subordinate Robert Toombs disobeyed orders and left a ford on the Rapidan entirely unguarded, a Federal cavalry column slipped through the gap unscathed, in fact unnoticed. The Yankees very nearly captured J. E. B. Stuart at Verdiersville. Stuart thought that the cavalrymen were Fitzhugh Lee's troopers, whom he expected to arrive soon. Although this relatively minor incident caused some inconvenience to the army, it hardly warranted the hyperbolic historiographical counteroffensive launched by Longstreet. He spread the word that Lee, who was among the victims of the malfeasance by Longstreet's friend Toombs, was really the culprit and escalated the result so egregiously that he later subscribed to the amusing premise that Lee "lost the Southern cause" on that largely forgotten morning. Longstreet later explained that all of the Virginia cavalrymen required guidance. Stuart in particular needed "an older head"—no doubt Longstreet had himself in mind—"to instruct and regulate him."[12]

Debate raged postwar about whether Longstreet disobeyed Lee in delaying his offensive at Second Manassas, where the armies met ten days after Fitz Lee "lost the war" at Verdiersville. Supporters of the First Corps commander continue to insist that his delay in executing Lee's wishes at Second Manassas was the right thing to do. But they can hardly cling to the notion that Longstreet was not dragging his feet, since he calmly admitted to doing so. "I failed to obey the orders of the 29th," he boasted, "and on the 30th, in direct opposition to my orders, made the battle from my position and won it." In describing tactical developments on the field, Longstreet gerrymandered them through an arc of nearly 180 degrees in a display of either extraordinary sloppiness or blatant dishonesty.[13]

Judging from his letter to Joe Johnston quoted above, Longstreet obviously believed from the early days of his association with Lee that he knew better

12. James Longstreet, *From Manassas to Appomattox: A Memoir of the Civil War in America* (Philadelphia: J. B. Lippincott, 1896), 196; James Longstreet to T. T. Munford, November 8, 13, 1891, Box 26, Munford-Ellis Family Papers, PLD. Amusingly, but hardly surprisingly, Longstreet fell out with the publishers of *Manassas to Appomattox*, alleging that "Lippincotts did not allow me . . . sufficient royalty" (Longstreet to General James G. Wilson, March 25, 1903, original sold November 3, 1998, by Alexander Autographs in Connecticut).

13. James Longstreet to Fitz John Porter, April 1878, Porter Papers, LC; Longstreet, *Manassas to Appomattox*, 187.

General Stuart's narrow escape at Verdiersville

how to run the army. That belief apparently had grown by the summer of 1863 to include warwide strategic concepts, according to Longstreet's postwar declarations. The corps commander claimed to have been brimming with unbeatable options for forays into Tennessee, Ohio, and other such exotic latitudes, but Lee was immune to reason. A contemporary letter from Longstreet to McLaws hints that the lieutenant general's hindsight was much crisper than his foresight. McLaws hoped to get back to the vicinity of Georgia and his family—the direction in which Longstreet's strategic vision was supposed to be gamboling. Longstreet thought he might be able to work it out, but if McLaws went south and west, he must remember that "we want every body here that we can get and . . . you must agree to send us every man that you can dispense with during the summer particularly."[14] That would seem to indicate that Longstreet's strategic vision about the poor chances in Lee's theater were somewhat more autobiographical than contemporary.

Longstreet's version of his dismayed abandonment of the various better ideas includes two remarkable words. After badgering Lee about Cincinnati, Vicksburg, and other such chimeras, Longstreet "found his [Lee's] mind made up not to allow any of his troops to go west. I then *accepted* his proposition to make a campaign into Pennsylvania, *provided* it should be offensive in strategy but defensive in tactics" (emphases added). That a corps commander would use words of that sort in describing the decisions of his army's head reveals a phenomenal degree of arrogant disrespect. Lee of course had not struck such a "bargain" and in the event behaved without respect to the nonexistent pact. Longstreet later professed to know somehow that Lee had missed his only real chance to breach successfully this pseudo-cartel when he overlooked a great opportunity at Brandy Station, "when he could have caught Hooker in detail, and, probably, have crushed his army."[15]

General Longstreet's corps fought one of the war's most desperate engagements on July 2, 1863, on the Confederate right at Gettysburg. Despite the corps' brave and stubborn performance, its commander came in for bitter criticism for his attitude and behavior on that crucial day. There was generously

14. James Longstreet to Lafayette McLaws, June 3, 1863, McLaws Papers, SHC.

15. James Longstreet, "Lee's Invasion of Pennsylvania," in Robert Underwood Johnson and Clarence Clough Buel, eds., *Battles and Leaders of the Civil War*, 4 vols. (New York: Century, 1887–88), 3:246; James Longstreet, "The Mistakes of Gettysburg," in *The Annals of the War Written by Leading Participants North and South* (Philadelphia: Times Publishing Company, 1879), 620. An important, and somewhat more moderate, statement of Longstreet's notions on the campaign is in his letter to McLaws, July 25, 1873, printed in *Gettysburg Magazine* 17 (1997): 14–16.

ample basis for such criticism, but as controversy swirled around the subject some of the general's detractors—most notably the Reverend William Nelson Pendleton—produced inaccurate and misleading testimony. The nature and processes of the controversy itself have become controversial, but this essay inquiring particularly into the nature of Longstreet's attitude must focus on primary evidence.

Longstreet did not want Lee to take the initiative on July 2. He made that unmistakably clear to his superior, but Lee determined that the army must find the best possible spot at which to seek a continuation of the striking success it had won the previous day. After an often-discussed series of conferences with Lee, some of them turbulent, Longstreet faced the simple fact that he must move to the right and attack. He accepted that responsibility with the poorest possible grace. Had Tom Goree been writing to his mother on this day he most certainly could have duplicated his December 1861 letter: when "something has not gone to suit him. . . . [He] merely looks grim." James Longstreet spent most of July 2 "without having much to say to anyone, and . . . as grim as you please," in accordance with Goree's earlier description.

One early and striking manifestation of Longstreet's sullen execution of his orders has not received much attention in the voluminous literature on Gettysburg. His two divisions faced a long and uncertain march to their intended destination. The march surely would take considerable time under the very best of circumstances. Inevitably such moves involved delays. Given the urgency of the situation, celerity (to use one of the favorite words of the sorely missed T. J. Jackson) clearly was in requisition. Longstreet ignored that patently obvious imperative from the outset. Evander M. Law's brigade of Alabama troops, one of eight brigades scheduled for the march, had not yet closed up to the point from which the march would begin. Longstreet insisted on waiting for its arrival. As he reported officially to Lee, "I delayed until General Law's brigade joined its division." Even then he was not ready, having "*after his arrival*" (emphasis added) to "make our preparations." While the clock inexorably ticked off moments potentially golden for the South, Longstreet lounged with division commander John B. Hood "near the trunk of a tree" and explained to Hood that General Lee "is a little nervous this morning; he wishes me to attack." Hood's description of this relaxed encounter, written after the war to Longstreet himself, concluded ominously: "Thus passed the forenoon of that eventful day."[16]

16. *OR* ser. I, 27 (2): 358; John Bell Hood to James Longstreet, June 28, 1875, in *SHSP*, 4:148.

Had Longstreet insisted on awaiting Law's arrival at the line of departure before launching his attack, he might have been able to make a weak case; though under the circumstances that afternoon, a delay in attacking to augment the force by one-eighth would not have made good sense, especially given the en echelon arrangement that was used. He was not waiting to attack, however, but merely to *begin* a complicated march—actually to begin "preparations" for it. Law of course would have arrived at the jump-off point for the march long before his turn came to fall in at the end of the column. Longstreet simply was dragging his feet.

Once the march finally began, on a dismally tardy schedule, the sulking corps commander put on a display of pettiness of heroic proportions by pretending to think that he could not direct his own troops. Captain Samuel Richards Johnston, engineer officer on Lee's staff, had reconnoitered early that morning in the area toward which Longstreet was grudgingly headed. Beginning at about 4 A.M., Johnston rode over the ground between Willoughby Run and Marsh Creek leading east toward the Emmitsburg Pike. He examined the terrain between the pike and the Round Tops, rode over the slopes and perhaps to the crests of those soon-to-be-famous knobs, crossed the Slyder farm, and returned. When the scouting captain reached headquarters, General Lee "was surprised at my getting so far, but showed clearly that I had given him valuable information." Lee suggested that Captain Johnston join Longstreet's column on its march; any other use of the man best informed about the ground would have been criminally negligent. The army commander of course gave his staff captain no special authority. In fact, he gave him "no other instructions" at all beyond joining Longstreet. Johnston thought it was about 9 A.M. when he joined Longstreet and added what everyone else well knew: "He did not move off very promptly—nor was our march at all rapid. It did not strike me that Genl Longstreet was in a hurry to get into position. It might have been that he thought hurry was unnecessary."[17]

Longstreet decided to play an ugly game with the misguided Lee—and with thousands of unfortunate soldiers and the destiny of a mighty battle—by taking the ludicrous position that Sam Johnston really commanded the march. He was Lee's man on the spot, and this wholly silly march and attack were Lee's idiotic idea, so let him have his way and then we'll just see who really

17. Undated transcript of Samuel R. Johnston's letter to McLaws, in the latter's hand, McLaws Papers, PLD; S. R. Johnston to Fitzhugh Lee, February 16, 1878, to Lafayette McLaws, June 27, 1892, and to George Peterkin, date illegible, all three in the Johnston Papers, VHS.

knows best! No episode in the army's long history, which included more than
a few displays of temper and spite and small-mindedness, can measure up to
this exhibition by Lieutenant General Longstreet. Johnston was a splendid
engineer and staff officer—Lee's chief engineer called him "the *best* [emphasis
in original] and most deserving . . . reconnoitering officer" in the entire army.
More than two hundred officers in the marching column outranked Sam
Johnston, however, if in fact his staff rank could be counted at all in the face of
line commanders. To make matters even worse, this tragicomic affair unfolded
without Johnston knowing that he was the stalking-horse for the pouting
corps commander. As the astonished Johnston put it years later when he heard
of Longstreet's fabrications: "I was ordered by Gen'l Lee 'to ride with Gen'l
Longstreet,' this is all the instructions that I received. I had no idea where he
was going."[18]

When the head of the marching column passed Black Horse Tavern it
quickly came to a point where the narrow road crawled over a high knoll. At
its top, the Confederates would come in clear view of Federals on Little
Round Top. Sam Johnston innocently told Longstreet that this would "discover your movements to the enemy," but Longstreet had no comment. He
watched as the column went over the crest into view of the Federals and
halted. The knoll with the naked crest actually extended only a short distance
in either direction. Porter Alexander moved his large artillery battalion around
the far (nominally southern) edge of the knoll without a second thought.
When he noticed the infantry not only failing to follow his example but also
halted in clear view of Little Round Top—thus abdicating *both* secrecy and
speed—he was astonished. The infantry never did follow Alexander's simple
and convenient route. Instead they retraced their steps and went on a great
looping detour that covered, Alexander noted disgustedly, "four miles to get
less than one" and cost "more than two hours."[19] The spectacle of a corps
under arms, groping its way without a commander at a crucial moment, makes
one of the most pathetic vignettes in the army's annals.

Longstreet's bitter game, with his own rules developed as he went, eventually allowed him to assume command of Hood's division but not that of

18. W. H. Stevens to J. F. Gilmer, October 11, 1864, in Samuel R. Johnston's official CSR,
M331, NA; Samuel R. Johnston to Fitz Lee, February 11, 1878, Johnston Papers, VHS.

19. Johnston transcript as cited in note 17; E. P. Alexander, *Fighting for the Confederacy: The
Personal Recollections of General Edward Porter Alexander*, ed. Gary W. Gallagher (Chapel Hill: Uni-
versity of North Carolina Press, 1989), 236; Alexander to J. Willard Brown in Brown's *The Signal
Corps, U.S.A., in the War of the Rebellion* (Boston: Press of B. Wilkins, 1896), 367–68.

McLaws. Under this system, Longstreet could declare that he "did not order General McLaws forward, because, as the head of the column, he had direct orders from General Lee [he unquestionably did *not*] to follow the conduct of Colonel [*sic*] Johnston: Therefore, I sent orders to Hood, who was in the rear and not encumbered by these instructions." All of this petty and dishonest posturing dramatically exacerbated the tendency of Longstreet's command to move with what some observers thought was unwonted sluggishness even under ordinary circumstances. A member of General Ewell's staff remarked of operations during July that "Longstreet was . . . himself notorious for moving slowly, & McLaws' Divn of his Corps was . . . the slowest of Longstreet's troops & a clog on the whole Army." An engineer officer who had nothing to do with Longstreet and expressed no opinion of any sort about him referred to him as "Old Snail" in a routine diary entry during July, as though that were his common nickname.[20] Troops with that marching tendency were particularly vulnerable to the sort of sulky delaying action that Longstreet employed on July 2.

Why did Lee not accompany his grumpy subordinate, insist on greater organization and speed of movement, and make his presence felt at the point of decision? Because he came to Gettysburg with two brand-new corps commanders and neither of them was James Longstreet. Lee had already had cause to be deeply concerned about Ewell, and Hill's inaugural attempt at corps command at Gettysburg left very little impact on the battle. It must have been easy for Lee to decide to stay near the sectors of his two tyros while leaving his one veteran to operate with greater independence, as was Lee's preferred system. Longstreet's admirer Porter Alexander concluded categorically: "There seems no doubt that had Longstreet's attack . . . been made materially sooner, we would have gained a decided victory"; but Alexander says Lee somehow should have done a better job of forcing Longstreet to conform to his will. We can of course recognize that Lee's presence with Longstreet was desperately needed, using hindsight, but that incomparable tool by definition was not in the army commander's arsenal. The wry conclusion of an analyst of a battle eight decades in the future obtained here as well: "At this period the Tables of Organization did not provide for any crystal-gazers at regimental level." Lee was left to ask, according to one of his staff, "in a tone

20. Longstreet, "Lee in Pennsylvania," 423; G. Campbell Brown memoir, 83, Brown-Ewell Papers, Tennessee State Library and Archives, Nashville; Henry Herbert Harris Diary, July 14, 1863, typescript at FSNMP from original owned by a descendant living in Fredericksburg.

of uneasiness, 'what *can* detain Longstreet? He ought to be in position now.'"
When Lee learned of the advance of Federal general Daniel E. Sickles to the
Emmitsburg Pike he "again expressed his impatience."[21]

When at last the marching comedy of errors reached the vicinity of the
Emmitsburg Pike opposite the Peach Orchard and the Round Tops, Longstreet for the first time could see the ground over which he was to attack. It
obviously offered strong advantages to the defenders, if they were present in
strength, but by the same token it offered equally alluring opportunity to the
Confederates if they could occupy the high ground by some means. Longstreet had been stubbornly opposed to fighting on the offensive under any circumstances. His churlish behavior all day had resulted from that general
conviction, not from any idea of the terrain, which he only now could see. As
Porter Alexander aptly commented: "The long & the short of the matter
seems to me as follows. Longstreet did not wish to take the offensive. His
objection to it was not based at all upon the peculiar strength of the enemy's
position for that was not yet recognized, but solely on general principles."[22]

As Longstreet's two strong and tested divisions neared action, the corps
commander adjusted his horizon to the point that he was willing to resume
his abdicated command of McLaws. Captain Sam Johnston would have been
relieved to relinquish the weighty responsibility, we can suppose, had he ever
known that he had it in the first place. It might have appeared that the lieutenant general was prepared to go back to work in the interests of his faithful
and trusting riflemen who were about to head into mortal combat, but in fact
his taste for charade and for self-fulfilling prophecy had only been whetted.
The most pressing question facing the corps, which should have occupied the
energies of its commander, was how to align the troops and commit them to
battle. Longstreet abdicated that responsibility and insisted that Lee's plan,
now long stale and necessarily only a general guide in any event, be rigidly
honored. It had become apparent that Lee knew far less well than Longstreet
how to win a battle, and here was an irresistible opportunity to prove it to
him.

The division and brigade commanders, together with some aggressive regimental officers, had looked at the zone of attack eagerly and with pragmatic

21. Alexander, *Fighting for the Confederacy*, 278; Frank O. Hough, *The Assault on Peleliu*
(Washington, D.C.: Headquarters Marine Corps, 1950), 84; A. L. Long, *Memoirs of Robert E. Lee*
(Richmond: B. F. Johnson, 1886), 281–82.
    22. Alexander, *Fighting for the Confederacy*, 237.

eyes. Some of them quickly discerned that the Federal left ambled amorphously through a large and vaguely defined region north of Round Top. John B. Hood, whose division stood on the far right, at once requested permission to turn that flank. Longstreet refused to entertain any such deviations from Lee's plan, which he now suddenly endowed with a categorical aura. To alter it would be to impair the lesson Lee needed to learn. Hood later reminded Longstreet how he had urged "that you allow me to turn Round Top and attack the enemy in flank and rear." Longstreet replied curtly, "Gen'l Lee's orders are to attack up the Emmettsburg [sic] road." A second heartfelt plea met a similar response. "A third time I dispatched one of my staff to explain fully," Hood recalled, "and to suggest that you had better come."[23] Longstreet refused to go look for himself or to consider any alternatives. To do so would have been to exercise corps command, and he was not yet ready to dismount from his high horse.

Moxley Sorrel confirmed Hood's account of his desperate attempts to operate intelligently. Hood "begged me to look at" his division's plight, Sorrel remembered, "report its extreme difficulty, and implore Longstreet to make the attack another way." The staffer complied but elicited the same answer from Longstreet. McLaws was not involved in the vain attempt to move around the right, but his superior found opportunity nastily to force him too into misguided positions as a means of venting his spleen. Longstreet in fact never denied having refused to consider alternatives. He actually reiterated his position as a means of clarifying Lee's bad plan; that was the point of the whole business. "General Hood appealed again and again for the move to the right," Longstreet confirmed.[24]

What Hood wanted to do, Longstreet insisted, "had been carefully considered by our chief [who of course actually knew nothing whatsoever about it] and rejected in favor of his present orders."[25] Longstreet had the genetic equipment to be naturally, as well as intentionally, obtuse. In this instance he certainly was employing a calculated density rather than his ample native supply. He and Lee had disagreed over whether it was desirable—to say nothing of practicable—to relocate the army in some miraculous fashion to a point between Gettysburg and Washington. That would have been more or less to the Federal strategic left (if not right in the midst of their approaching col-

23. John Bell Hood to James Longstreet, June 28, 1875, in *SHSP*, 4:149.

24. Sorrel, *Recollections*, 169; Longstreet, *Manassas to Appomattox*, 368.

25. Longstreet, *Manassas to Appomattox*, 368.

umns). In rejecting that visionary notion, Lee of course was offering no comment of any sort about moving against the Federals' tactical left on the
battlefield. The whole movement of July 2 was aimed toward just that target.
Lee always left the means of committing a corps to action up to its commander, certainly when out of his presence and almost invariably even when
he was nearby. He had refused to attempt to relocate his army southeastward
into a different county; that had nothing at all to do with relocating its tactical
arrangements in the same direction—or in any other—by the width of a pas-
ture or two or a few hundred yards of woods.

Among the most telling indictments of Longstreet's behavior are the words
of two of his intimates, one who remained so for life and one who broke with
him on the spot. Both Moxley Sorrel and Lafayette McLaws commented
pointedly on their superior's attitude on this dark and bloody day. Sorrel
stayed on close terms with his chief to the end of his life but could not conceal
some surprise about how Longstreet acted on July 2. The lieutenant general
"failed to conceal some anger. There was apparent apathy in his movements.
They lacked the fire and point of his usual bearing on the battlefield." Sorrel
admitted to imagining Lee's horror about "what was going on to the disadvan-
tage of the army," then reined himself in with a discernible jolt: "This is all I
shall permit myself to express on this well-worn . . . subject."[26]

Lafayette McLaws stood high among James Longstreet's favorites on July
1. Just a few weeks before, he had been Longstreet's candidate for a lieutenant
generalcy and command of one of the new corps. To the end of his life Longstreet grumbled about the dark Virginian plot that gave those billets to Ewell
and A. P. Hill instead of to McLaws. By the end of July 2, however, the veteran division commander had been so revolted by his chief's behavior that
he was unable to abide his further patronage. The two generals remained at
loggerheads and wound up in open conflict later in the war. Their hostility
extended unabated through McLaws's life, despite some periods of superficial
postwar rapprochement. After the feud erupted, McLaws's testimony must be
viewed in that context, though it remains more important than would be admitted by the school of thought that suggests that no one could effectively
criticize Longstreet because so many hated him.

The misbegotten tendency to flick away attacks on Longstreet's behavior
as the work of a dishonest postwar cabal just will not stand up in considering
McLaws's most pointed description of July 2. It came in the intimate forum

26. Sorrel, *Recollections*, 157–58.

of a letter to his wife and was written not in the grip of some 1880s political frenzy but on July 7, 1863. "General Longstreet is to blame for not reconnoitering the ground and for persisting in ordering the assault when his errors were discovered," he told Mrs. McLaws. "During the engagement he was very excited, giving contrary orders to every one, and was exceedingly overbearing." In consequence, McLaws said, "I consider him a humbug, a man of small capacity, very obstinate, not at all chivalrous, exceedingly conceited, and totally selfish."[27] A stronger bill of particulars would be difficult to contrive. If McLaws's description is in any wise accurate, and it seems to be substantially correct, James Longstreet's deportment stands in stark and ugly contrast next to the selfless devotion shown by the thousands of men who were bleeding and dying that afternoon under his direction—or, more accurately, his lack of direction.

A striking and fascinating comparison can be made between the actions of James Longstreet on July 2 and those of Stonewall Jackson on May 2 at Chancellorsville. On May 2, 1863, Lee chose to send his ranking subordinate on an extended march toward his enemy's most exposed flank on the second day of battle. Lee remained with the fixing element of his army to supervise its less experienced leaders, assigned to the maneuver element the key tactical responsibility, and instructed the commander of the maneuver element to attack the enemy flank at a specific point at which it apparently rested. In the event, Jackson managed his march with his accustomed energy and skill; Lee remained with the static element of the army and succeeded in bemusing the Federals opposite him; Jackson accepted the tactical responsibility eagerly; and, most significantly, when Jackson reached the enemy flank and found the situation somewhat different than what had been expected, he altered the tactical plans without a moment's hesitation and realized in consequence a victory of staggering proportions.

The situation facing Lee at Gettysburg two months later to the day was not precisely identical, but it was analogous to an interesting degree. He again chose on the second day of battle to send his ranking subordinate toward what he believed to be the most vulnerable enemy flank. He remained with the static element of his army to supervise its inexperienced leaders; expected the point of decision to be where his maneuver element struck; and surely expected the lieutenant general on the scene to seek the best possible terms when he attacked at the end of a careful and rather risky march. Longstreet,

27. Lafayette McLaws to My Dear Wife, July 7, 1863, McLaws Papers, SHC.

General Lafayette McLaws

of course, prosecuted the march execrably (or Captain Johnston unwittingly did, if you will). The most arresting parallel between the two days is the way in which Jackson, as was his custom, sought—and found—the best way to accomplish the purpose for which so much effort and risk had been incurred. In doing so Jackson received timely advice from several subordinates, most notably Fitzhugh Lee. Longstreet not only sulkily failed to seek out the best means of accomplishing his assigned task but also refused to countenance intelligence toward that end voluntarily supplied by subordinates. When he ostentatiously announced to all listeners, then and later, that Lee's bad plan must be followed, Longstreet was delineating as starkly as any critic ever could the chasm that separated his attitude from that of Stonewall Jackson. The contrast is an unpleasant one, not only in theoretical fashion but particularly because it was drawn in the blood and suffering of thousands of his own men and at a time that caused immense damage to his country.

Longstreet's demeanor on July 3 affecting the major assault on that day is another subject and beyond the scope of this essay. Later on the third, as the army contemplated disengagement, the general displayed further confusion and pique affecting McLaws. In an episode that has not received much attention, Longstreet again thrashed angrily about, giving more of what McLaws had called "contrary orders to everyone." McLaws promptly obeyed the first set of new orders, although he remonstrated against their pertinence with Moxley Sorrel; this obviously was not the week to seek sweet reason from Longstreet. After a time Sorrel came back and asked whether McLaws could resume his original position. McLaws of course reminded the staff officer of their earlier discussion. Sorrel responded, "Yes, I gave you the order to retire and it was given to me by Genl. Longstreet himself, but he now denied having given it!" Generals Law and Henry L. Benning were also victims of this unusual proceeding and compared disgruntled notes with McLaws. A few weeks later, McLaws recalled, he wrote to Longstreet seeking an explanation and received the response that the corps commander "had no recollection concerning the orders."[28]

No better credo could be imagined for a subordinate in disagreement with his superior than one Longstreet himself wrote, or claimed to have written, on July 24, 1863. In a letter that Longstreet published as written to his uncle, he declared: "I consider it a part of my duty to express my views to the commanding general. If he approves and adopts them, it is well; if he does not, it is my duty to adopt his views, and to execute his orders as faithfully as if they were my own."[29] It is difficult to imagine a more prudent guideline for application to circumstances such as Longstreet faced at Gettysburg. Only the most intransigent of the general's supporters can cling to the notion, however, that he executed Lee's orders in Pennsylvania "as faithfully as if they were my own." Was his July 24 letter the special pleadings of a guilty conscience?

In terms of strategy and tactics, Lee's army suffered most at Gettysburg because of the unwonted absence of J. E. B. Stuart and his skilled mounted men. It suffered next, both chronologically and with regard to impact, from the sloth and equivocation of Richard S. Ewell on July 1. Longstreet's uncertain opportunities lost in the midst of an unseemly sulk on July 2 can only be reckoned as third behind those more crisply defined shortcomings. The salient

28. For considerable detail on this episode, see Lafayette McLaws to I. R. Pennypacker, July 31, 1888, A. K. Smiley Public Library, Redlands, Calif. After the war, when it suited him again, Longstreet reclaimed these orders to withdraw as his own.

29. Longstreet, "Lee in Pennsylvania," 414.

difference is that Stuart and Ewell were not displaying petty personality traits as they strove in vain.

A peculiar footnote to the Gettysburg controversies cropped up late in the nineteenth century when General Cullen A. Battle publicly reported that a formal court of inquiry actually convened to examine the campaign. General William Mahone presided, according to Battle, who claimed to have been appointed recorder for the court. In its verdict the court "censured both Stuart and Longstreet, but General Lee suppressed the report, and took the blame upon himself."[30] General Battle's account must be classified as falling among the bizarre satellite claims that cluster tenaciously around the larger Gettysburg controversies.

Longstreet's career after Gettysburg included further refinement of his blame-shifting techniques. It also included what must have been for him the startling lesson that fondness for the tactical defensive cannot be readily translated into battlefield results. Twice during the war, Longstreet had the chance to operate on a large scale independent of Lee's oppressive damper on his creative skills. Not long before Gettysburg the ambitious corps commander had led a strong force in a campaign around Suffolk. Such initiatives as Longstreet found occasion to use included no tactical defensive; cooperative Federals proved to be in short supply. Federal general John G. Foster, who faced Longstreet, was hardly a commander of legendary proportions, but he was able to restrain any impulses he might have had to cooperate with Longstreet. The Suffolk command produced no striking results for Longstreet and might be classified as an embarrassment rather than a humiliation. Longstreet earned humiliation in ample doses in Tennessee later in the year.

During the last week of November 1863, Longstreet tasted the bitter dregs of total defeat around Knoxville. His attack on Fort Sanders—not only a tactical offensive but a brutal frontal assault—cannot be adjudged anything other than a pathetic exhibition of ineptitude. No large veteran contingent of Army of Northern Virginia troops experienced anything so grotesque during the war, even during its closing hours. The few dozen Federals in the fort routed the thousands of attackers with great slaughter. The northern assaults on Marye's Heights on December 13, 1862 (probably the only battle that really suited Longstreet, first and last), look like classic practice of military science compared to Fort Sanders. It is impossible to imagine R. E. Lee or T. J. Jack-

---

30. Undated newspaper clipping, Roll 59, Frame 83, Hotchkiss Papers, LC. Several similar clippings are in adjacent frames of the same source.

son—or Robert E. Rodes, William Dorsey Pender, S. Dodson Ramseur, John B. Gordon, or William Mahone, for that matter—caught up in so ghastly a tactical situation.[31]

After Knoxville even Longstreet must have admitted to himself that his cherished dreams of independent success were only cloud castles. He had been rebuffed by the unknown and undistinguished John G. Foster at Suffolk and then humiliated by Ambrose E. Burnside, of all people, for it was the inept Burnside who tormented Longstreet at Knoxville. The solution, once again, was to distribute blame among whatever targets came to mind. It seemed obvious to blame them for lack of enthusiastic support of their commander; after all, Longstreet knew with conviction, from his own career, how subordinates who lacked enthusiasm could foul up operations pretty thoroughly. The general put in arrest Generals McLaws, Evander M. Law, and Jerome B. Robertson. These sweeping arrests outstripped the record of the notoriously litigious Stonewall Jackson, who, though harsh and fond of courts, had no need of scapegoats.

Writing at the time, McLaws declared: "The charges were forced on him by public opinion & he attempts to make me a blind to draw public inquiry from his complete failure in the whole Tennessee campaign. . . . When it is considered that Gen. L . . . has nothing to recommend him as a commander, but the possession of a certain Bullheadedness, it is mortifying when one feels that he is allowed to tyranise, as he is doing." After the war McLaws summarized Longstreet's conduct of the campaign harshly but essentially accurately: "He was so out-witted and his movements so timid and managed as to conform exactly to those of the enemy, and as the enemy must have wished him to order, so as to give them every success and bring disaster and shame upon us."[32]

Longstreet sought to avoid charging McLaws formally, which he must have known would lead to embarrassment. He attempted merely to arrest his subordinate without either charges or a trial. McLaws insisted on being charged and tried, and Longstreet was indeed embarrassed by the results. The court ruled against McLaws on one single issue of the six posed by Longstreet and in his favor on the other five; but the War Department overturned even that vague stricture and censured Longstreet for his fiddling with the proceedings of the court.[33]

31. See Chapter 4 in this book, "Longstreet Versus McLaws—and Everyone Else—About Knoxville."

32. Lafayette McLaws to Lizzie Ewell, February 29, 1864, Ewell Papers, LC; Lafayette McLaws to Charles Arnall, February 2, 1897, Roll 34, Hotchkiss Papers, LC.

33. The only published summary of the charges before the publication of the present book was

Tactical offensives in the Civil War, and perhaps in most military epochs, required a good deal more from their commanders than did defensive arrangements—more coordination, diligence, moral force, breadth, grasp, and strength of purpose and mind. That is not to postulate that they were the preferable alternative, because they surely were not. A cooperative foe such as Burnside at Fredericksburg, however, turned up only intermittently. Meanwhile, the initiative regularly required taking the offensive; witness even the defensive oracle Longstreet staggering helplessly into an offensive mode at Knoxville. The most-studied, most-cited military thinkers of the Civil War era often are quoted in connection with modern analyses of almost everything from the 1860s, usually without acknowledging their awareness of the defects inherent in passivity. Among the mots of Clausewitz and Jomini on defensive roles are these apposite observations: "Never be enticed into passive defense by a strong terrain" and "A swift and vigorous transition to attack . . . is the most brilliant point of the defensive"; and "The passive defense is always pernicious."[34]

Neither Longstreet nor his special hero Joe Johnston ever managed an offensive well in independent campaigning. When the two kindred spirits collaborated at Seven Pines, "no action in the war was planned with such slovenly thinking or prepared so carelessly," in the apt words of Clifford Dowdey (who may have overlooked Knoxville in choosing his superlative). "Johnston's aversion to details . . . was typical of him" and also of Longstreet's feeble offensive gesture. As Charles Marshall of Lee's staff wrote, in mixed disgust and amusement over Johnston's published memoir: "If books [that] large . . . are to be written to explain why things were *not* done, what room will be left in our libraries for the lives of those who actually did something deserving of record, and need no apology or 'agility' of explanation?"[35] Lassitude and whatever else went into the defensive-only formula left Longstreet incapable of managing an offensive campaign when he—even he—recognized no alternative. That may well have affected his attitude throughout the war.

On the eve of the 1864 Wilderness campaign, Longstreet rejoined Lee's

---

in Robert K. Krick, "The McLaws-Knoxville Court Martial," a short article without notes in *A Collection of Essays Commemorating the 125th Anniversary of the Siege of Knoxville* (Knoxville: Knoxville Civil War Round Table, 1988), 11–14.

34. Clausewitz and Jomini, on either side of the semicolon, from Robert Debs Heinl, Jr., *Dictionary of Military and Naval Quotations* (Annapolis: United States Naval Institute, 1966), 82–83.

35. Clifford Dowdey, *The Seven Days: The Emergence of Lee* (Boston: Little, Brown, 1964), 84; Charles Marshall to G. W. Mindil, April 26, 1875, copy at Richmond National Battlefield Park.

army with far more relief and gratitude than he could have imagined when he left to attempt great things on his own. The McLaws results, which must have embarrassed Longstreet, were published in Richmond the day Grant crossed the Rapidan. At the same time, General Law, one of McLaws's fellow sufferers, was preparing to file formal charges against Longstreet on several counts, including "conduct unworthy of an officer and gentleman in making a false report of the fight" at Wauhatchie. Law had caught Longstreet in another "infamous lie," and he told McLaws, "If you will cover the Knoxville Campaign in your charges, I believe we can oust him." "Longstreet," Law insisted, "is most certainly on the wane

Wounding of
General Longstreet
by his own men.

both in, and out of the army."[36] In fact the general was on his way out of the army by means of convalescent leave, to the army's considerable loss.

Longstreet arrived in the Wilderness on the second day of battle, May 6, 1864, from a bivouac far to the southwest. Some sources suggest that Lee was dismayed over the tardiness of that arrival, including G. W. C. Lee quoting his father, C. S. Venable to Longstreet himself, and H. B. McClellan of Stuart's staff. The morning of the sixth proved to be Longstreet's last with the army for many months, as he fell dangerously wounded, the victim of a mistaken volley fired by Confederates in the tangled thickets of the Wilderness.[37]

When Longstreet returned to duty during the autumn of 1864, Lee must have eagerly welcomed the return of his seasoned lieutenant and best available corps commander. Whether Longstreet ever recovered his full ability to control his corps remains uncertain. Early in 1865 (on Lee's fifty-eighth birthday, in fact), the commanding general sent an inspection summary to Longstreet that expended nearly one thousand words in criticism of the condition of the First Corps. Although it no doubt was primarily a staff-to-staff communiqué, the document bore Lee's signature and was addressed to the corps commander. It cited "unsatisfactory" reports, officers who "have failed to do their duty," and units "lax in discipline" and "unsoldierly & unmilitary." The letter exhorted Longstreet in stern phrases: "Prompt measures must be taken"; "I desire that you will give particular attention . . . and exact unceasing effort"; "I desire you to correct the evils . . . by every means in your power"; "I beg that you will insist upon these points"; and "this should be at once corrected."[38]

As Lee's senior subordinate, Longstreet enjoyed the applause of most officers and enlisted men, but at least a few of them felt that his late-war performance let them down. A novice artillerist declared on March 19, 1865, that he considered Longstreet "the poorest general we have." Another man in the same eighty-man battery wrote later, "For a few months near the close of the war . . . to our great regret we had to serve under Longstreet."[39] Neither artil-

36. Evander M. Law to Lafayette McLaws, April 29, 1864, McLaws Papers, SHC.

37. Despite the complaints about Longstreet's march to the Wilderness, it is difficult to see how he could have done any better than he did. For details about the general's wounding on May 6, see Robert E. L. Krick, "Like a Duck on a June Bug, James Longstreet's Flank Attack, May 6, 1864," in Gary W. Gallagher, ed., *The Wilderness Campaign* (Chapel Hill: University of North Carolina Press, 1997), 236–64.

38. R. E. Lee to James Longstreet, January 19, 1865, MS 1F1613a2, VHS.

39. Thomas Miller Ryland Diary, March 19, 1865, typescript in the author's possession from original owned by a descendant in Warsaw; Charles B. Fleet memoir in Elizabeth M. Hodges, *C. B. Fleet: The Man and the Company* [Lynchburg, Va.?, 1985?], 42.

lerist ever earned an epaulet as military critic, but their unease suggests that Longstreet's 1865 aura as seen from the ranks was not quite what it once had been.

James Longstreet spent nearly four decades after the war assailing his former comrades in arms, beginning just slowly enough to avoid open assaults on Lee until after the death of the former army commander in 1870. When Lee heard the first mutterings about Longstreet's fabulous assertions and criticisms, he simply refused to believe that his former subordinate had said such "absurd" things.[40] Longstreet reached vitriolic high gear soon after Lee's death and maintained his momentum ever after. When the aging general's first wife died (she had been a Virginian, remarkably enough), he married a young woman—born the year of Gettysburg—who was herself a born controversialist and who acted on the general as kerosene would on a raging blaze.

At his death in 1904, Longstreet was one of the most thoroughly loathed men in the South. Many who found Longstreet's behavior distasteful would have echoed the mature judgment of Dr. Hunter Holmes McGuire, who read the general's mean-spirited memoir "more in sorrow for the man than indignation at his bad taste and temper." A considerable body of observers also shared McGuire's empirical conclusion: "If Longstreet . . . says so, it is most likely not true."[41]

Had General Longstreet died at the head of his corps on May 6, 1864, he surely would stand tall in the pantheon of Confederate heroes. We would see him in bronze on more than one battlefield and probably in Richmond as well. The mortal wounds inflicted on Longstreet's reputation therefore seem to some observers to be the result of what he did after the war. The hurtful impact, however, came not so much from postwar deeds as from the vistas Longstreet unveiled in the long life left to him. His longevity gave him numerous opportunities to bare his soul—the same one with which he had been saddled during the war—and the view was not a savory one.

Lieutenant General Richard Taylor surveyed the Gettysburg controversy a few years after the war with interest and some detachment. As a son of a president of the United States, a brother-in-law of the president of the Confederate States, and a general officer who served in the Virginia theater, Taylor was

40. Transcript of conversation between R. E. Lee and William Allan, April 15, 1868, p. 15, William Allan Papers, SHC.

41. Hunter H. McGuire to Jedediah Hotchkiss, March 30, 1893, January [day illegible], 1897, Roll 34, Hotchkiss Papers, LC.

blessed with exemplary connections in high circles. He had gone west well before Gettysburg so had no vested interest in the specific details under debate. He did know the principal figures well enough, however, to offer a lively and apposite comment: "A recent article in the public press, signed by General Longstreet, ascribes the failure at Gettysburg to Lee's mistakes, which he [Longstreet] in vain pointed out and remonstrated against. That any subject involving the possession and exercise of intellect should be clear to Longstreet and concealed from Lee, is a startling proposition to those having knowledge of the two men."[42]

42. Richard Taylor, *Destruction and Reconstruction* (New York: D. Appleton, 1879), 231.

4

Longstreet Versus McLaws—and Everyone
Else—About Knoxville

On November 6, 1863, James Longstreet led some twelve thousand troops out
of the Confederate lines besieging Chattanooga and joyfully moved away from
the Byzantine politics and inefficiencies of the Army of Tennessee. As he
moved northeastward toward Knoxville and away from General Braxton
Bragg, Longstreet was embarking on his second independent campaign. The
general's militantly self-confident attitude and his disdain for what seemed to
him to be the tactical and strategical ineptitude of his superiors, notably R. E.
Lee, made him eager to succeed on his own. His first opportunity a few
months earlier in Southside Virginia had yielded vague and disappointing results. Now, however, with freedom of maneuver and facing a hostile force led
by the spectacularly maladroit Ambrose E. Burnside, Longstreet could perform on his own terms. A more attractive stage upon which to strut would
have been hard for the disgruntled general to create.

A few weeks later Longstreet's force retreated in dejection from the outskirts of Knoxville, having missed several opportunities and accomplished
nothing whatsoever. The Confederates closed around Knoxville on November
18, but for ten days Longstreet equivocated while Federal fortifications steadily swelled in number and size. Finally, early on November 29, he threw several brigades against Fort Sanders in an assault scheduled days before but
drastically revised at the last minute. The attack by a substantial body of the
finest shock troops in the Army of Northern Virginia was easily and bloodily
repulsed by fewer than 150 Federal soldiers within the fort. What should have
been an epiphany for Longstreet had turned into humiliating, unredeemed

General Lafayette McLaws during the war.

disaster. The restless corps commander had fallen victim to the truth in the homely old maxim: "Be careful what you wish for—else you may get it."

In the aftermath of his fiasco in Tennessee, Longstreet spent the winter of 1863–64 casting about for scapegoats. He arrested and filed charges against General Jerome B. Robertson, commander of the famous Texas Brigade. He did the same to General Evander M. Law, the seasoned and well-respected brigade commander who happened to be harshly at odds with Longstreet's protégé, Micah Jenkins. The embittered general's highest-profile target was Lafayette McLaws, who for more than a year had been Longstreet's highest-ranking subordinate and, until disgust with Longstreet's demeanor turned him around, had been the corps commander's favorite candidate for promotion to the rank of lieutenant general.

The records of the court-martial, on which McLaws insisted despite Longstreet's patently obvious eagerness to avoid such a hearing, have never been published nor apparently even examined in detail by historians. In fact, a recent biography concerning one member of the court declares, in egregious error, that the government in Richmond sought to avoid controversy and thus the court never convened.[1]

The court actually met and began deliberations near New Market, Tennessee, in early February 1864. Obstructionism by Longstreet thwarted the proceedings after a few days. With help from the War Department in Richmond, McLaws managed to arrange a renewal of the court at Midway, Tennessee, in mid-March. Its proceedings unveil one of the most remarkable cases in American military history. The court testimony revealed that Longstreet's arrant failures near Knoxville unfolded without the commanding general understanding what was happening—before, during, or after the fighting. As a result, Longstreet's attempt to blame McLaws met with ludicrous failure. It seems apparent in retrospect that the lieutenant general was not lying as he filed spurious charges, although such behavior was well within his character; instead, he was simply utterly befuddled.

Official copies of Confederate court-martial transcripts did not survive the war. They probably went up in flames when Richmond burned on April 3, 1865. The only copies of such proceedings available today, and they are very few in number, are ones retained by participants. Fortunately, the fascinating trial in which Longstreet displayed his startling confusion about the assault on Fort Sanders is one such. This description of the trial is based almost entirely on those manuscripts, which provide rich and ample grist for historical inquiry.

The central figure in Longstreet's Knoxville witch-hunt was Lafayette McLaws—the Army of Northern Virginia's highest-ranking division commander for longer than any other officer. He was senior to A. P. Hill, Richard H. Anderson, John B. Hood, George E. Pickett, Jubal A. Early, J. E. B. Stuart, and many others during their tenures as major generals. Only D. H. Hill and Richard S. Ewell held commissions at that rank senior to McLaws's—and both of those men were with the army in division command for relatively short periods (only a few weeks in Ewell's case). McLaws deserves a bit of attention.

The lifelong Georgian was born in Augusta on January 15, 1821. He attended the University of Virginia in 1837, where he took mathematics, modern languages, and natural philosophy, then went on to West Point the next

1. Evans J. Casso, *Francis T. Nicholls* (Thibodaux, La.: Nicholls College Foundation, 1987), 93–94.

year. After a solid first year at the Military Academy, standing 23rd out of 85 cadets, McLaws's scholarship and deportment both slipped markedly. He finished 48th out of 56 graduates in 1842 and stood 198th of 217 cadets throughout the institution in conduct. Even that standing marginally out-shone class dullards James Longstreet (54th) and Earl Van Dorn (52nd). Not surprisingly, given his ribald Confederate career and death by cuckold, Van Dorn ranked within a half-dozen of the bottom in conduct among the 217 cadets in all four classes. McLaws scored his best in ethics and engineering. Longstreet (next to last) and Van Dorn (only three above Longstreet) an-chored the bottom of the list in ethics.[2]

Most of Lafayette McLaws's antebellum career in the U.S. Army consisted of the same frontier drudgery and sluggish promotion that is familiar from the biographies of his fellow officers. On March 16, 1844, he became a second lieutenant—after two years holding only a brevet in that lowest commissioned rank. McLaws inched up to first lieutenant on February 16, 1847, and to cap-tain on August 24, 1851. A decade later he resigned at that rank. Frontier army postings before the Mexican War included Fort Gibson, Indian Terri-tory; Pass Christian, Mississippi; Baton Rouge; and Fort Pickens, Florida.[3]

In the early stages of the Mexican War, McLaws served on the northern frontier with Zachary Taylor. He helped defend Fort Brown and capture Monterey, then transferred to Winfield Scott's army and was present at the capture of Vera Cruz. A bout with sickness drove First Lieutenant McLaws home from Mexico City for a tour of recruiting duty. In 1849 he married Emily Allison Taylor, a niece of his former chief. Emily was nine years Lafay-ette's junior. McLaws thus became a cousin by marriage of Jefferson Davis's first wife and also of Richard Taylor, who was destined for a stellar Confeder-ate career.

McLaws went back to the frontier with the post–Mexican War army, to Jefferson Barracks in St. Louis; Santa Fe; Fort Gibson again; Fort Smith, Ar-kansas; and as acting adjutant general of the Department of New Mexico. In 1858 Captain McLaws served in the Utah expedition, and he spent 1859

2. University of Virginia matriculation book, 1826–56, Alderman Library at the university; *Register of the Officers and Cadets of the U.S. Military Academy, West Point, N.Y., June, 1839* [West Point, 1839], 15; *Official Register of the Officers and Cadets of the U.S. Military Academy, West Point, New-York, June, 1842* (New York: J. P. Wright, 1842), 8, 21. McLaws and John C. Breckinridge shared the same birth date.

3. Francis B. Heitman, *Historical Register and Dictionary of the United States Army*, 2 vols. (Washington, D.C.: GPO, 1903), 1:675.

"protecting emigrants and escorting Mormons to California." During the following two years he served on a march to New Mexico, held posts at Fort Craig and Fort Defiance, and went on an expedition against the Navajos.[4]

Emily evidently accompanied her husband through much of this campaigning, since children were born to her through the 1850s. The couple eventually had three boys and four girls. One of the latter became the wife of General Edward P. King, Jr., who surrendered Bataan in 1942. Lafayette McLaws's son Uldrich named one of his daughters Lafayette; that granddaughter of the general wrote several novels on Confederate and other historical themes. The family owned no slaves.[5]

Captain McLaws, U.S. Army, became Major McLaws, C.S. Army, soon after Georgia seceded, to take rank from March 16, 1861. Four days later his brother wrote to the Confederate secretary of war, because Lafayette was too sick to do so, pleading for a furlough before reporting for service. Incredibly, McLaws had not seen his family for three years—during which time Emily apparently had grown fat; Lafayette was impolitic enough to recall lifting her over muddy spots during their honeymoon, but now "I fear tis not in my power." Through April and May, Major McLaws served as a quartermaster and then adjutant general in the District of Savannah, where his Confederate service would end four years later. Four months after he left Savannah, poor McLaws learned the sempiternal truth that bureaucracy overrides every emergency. The secretary of the treasury sent him a demand for reimbursement of $800 expended during his stint as a fill-in quartermaster. There was no question about the funds being misspent; the problem was that McLaws had not been bonded properly when he performed the job. The exigencies of a revolutionary experiment be damned: get the paperwork done![6]

4. Dumas Malone, ed., *Dictionary of American Biography*, 20 vols. (New York: Charles Scribner's Sons, 1928–36), 12:120–21.

5. Lafayette's books include *Jezebel, A Romance in the Days When Ahab Was King of Israel* (Boston: Lothrop, 1902); *The Welding* (Boston: Little, Brown, 1907); *When the Land Was Young, Being the True Romance of Mistress Antoinette Huguenin . . . in the Days of the Buccaneers* (Boston: Lothrop, 1901); and *Maid of Athens* (Boston: Little, Brown, 1906). *The Welding* has a Civil War theme. Miss McLaws also prepared sketches of Mrs. Jefferson Davis and other prominent southerners for the Federal Writers Project. When General King was released from Japanese irons in 1945, he managed to recover the Savannah silver service belonging to his wife, Betty, from a vault at the Bank of Manila. Another daughter was Virginia McLaws, a maiden lady who taught art at Sweetbrier College for many years (family information from Carlton Jones of the *Baltimore Sun*, who knew both Betty and Virginia).

6. W. R. McLaws to Leroy Pope Walker, March 20, 1861, "Letters Received by the Confederate Secretary of War," document 100–1861, M437, NA; McLaws to Emily, June 10, 1861,

On June 17, 1861, McLaws was commissioned colonel of the 10th Georgia Infantry. He commanded infantry at that rank, and the next two higher, for the rest of the war—no doubt shaking the dust of the quartermaster bureaucracy from his garments with real satisfaction. Three months later (September 25), McLaws received promotion to brigadier general, and on May 23, 1862, he advanced to major general.[7]

General McLaws fought under the unbalanced John B. Magruder on Virginia's Peninsula with some success. During the Maryland campaign, his capture of Maryland Heights, wrought with real determination and style, was the key to the capture of Harpers Ferry. At Sharpsburg on September 17, it was McLaws's division that won the most ringing (albeit fortuitous) Confederate victory of the day, against Federals under John Sedgwick and Edwin V. Sumner in the West Woods. The campaign in Maryland also embroiled McLaws in two controversies: with General Howell Cobb, who had behaved badly near Crampton's Gap; and with John B. Hood, over a Texas Brigade book critical of McLaws. Both Hood and McLaws remained privately bitter over this matter, despite an ostensible reconciliation for public consumption.[8]

Fortunately for our perspective on Lafayette McLaws, his correspondence survives in really tremendous bulk. That with Emily McLaws, which constitutes the largest volume, is of very warm tenor, often touching in content and expression—but is discouragingly domestic for historical purposes. All of the general's writing is less accessible than it otherwise would be because of absolutely execrable penmanship. A great deal of practice, and even more patience, is wonted to decipher the flat lines and arcane squiggles of what often resembles the electrocardiogram wave of a nearly moribund patient.[9]

The general's scribbling to his wife—as so often is the case with private correspondence—reveals a man of more soulful mien than his public persona

---

McLaws Papers at SHC/UNC (see note 9 below for collection); Secretary of the Treasury Memminger circular letter dated September 7, 1861, "Letters Received by the Confederate Secretary of War," document 5378–1861, M437, NA. McLaws's first appointment actually came in the short-lived Army of Georgia, with rank as captain tendered to him on January 29, 1861, by the governor (McLaws's official Compiled Service Record with the 10th Georgia, M266, NA).

7. McLaws's CSR, M331.

8. Correspondence about both controversies is in the McLaws Papers cited in the next note. The Texan book that triggered the tiff between McLaws and Hood was Nicholas A. Davis, *The Campaign from Texas to Maryland* (Houston: E. H. Cushing, 1863).

9. The largest groupings of McLaws manuscripts are in the McLaws Papers, SHC and in the McLaws Papers, PLD.

suggested. The intimate letters also display a decidedly negative attitude toward Yankees. In a modern world ostentatiously tolerant of everyone and everything, Lafayette's regional chauvinism would be condemned. In 1862, though, disliking Yankees and their demeanor was an entirely acceptable notion at some latitudes, and McLaws indulged the chance. He wrote of "the vulgarities of the Yankee" and of "utter loathing for the depraved wretches, totally devoid as they are of all delicacy and decency and refinement." Yankee women, he declared, "were not ladies in the Southern acceptations of the word." Northerners seemed to him to be "a very different race from the Southerners. There is a coarseness in their manners and looks and a twang in their voices, which grates harshly." Furthermore, Yankees treated blacks, poor people, and even the sick in uncivilized fashion.[10]

Mrs. McLaws wrote less frequently and ardently to her husband, to his chagrin. Typical of the letters to Emily is one that McLaws penned in the fall of 1862, damning her dilatory writing habits. "No letter for me to night?" he complained, having himself sent six letters in seven days. "Must I again exclaim without any response on the other side 'What an affectionate husband I am; and what an affectionate wife I deserve to have!' " The general's plea for attention insisted that it would be much better to receive a note saying, " 'Dear husband you are indeed a good and affectionate one' than to be forced to write it myself, it would be much more consoling."[11]

A few months later, at the height of the doldrums in winter encampments, he mused wistfully about the joyful prospect of becoming a civilian husband again. "I have a very great longing to quit the army & live in a quiet secluded place," he ruminated. Such an existence would enable the couple "to educate our children and teach them a home feeling, which they must be strangers to now." The restless major general proposed becoming a farmer, a carpenter ("it is clean and neat . . . and requires a head and good thoughts"), teaching, clerking, or (tongue clearly in cheek) inventing something valuable. He rejected blacksmithing ("I do not like Blacksmithing, so will not discuss it"), painting ("not knowing colors"), and architecture and engineering. Waxing waggish with his wife of a dozen years, McLaws admitted being "too old to be a dancing master, though graceful enough in all conscience!" and being "good enough to be a preacher but could not preach." A role near the top of his

10. McLaws to wife, December 3, 1862, June 28, 1863, McLaws Papers, SHC.
11. McLaws to wife, November 16, 1862, McLaws Papers, SHC.

lifelong profession, as one of the highest-ranking officers in a world-famous army, obviously did not seem as attractive to Lafayette McLaws as might have been expected.[12]

Events during the two years after that plaintive letter cannot have increased McLaws's contentment with his military lot. He shared the army's fondness, approaching reverence, for R. E. Lee—but ran afoul of the army commander's displeasure. A fortnight before the Battle of Chancellorsville, McLaws told his wife that Lee had been sick for ten days, "but is getting better . . . much to my pleasure . . . it would be a real misfortune for him to be away from us." Soon thereafter, in the backwash of Lee's greatest victory, the commanding general lost his temper for one of the few times recorded during the war. On May 2, 1863, Lee had been displeased with McLaws for a lack of vigor near the Orange Turnpike. Again near Salem Church on the afternoon of May 3, "the old man seemed to be feeling so real wicked" that his subordinates avoided him. Lee's anger arose from wasted time and a lack of reconnaissance and preparation, in a sector under McLaws's control. McLaws probably lost on that afternoon any chance at one of the new lieutenant general billets assigned later during the month.[13]

Neither of the two new lieutenant generals, who between them replaced Stonewall Jackson—or attempted to—carved out a successful record in corps command. It is far from certain that McLaws would have done better. His considerable skill in leading a division grew out of his calm, methodical approach to military details, unleavened with any notable flair. Thoroughness played well at the division level; more than that would be required from an accomplished corps commander. It would be hard to improve on the deft summary of McLaws's military characteristics left by Moxley Sorrel of Longstreet's staff: "He was an officer of much experience and most careful. Fond of detail, his command was in excellent condition, and his ground and position well examined and reconnoitered; not brilliant in the field or quick in movement there or elsewhere, he could always be counted on and had secured the entire confidence of his officers and men."[14]

12. McLaws to wife, February 2, 1863, McLaws Papers, SHC.

13. McLaws to wife, April 13, 1863, McLaws Papers, SHC; Randolph Barton to A. C. Hamlin, July 3, 1893, Hamlin Papers, Harvard University, Cambridge, Mass.; Gary W. Gallagher, ed., *Fighting for the Confederacy: The Personal Recollections of General Edward Porter Alexander* (Chapel Hill: University of North Carolina Press, 1988), 213.

14. Gilbert Moxley Sorrel, *Recollections of a Confederate Staff Officer* (New York: Neale, 1905), 135.

The First Corps's artillerist par excellence, Porter Alexander, delivered a judicious summary of McLaws's sturdy performance that nicely complements Sorrel's analysis: "Few of our generals equaled him in his care for [the soldiers'] comfort & the pains he took in many matters of little detail. . . . [He had] his division always in the best possible condition. . . . McLaws was about the best general in the army [for defensive alignments]. He had fixed up his sharpshooters [at Fredericksburg] all along the river to the Queen's taste. . . . with his usual painstaking care & study of detail. . . ."[15]

Lafayette McLaws marched his division north toward Pennsylvania in June 1863 as an accomplished troop leader, reliable, careful, painstaking, and efficient—and as James Longstreet's recognized protégé: he came back to Virginia in July a pariah at First Corps headquarters. The revolution in McLaws's status resulted from Longstreet's behavior at Gettysburg and his subordinate's distaste for what he saw in that connection. A separate chapter in this book is devoted to Longstreet's behavior on July 2, 1863, at Gettysburg, and its impact on the unfortunate McLaws. The distraught and disillusioned division commander told his wife of the mess in a letter dated July 7 ("I consider him a humbug, a man of small capacity . . .") and concluded firmly: "It is my intention to get away from his [Longstreet's] command." He recognized his consignment in Longstreet's eyes to a point beyond the pale: "After this the scheme was to get rid of me in order that Kershaw might get my Division and Jenkins could then get Hood's without opposition."[16]

McLaws's yearnings to be free from Longstreet were entirely in vain. Two months later the two generals were en route to Georgia and Tennessee, for attachment to General Braxton Bragg's Army of Tennessee. McLaws's division did not arrive in time to take part in the great Battle of Chickamauga, but it made up the largest element of Longstreet's force when that general moved from Chattanooga toward Knoxville on November 6. Free at last, free at last, Longstreet set out to engrave his mark upon the war and upon the inept Ambrose E. Burnside, who commanded a modest Federal force in east Tennessee. Longstreet's attitude toward McLaws on the eve of the campaign included some uncertainty. He responded positively to Bragg's suggestion that McLaws go on an independent foray ("it may be well to give him a trial") but added the caveat that McLaws sometimes was indolent and "should hush up."

15. Gallagher, ed., *Fighting for the Confederacy*, 136, 170, 176.

16. McLaws to wife, July 7, 1863, McLaws Papers, SHC; draft article by McLaws in his papers, SHC.

Obviously McLaws was not being subservient enough for Longstreet's tastes six weeks before the Fort Sanders fiasco unfolded.[17]

Longstreet's mission was clear: he must destroy, or at least damage, Burnside in the vicinity of Knoxville; he must achieve that goal promptly; and then he must return to aid Bragg, who had General U. S. Grant bottled up in Chattanooga (or at least thought he did). Burnside's goal was similarly clear, and of course the precise reciprocal of Longstreet's: he must delay Longstreet as long as possible to leave Grant free to deal with Bragg unhindered. The Confederate purpose required decisiveness, alacrity, aggression, and initiative. None of those things were among Longstreet's particular strengths. He had, in fact, hewn out a military philosophy position stridently opposed to aggression and initiative. The man and the hour had *not* met. That awareness sooner or later must have dawned on Longstreet himself. Perhaps it was stirring in his mind even before his departure, because at the end of September he wrote to the secretary of war plaintively: "Can't you send us Gen. Lee? . . . We need some such great mind as Gen. Lee's." Longstreet spent a third of a century after Lee was dead explaining how much deeper his (Longstreet's) own understanding of military affairs had been than Lee's, but in Tennessee in 1863 he experienced some obvious yearnings for the guiding hand that had so long controlled his military environment. After the war, McLaws suggested that Longstreet's plea to Richmond had been designed either to secure the army's command to himself or to gain command of the Army of Northern Virginia if Lee went west. The wording, however, has the clear odor of genuine dismay, not of Machiavellian manipulation.[18]

Expecting one's enemy to do what you *want* him to do is precisely counter to the basic military maxim that suggests the prudence of expecting him to do what he *should* do. Things work out the delightfully easy way only rarely in military affairs—or in human affairs in general. R. E. Lee might well have sent to Longstreet a copy of a letter he had written to an ineptly visionary subordinate a few months earlier, responding to an elaborate proposal built on wishful thinking: "I know the pleasure experienced in shaping campaigns [and] battles, according to our wishes, and have enjoyed the ease with which obstacles to their accomplishment (in effigy) can be overcome."[19] Longstreet

17. Longstreet to Bragg, October 16, 1863, Frederick Dearborn Collection, Folder 568, Houghton Library, Harvard University, Cambridge, Mass.

18. Lafayette McLaws, "After Chickamauga," *Addresses Delivered Before the Confederate Veterans' Association, Savannah, Ga.* (Savannah: The Association, 1898), 54–55, 59.

19. Lee to Isaac R. Trimble, March 8, 1863, in *OR* ser. I, 25(2):658.

really would have liked Burnside to attack him in feckless fashion, in a sort of Fredericksburg Redux. By now, though, even the bewhiskered Ambrose knew better, and the Confederate commander was left to fashion effigies. After much aimless fiddling, Longstreet found no option but to attack, and he did it in pathetically inept fashion.

View from Fort Sanders

The Confederate force lost its best chance to harm Burnside in the open field on November 16 around Lenoir Station, whether or not through any fault of Longstreet himself. Two days later he approached Knoxville and began a painful attempt to decide what to do. An aide, friend, and apologist of Longstreet's admitted: "An energetic movement, without the slightest delay, would have carried us into town and brought Burnside to terms."[20]

What had been at the outset a very rudimentary curtain of Unionist rifle pits developed into a stout defensive line, two tiers deep in most places, more than that in others, as Longstreet stood by impassively. McLaws in vain "*volunteered* to assault the city . . . that the enemy were busily fortifying before our eyes [while] the works were incomplete." Impressed black laborers lined the parapets with cotton bales and then covered them with rawhide. While Longstreet did nothing, day after day—not even a notable demonstration—the blue-clad defenders steadily improved their positions. They erected cheveaux-

20. Sorrel, *Recollections*, 212–13. McLaws, in a draft article in his papers at SHC, reported that he proposed a practicable turning movement to Longstreet on November 16, but that "rapid Movements" were "not in his programme."

de-frise in front of the lines to snarl the approaches and strung telegraph wire
taut between tree stumps. Desperately eager to avoid the offensive measures
so alien to his nature, Longstreet fell upon the ludicrous notion of starving
out Burnside—this by an army utterly tied to movement for success, both by
its orders and by pragmatism! Local citizens reminded him that the nature of
the river corridors gave the Federals plenty of obvious supply access points.
Longstreet called the citizens liars, in a sort of a priori warmup for his pending
attack on McLaws's performance: if it did not come up to the general's wishes,
it simply must be untrue. The dithering lasted until the twelfth day of the
"siege," when orders came from Bragg to attack immediately. An assault on
Fort Sanders would be launched on the twenty-eighth. The day proved to be
dark and foggy and cold, so the schedule fell back yet one more day. Longstreet's lone tactical offensive of the war, launched as an independent commander, would step off on the morning of November 29.[21]

Fort Sanders covered just a bit more than two acres of hilltop west of Knoxville. Its earthen walls loomed a dozen feet or more high. A ditch on the Confederate side averaged twelve feet wide and six or eight feet deep but as much
as eleven feet deep in places. Thoughtful Yankee engineers had plowed the
open space opposite the vulnerable northwest bastion with furrows that chan-
neled toward fields of artillery fire. Telegraph wire obstructions covered that
sector especially thickly. Federal unease about the northwest salient arose in
large part from the ample defilade available to attackers in a swale barely one
hundred yards from the fort's walls. That "remarkable" feature, which Porter
Alexander called "a big limestone sink," would save many Confederate lives—
but it could not offset the fort's inherent strength unless the southerners sup-

21. McLaws to Marcus J. Wright, June 7, 1882, copy in the author's possession (I have the
admirable historian of the campaigns in those environs, William Glenn Robertson, to thank for a
copy of this fine letter). The best summary of the Knoxville campaign is Digby G. Seymour, *Divided Loyalties: Fort Sanders and the Civil War in East Tennessee* (Knoxville: East Tennessee Historical Society, 1982). A brief monograph of thoroughly anti-Longstreet tenor is Judith Lee Hallock,
General James Longstreet in the West: A Monumental Failure (Fort Worth, Tex.: Ryan Place Publishers, 1995). A logical place to seek the pro-Longstreet side would seem to be in the slavishly adula-
tory book by W. G. Piston, *Lee's Tarnished Lieutenant: James Longstreet and His Place in Southern
History* (Athens: University of Georgia Press, 1987), but that dreadful work, amusingly, elects the
comfortable option of all but ignoring what happened at Knoxville. Gallagher, ed., *Fighting for the
Confederacy*, 318–29, provides wonderful insights on Longstreet's repeated equivocations, from the
perspective of a high-ranking First Corps officer of exceptional intelligence. For the impact of
Longstreet's dithering on the army, see Robert K. Krick, *Parker's Virginia Battery* (Wilmington,
N.C.: Broadfoot, 1989), 230–39.

pressed its fire. Suppressing that fire should have been easy because only 105 northern artillerists manned Fort Sanders. Their commander was a mere first lieutenant. A few score Federal infantry supported the position. Against that handful, Longstreet would throw thousands of the best battle-tested veterans of the Army of Northern Virginia.[22]

Porter Alexander superintended a detailed assault plan that ensured, he felt certain, a thorough success. It featured careful preliminary fires from an array of Confederate ordnance. A final barrage of twenty minutes' duration would ensure suppression of Federal resistance, even if it did not kill the enemy or damage the fort. Then, no matter how formidable the enemy ditch and parapet were found to be, they could be "deliberately examined, undertaken, & overcome," even if it should be necessary to carve out steps or shallow ravines into the face of the works. "If our infantry once scaled the parapet, the fort was ours," Alexander declared. "And the Federal lines became untenable when we held the fort." It is hard to argue with those conclusions. Longstreet, however, abandoned the entire plan shortly before the attack was launched. Alexander—no Longstreet foe usually—referred to the change as the "absurd & fatal idea of converting his attack into a surprise." The new plan, he fumed, was full of "absurdities . . . Some of its features were crazy enough to have come out of Bedlam."[23]

The "absurd & fatal idea" canceled the artillery feature almost completely, substituting instead an infantry-only surprise attack to be pressed home in the predawn darkness as a surprise. Incredibly, the "surprise" was emasculated by another Longstreet stratagem: after dark on the twenty-eighth, Confederate sharpshooters were sent to drive away northern skirmishers and take up position within rifle range of Fort Sanders. The surprise therefore was many hours stale by the time of the actual assault. McLaws's four brigades, under Generals Benjamin G. Humphreys, Goode Bryan, Joseph B. Kershaw, and William T. Wofford, made up the main attacking column. Three other brigades under General Micah Jenkins were to move in close support. Several other brigades hovered near the flanks to assist as needed. In his usual methodical fashion, McLaws outlined responsibilities in a detailed order. It specified brigade alignments; formation in columns of regiments; an assault "with fixed bayo-

22. Gallagher, ed., *Fighting for the Confederacy*, 325; Seymour, *Divided Loyalties*, 177–82.

23. Gallagher, ed., *Fighting for the Confederacy*, 325–26. Longstreet's own explanation of this unhappy mess appears in his memoir, James Longstreet, *From Manassas to Appomattox: A Memoir of the Civil War in America* (Philadelphia: J. B. Lippincott, 1896), 497–508.

nets, and without firing a gun"; focus on the key "northwest angle of Fort . . . Sanders"; that "the men should be urged to the work with a determination to succeed, and should rush to it without hallooing"; and finally that the sharpshooters must suppress fire from the fort.[24]

Most ranking Confederate officers shared Porter Alexander's scorn for the last-minute revision. Both of the plan's primary executors, McLaws and Jenkins, attempted to convince the army commander of his mistake. McLaws wrote a thoughtful and thoroughly rational note to Longstreet based on the rumors cascading in from Chattanooga that Bragg had just fought a major battle (he had, and of course had been defeated). If Bragg had won, McLaws pointed out, "do we not gain by delay at this point?" If Bragg had lost, McLaws argued irrefragably, the Confederates around Knoxville must reorient their line of communications toward Virginia. A battle at Chattanooga, whatever the result, would make an attack on Fort Sanders needless bloodshed and a pointless operational risk. Longstreet replied that he did not think Bragg had fought a big battle and that if Bragg had lost, honor required that they go to his succor or be "disgraced" (less than a week later, Longstreet was marching in the direction of Virginia). Jenkins's vain appeal to Longstreet was based on new intelligence about the depth of the ditch around Fort Sanders. Any thought of constructing ladders or fascines for crossing the moat foundered on the total absence of wood, even trees, in the vicinity. Longstreet responded, in the same wishful vein as his rejection of the civilians who had pointed out basic facts about local geography: "The work of the enemy is not enclosed. The ditch is probably at some points not more than three feet deep, and five or six feet wide. . . . I have no apprehension of the result of the attack. . . ."[25]

McLaws later expressed his conclusions about the fatal change most emphatically. He blamed the revision on "the effect of a panick in the mind of Genl L, that he now realised how much he was to blame for the delay of the last two weeks in doing nothing & making no preparation. . . . He felt that his hitherto non-action was near akin to criminality, that he ought to have done something. . . . Every one could see the numerous chances we had for failure and the very few we had for success." In the face of "facts patent to

24. Seymour, *Divided Loyalties*, 184–87.

25. Longstreet, *Manassas to Appomattox*, 504–5; Henry S. Burrage, *History of the Thirty-Sixth Regiment, Massachusetts Volunteers* (Boston: Press of Rockwell and Churchill, 1884), 116. A transcribed copy of Longstreet's reply, supplied to the judge advocate of the subsequent court-martial, is in the Garnett Andrews Papers, SHC.

every thinking officer and man under me," McLaws "shrank from making what was a useless sacrifice of the lives of so many brave and patriotic men." His note full of careful ratiocination left Longstreet unmoved, as such things so often did.[26]

For more than a week, Longstreet had forged a litany of excuses for delaying an attack, despite his subordinates' wishes. Now he was determined suddenly to launch an assault, again despite his subordinates' advice. Perhaps contrariness dictated the need to override advice. Perhaps Longstreet actually did believe the ample evidence that Bragg had fought a battle and was spurred to action by the realization that his long-awaited chance at independent command was waning. Perhaps he actually thought this ill-prepared pseudo-surprise really was the answer. McLaws wrote emphatically (but probably unfairly) after the war that the entire campaign had been driven by "gratification of [Longstreet's] personal malice only"—winning early at Knoxville would have helped Bragg, whom Longstreet was "determined to break down . . . let it cost what it may."[27] Whatever the trigger, Longstreet at last was about to launch a crucial attack on his own, without interference from Lee and the others who for so long had been unwilling to accept his ostensibly superior tactical wisdom.

Ten thousand Confederates suffered a miserable night in freezing mud awaiting the signal to attack. Just before dawn they moved out, toward the crackling musketry of the advanced sharpshooters and under some covering fire from artillery. The heart of the advance made straight for the northwest salient of Fort Sanders. Longstreet's chief of staff called the assault "vigorous," "shoving everything aside." Then the converging furrows slowed them down. Telegraph wire tripped some of the front files, and their comrades behind them tumbled into the same heap. Even so, the sturdy southern infantry poured into the ditch, chased away enemy skirmishers, and silenced the Federal cannon by firing through the embrasures. The fort would be theirs, easily won, if they could get into it. Longstreet's three-foot ditch would have made that easy. A ditch four times that deep proved a death trap, especially with a parapet rising that far again above it and cotton-bale redoubts above that. The walls, furthermore, were slippery and icy: only "six or eight" Confederates managed to scramble over the barrier. No Federal dared lean through an opening to fire down. Confederates watching from afar assumed that Fort Sanders

26. McLaws to Marcus J. Wright, June 7, 1882, copy in the author's possession.
27. Ibid.

The assault on Fort Sanders, Knoxville

had surrendered, since no resistance was evident. At closer range, one South Carolina colonel summarized the southerners' plight as "like rats in a cage-trap." One of Bryan's Georgians wrote succinctly: "We planted our colors on the fort but could not get into it." A few of the bravest and hardiest attackers clawed their way up the towering slick walls, only to be knocked back by fire from Yankees crouching under cover. Lieutenant Colonel George Hunter Carmical was hit by four bullets within a few moments—but lived until 1929.[28]

Confederate soldiers stumble on the wires as they charge uphill.

28. Sorrel, *Recollections*, 214–15; Seymour, *Divided Loyalties*, 191–204; Frank Huger to father, January 1, 1864, copy in the author's possession; Asbury Coward, *The South Carolinians* (New York: Vantage Press, 1968), 101; Grant D. Hurley (53rd Georgia) letter, December 14, 1863, Bell Wiley Collection, Box 3, Folder 50, Emory University, Atlanta, Ga.; Mamie Yeary, comp., *Reminiscences of the Boys in Gray* (Dallas: Press of Wilkinson Printing Company, 1912), 690; Robert K. Krick, *Lee's Colonels: A Biographical Register of the Field Officers of the Army of Northern Virginia* (Dayton, Ohio: Morningside, 1992), 83.

Emerging daylight revealed an amorphous mass of humanity in the ditches, with no means to get out. Unionists in adjacent positions brought fire against the ditch, especially from the unthreatened Confederate left. Men inside Fort Sanders lit shells and rolled them over the parapet as sort of immense hand grenades. Eventually the Confederates climbed back out and ran rearward to cover, taking losses the whole way—far more than during the forward movement. A few minutes later, Longstreet received a telegram with formal notice of the news already current throughout the army: Bragg had been defeated at Chattanooga. In a meaningless attack that lasted less than half an hour, Longstreet's ill-aimed effort had suffered nearly one thousand casualties. The Federal lieutenant in the fort, who had whipped an entire army, reported Federal losses in the fort as five killed and eight wounded. The Yankees also captured three flags and picked up more than one thousand rifles that the ordnance-poor Confederates could ill afford to lose. A northern officer wrote, entirely aptly, that "this assault on Fort Sanders was Fredericksburg reversed. . . . Never was a victory more complete and achieved at so slight a cost." Given the presence of both Burnside and Longstreet, in reversed roles, the parallel was indeed striking. Casualties near the proportion of one hundred to one at Fort Sanders suggest, in fact, that the hopeless assaults at Fredericksburg in December 1862 were relatively a far less unmitigated military fiasco.[29]

Five days later, Longstreet's beaten army began a sullen retreat away from Knoxville, away from Bragg, toward Virginia. Ahead of them lay months of hardship and a winter of discontent. Ahead of Longstreet loomed the task of finding suitable scapegoats. On December 4, McLaws submitted an enormous requisition for stationery: he apparently had an inkling of what was to come. On the seventeenth, Longstreet ordered McLaws relieved of command and told him to go to Georgia. When the victim, understandably, asked why ("I respectfully request to be informed of the particular reason"), he was told that he had "exhibited a want of confidence in the plans and efforts [of] the Commanding Genl." That was, of course, unmistakably true—albeit a failing all but universal among observers of the operations around Knoxville. Not a word of that complaint would appear in the formal charges, however, when finally they were levied; nor was there any hint of what eventually would be the for-

29. Longstreet, *Manassas to Appomattox*, 507; *OR*, ser. I 31(1):341–43, 475; Henry S. Burrage, "Burnside's East Tennessee Campaign," *Papers of the Military Historical Society of Massachusetts*, 14 vols. (Boston: Military Historical Society of Massachusetts, 1895–1918), 8:595–96.

mal charges in this preliminary summary of McLaws's malfeasance. Initially, Longstreet simply sought to be rid of McLaws by executive fiat, but McLaws of course "would not retire on his dictum" and demanded that he be charged formally. President Davis supported McLaws's demand, although prevailing military law eventually would have forced the same result. Longstreet would have been better served by adhering to the broader subjective complaint, which was beyond argument, when he made up his charges. McLaws admitted wryly: "As the campaign . . . up to the time . . . had been a complete failure, my want of confidence in the plans & efforts of the commanding general, was rather complimentary than otherwise."[30]

Pressed by McLaws for precise charges, Longstreet delivered a bill of particulars on the last day of 1863. He buttressed a single charge of "Neglect of Duty" with three specifications. The contents of those three mounted up to six actual grounds for trial—five of them of truly remarkable foolishness, the sixth perversely deceitful. McLaws knew at a glance that his defense would be easy to support with the testimony of any of hundreds of witnesses. In a letter to General D. H. Hill three weeks later, McLaws summarized his view of the behavior of his superior, who "has no scruples": "The truth is Genl L. had failed in his campaign, and thought to divert attention from his great want of capacity by charging me with neglect of some minor details." He used similar words in describing the genesis of the charges in a letter to another Confederate general: "Longstreet saw that he had blundered & was continually blundering, and thought it high time to do something to relieve himself."[31]

A few weeks later, General McLaws delivered the most detailed surviving private summary of his view of Longstreet's efforts to make him a scapegoat. In a letter to a young female acquaintance, McLaws traced the roots of the Knoxville court not all the way back to Longstreet's sulk at Gettysburg but rather to the turbulent affairs at Bragg's headquarters in more recent months. "The difficulty with Gen. L. and myself commenced," he wrote, "when I not believing he was a greater man than Genl Bragg kept aloof from the coalition which was forming against him, headed by Gen L." The tawdry business seemed to McLaws, aptly enough, to display both "the want of delicacy" and

30. Requisition dated December 4, 1863, McLaws's CSR, M331, NA; Sorrel, *Recollections*, 293; McLaws to D. H. Hill, January 23, 1864, D. H. Hill Papers, NCDAH; G. M. Sorrel to McLaws, December 17, 1863, McLaws's CSR, M331, NA; McLaws to Marcus J. Wright, June 7, 1882, copy in the author's possession.

31. McLaws to Hill, January 23, 1864, D. H. Hill Papers, NCDAH; McLaws to Marcus J. Wright, June 7, 1882, copy in the author's possession.

a potentially deadly lack of ethics: "It was not time to be spreading dissentions among the troops by the ambitious movements & aspirations of the chief commanders." Longstreet was itching and yearning for army command (again) and "has never forgiven my not joining that clique." After considering Longstreet's egregious failure at Knoxville "& that he has nothing to recommend him as a commander, but the possession of a certain Bullheadedness," McLaws simmered angrily, "It is mortifying when one feels that he is allowed to tyranise, as he is doing."[32] In that restless spirit the general approached a court-martial that he clearly should win readily.

Longstreet's orders to McLaws were to go to Augusta, Georgia, and report from there by letter to Richmond for orders, even though Richmond itself was a far shorter trip from east Tennessee. Public reaction included a good deal of surprise and dismay. A South Carolinian journalist wrote: "This army parts with one of its most gallant commanders, and most efficient officers. . . . To be relieved from his command, who are so much devoted to him, is nothing less than a calamity. If the General did dissent [from Longstreet's designs] it is nothing more than what a great many others did, and that on reasonable grounds."[33]

The Confederate Adjutant and Inspector General's Office (A&IGO) announced McLaws's court-martial in general orders dated January 26, 1864. The court was to convene at Russellville, Tennessee, on February 3, and consist of Generals Simon B. Buckner, Charles W. Field, James L. Kemper, John Gregg, Francis T. Nicholls, George T. Anderson, and Benjamin G. Humphreys. The last two were later excused from the duty. Major Garnett Andrews drew the assignment of judge advocate for the trial.[34]

Meanwhile, McLaws had obeyed his orders to go to Augusta, taking along "horses, servants, and baggage." With the court now scheduled for a venue in east Tennessee, the general hurriedly headed in that direction, taking along

32. McLaws to Lizzie Ewell, February 29, 1864, Ewell Papers, LC.

33. *Camden (S.C.) Journal*, January 22, 1864.

34. Special Orders No. 21/27, Adjutant & Inspector General's Office (A&IGO), January 26, 1864, manuscript copy in McLaws's CSR, M331, NA. The McLaws paragraph in the special orders as printed in a War Department compendium in the 1890s for some reason is paragraph 26 rather than 27. General Nicholls is spelled "Nichol" in the original. An excerpt from the proceedings of the court as convened—very briefly—on February 13, in McLaws's CSR, M331, NA, shows the court without Anderson or Humphreys present. Garnett Andrews forwarded the specifications to McLaws under a letter dated January 28, which also is in McLaws's CSR.

only enough clothing for a few weeks. The rest of his establishment went off to Sparta, Georgia.[35]

Getting the court to convene proved to be a considerable ordeal for McLaws. Longstreet "kept me for months without trial," he wrote in retrospect. The army commander "would give a member of the court leave & then another, would send away any officer I selected to defend me." Furthermore, the necessary "subserviency" of the court's officers to Longstreet and "the jesuitical character" of Buckner made McLaws fear having "sentence passed without a hearing."[36]

The day before the trial was scheduled to convene, the A&IGO issued a Special Orders designed to avoid interference with the proceedings by the exigencies of the service—both real emergencies and those that might be contrived by Longstreet to keep the court from going forward in what must have been obvious, even to him, would be embarrassing proceedings. The February 2 order authorized the court "to adjourn from place to place as circumstances may render necessary." When Longstreet assumed the authority to cancel the trial "indefinitely" on February 13 (holding the trial would "prejudice my operations," he wrote), McLaws left at once, this time for Richmond; most of his gear remained in Sparta. He covered 417 miles and reached the capital city on the seventeenth.[37]

The press of operations that ostensibly necessitated canceling the court did not keep Longstreet from granting extended leaves of absence to several officers who had been given subpoenas to appear. Those leaves of course resulted in yet further continuances. When at last Longstreet ran out of delaying tactics, the trial was complicated by weather. The army's units were necessarily widely scattered to take advantage of forage and subsistence across the countryside, and deep snow made travel extremely difficult. McLaws went into court despite having had only a few difficult contacts with his counsel and having had no chance whatsoever to interview witnesses in advance.[38] None

35. McLaws to General S. Cooper, March 9, 1864, McLaws's CSR, M331, NA.

36. McLaws to Marcus J. Wright, June 7, 1882, copy in the author's possession.

37. Special Orders No. 27/11, A&IGO, February 2, 1864; mileage voucher for travel on February 13–17, 1864, McLaws's CSR, M331, NA; Longstreet to "Major" [obviously Garnett Andrews], February 13, 1864, McLaws Papers, SHC; Benjamin G. Humphreys letter, February 16, 1864, McLaws Papers, SHC.

38. McLaws to Marcus J. Wright, June 7, 1882, copy in the author's possession; notes on difficulty with leaves granted to witnesses in McLaws Papers, SHC.

of that mattered much in the long run, as the witnesses could do nothing but tell the obvious facts—and that was all McLaws really needed.

On February 27, writing from Abingdon, McLaws wistfully expressed the hope that the court "will be assembled soon" and listed eighteen officers whom he wished to have on hand to testify. McLaws worriedly asked Major Garnett Andrews whether he might hold those officers on duty for the court: Longstreet was granting leaves of absence "so profusely" that the chances of having the men he needed on hand were dwindling steadily. In frustration, McLaws began drawing up charges of his own against Longstreet for subverting the intent of the War Department by granting leaves to members of the court and witnesses, without advising either the Richmond office that had ordered the court or the trial's judge advocate. Longstreet was, McLaws wrote, "using his official position to injure [me]."[39]

Complaints to the War Department brought action. On March 12, General Buckner received a brusque telegram from the A&IGO admonishing Longstreet for granting leaves that interfered with the trial. "Longstreet has no control over" the court, the wire read. At last the court convened in earnest at Midway, Tennessee, on March 16, 1864, and for three days listened to a procession of witnesses who without exception proclaimed facts that ran diametrically opposite to Longstreet's bewildered allegations. Continued attempts by Longstreet and his friends to postpone the trial occupied much of the formal transcription; but this time the pleas for adjournment failed. Poor Major Andrews grumbled with some asperity in the official transcript about his inability to persuade either General Jenkins or General Longstreet to appear, despite repeated requests over many weeks.[40] Jenkins probably had understood from the first that nothing but discomfort could result from appearing. By this time Longstreet too surely must have been suffering

39. McLaws to Andrews, February 27, 1864, Garnett Andrews Papers, SHC; draft charges against Longstreet in McLaws's hand, McLaws Papers, SHC.

40. The McLaws Papers, SHC, include thirty-five pages of testimony from March 16–18, 1864. In many instances, it is less detailed than the depositions and letters supplied in the same papers. In these notes, material from the thirty-five pages of official transcripts is identified as "testimony," with the affiant's name (e.g., "Hutchins testimony"). The other documents are identified as "deposition" or "letter," based on format and content. The language of the firm War Department telegram to Buckner is from the court testimony. Much detail about Longstreet's use of staggered leave for members of the court and witnesses also survives in the transcribed testimony. The nature of the transcription is such that there remains a possibility that the court convened shortly before the sixteenth.

through a dawning awareness of how grotesquely absurd most of his accusations were going to appear.

Longstreet's charges covered six areas. Most witnesses testified on more than one of the charges; some answered questions about all of them. For clarity, the summary of the proceedings that follows arranges testimony under six specifications, rather than following individual witnesses in their appearance chronology.

Witnesses for the prosecution had but little to say. What they did testify focused on establishing the most rudimentary facts. Osmun Latrobe of Longstreet's staff supplied the date of the attack (Longstreet had somehow not confused that) and, in response to a question, answered succinctly: "The assault failed."[41]

The first charge insisted that McLaws, having been ordered to advance his sharpshooters "to within good rifle-range . . . so as to give [them] play upon the enemy . . . did fail to arrange his sharp-shooters so as to meet this view . . . thus failing to give his assaulting columns the protection . . . during their advance and attack." McLaws told the War Department, with obvious frustration, that he not only had aligned the skirmishers, but their employment actually was "made at *my request and on my suggestion*."[42]

Evidence delivered to the court easily established the absolute inanity of Longstreet's accusation about sharpshooting negligence. Lieutenant Colonel Willis C. Holt of the 10th Georgia received orders to advance pickets "far enough to command the Fort," and he did so. "The Yankee works were completely commanded by our line," Holt told the court, "and there was no portion of our line but commanded them." General Joseph B. Kershaw testified about his orders to set up the skirmish line, which he did "about 11 o'clock P.M." with "complete . . . success." During the attack, his sharpshooters achieved "the complete silencing of the enemy's guns." "The operation of the rifle pits . . . was quite a success," Kershaw reported. Captain Lewis Dortch

---

41. Latrobe testimony, McLaws Papers, SHC.

42. R. C. Gilchrist, comp., *General Orders from the Adjutant and Inspector-General's Office, Confederate States Army, from January 1 to June 30, 1864, Inclusive* (Columbia, S.C.: Evans and Cogswell, 1864), 89–90. The general orders that published the charges and results was No. 46, dated May 4, 1864. Citations hereafter use page numbers from the compendium of general orders, but all refer to No. 46. See also McLaws to Samuel Cooper, January 17, 1864, McLaws Papers, SHC; McLaws to D. H. Hill, January 23, 1864, NCDAH. A manuscript copy of the charges and specifications against McLaws, attested by Garnett Andrews, is in the McLaws Papers, Duke. Another copy is in Andrews's own papers, SHC. Those vary from the printed version in only minor details. The printed version is cited hereafter because it is much more accessible.

of the 24th Georgia got his orders at 8:45 P.M., "drove the enemy pickets" away, and dug new rifle pits at least sixty yards closer to the fort than the Federals had been. Dortch "regarded my whole line as within easy rifle range of the parapet."[43]

The parade of witnesses offered dozens of testimonials (most of which are not adduced here for lack of space) to the care with which they were posted and the success of their efforts. Captain John F. Martin of the 3rd Georgia Battalion carefully explained the meticulous preparations and the result: "This we did, not a gun was fired by the enemy until after the column passed our line." Captain Ezekiel Fuller of the 24th Georgia said under oath that "the line of rifle pits . . . completely commanded the Fort in front." A procession of officers entered the docket and delivered the same testimony over and over, with but little variation. Longstreet was egregiously, embarrassingly, misinformed.[44]

Only one corner of the assault faced unsuppressed fire, and that came from the left flank, not from in front. Without being starkly pejorative, some witnesses suggested that Micah Jenkins's troops might have done more to interrupt the enemy in that direction; but Jenkins of course was a Longstreet favorite and would not suit as a scapegoat (nor is there solid evidence that he *should* have been one).[45]

In addition to the court-martial testimony, there is ample unofficial evidence from men in the ranks of the extent and vigor of the sharpshooters' endeavors. A 10th Georgia soldier, for instance, described the evening attack on Federal outposts in front of the fort to establish the Confederate sharpshooter line. The attackers were supposed to approach stealthily, but the bitter cold had them "coughing, sneezing [and] stumbling" in noisy fashion. Even so, they drove off the enemy with almost no loss to themselves and even captured some Federal pickets who had managed to sleep through the onset. A

43. Holt, Kershaw, and Dortch depositions, all in McLaws Papers, PLD. Even the prosecution's witness, Lieutenant Thomas Adams of the 10th Georgia, described thorough suppression of the Federal fire from the fort (Adams testimony, McLaws Papers, SHC).

44. Martin and Fuller depositions, McLaws Papers, PLD. The same collection contains other manuscripts that record evidence on the point; those of General Goode Bryan and Major E[llison] L. Costin are particularly effective. Major James M. Goggin's letter of February 17, 1864 (McLaws Papers, SHC), describes in detail how McLaws used Costin and Captain G. B. Lamar to superintend this phase of the operations. The testimony of the prosecution's own witnesses (for instance, N. L. Hutchins testimony, McLaws Papers, SHC) supported McLaws unswervingly.

45. General B. G. Humphreys, in his letter of February 16, 1864 (McLaws Papers, SHC), was one who wondered if Jenkins might not have done more.

member of the 20th Georgia wrote of driving the enemy skirmishers to within "about seventy-five yards" of the "great walls of the fort," where he and his comrades spent all night entrenching. At early daylight, the Georgians were ready "to sharp shoot into the port holes of the fort . . . so as to prevent . . . firing on our line of battle as it advanced. . . . We performed this duty successfully."[46]

Longstreet's second charge declared that McLaws "did fail to organize a select body of men to lead in the assault as is customary in such attacks." The army commander did not claim to have *ordered* that procedure, he only suggested that it was customary; even so, McLaws was easily able to refute the allegation. The choice of the Phillips Legion as one of the units at the forefront of the attack, its commander testified, had been "a compliment" to the Georgians' reputation and prompted the men to advance "in fine spirits and beautifully." Major James M. Goggin, a staff officer destined to become a general within a few months, asserted that the Legion and the 13th Mississippi were selected for the position of honor "with special reference to their fitness for that duty."[47]

McLaws himself attested to his amazement at the second charge. He wondered whether Longstreet "meant a 'forlorn hope' " when he spoke of "a select body." If so, the charge was "far fetched"; if not, the charge simply was untrue. The units chosen, McLaws said, "were select bodies . . . distinguished for coolness and courage." In a letter to the adjutant and inspector general of the Confederacy, McLaws called the two leading regiments "as fine bodies of men and as well commanded as can be found any where."[48]

The next (third) accusation against McLaws was that he "did allow his three brigades to advance to the assault without definite and specific instructions." In response, General Kershaw reported on a meeting of the brigade commanders with McLaws to discuss the new attack orders. General Goode Bryan also testified under oath about the brigadiers' meeting with McLaws

46. D. I. Walden, "The 10th Georgia at Knoxville," *Atlanta Journal,* January 11, 1902; George McRae, "20th Ga. Regiment Took Part in Attack on Fort Saunders," *Atlanta Journal,* January 25, 1902.

47. Gilchrist, comp., *General Orders,* 90; John S. Norris and Goggin depositions, McLaws Papers, PLD. Norris was captain commanding the Legion at Knoxville.

48. McLaws's summary, in his own hand, bearing the internal date of February 29, 1864, McLaws Papers, Duke (cited hereafter as McLaws deposition, PLD). In his letter to Samuel Cooper, January 17, 1864, McLaws called the Mississippi regiment the 17th (McLaws Papers, SHC). General Humphreys, from whose brigade the units came, said in his letter of February 16, 1864 (McLaws Papers, SHC), that the 13th led the column.

and added somewhat quaintly: "I received instructions from Maj Genl McLaws. . . . This was all I required of him." General Benjamin G. Humphreys remembered receiving both written and verbal orders.[49]

McLaws countered Longstreet's charge of negligent leadership with a telling account of the corps commander's own demeanor. "No officer of Genl Longstreet's nor was the Genl himself on the ground before the assault. . . . No one was sent to enquire Are You ready?! Is everything prepared? What arrangements have been made? No other instructions were given, but 'to make the assault with three of your Bri-

Confederates struggle with the deep ditch and steep walls, in an 1890s engraving.

gades, Jenkins to follow & Johnson to support.'" In retrospect, McLaws declared himself "at a loss to conceive" what further instructions he could have given his brigadiers.[50]

Incredibly, Longstreet actually accused McLaws (*fourth*) of not doing what

49. Gilchrist, comp., *General Orders*, 90; Kershaw and Bryan depositions, McLaws Papers, PLD; Humphreys letter, February 16, 1864, McLaws Papers, SHC.

50. McLaws deposition, McLaws Papers, PLD; McLaws to Samuel Cooper, January 17, 1864, McLaws Papers, SHC.

ten thousand men knew he had done—attack the northwest corner of Fort Sanders. Though having been "ordered to assault the enemy's position at the northwest angle of his works," McLaws attacked elsewhere, Longstreet imagined, and the craven division commander "did fail to inform his officers that the ditch on the west side of the fort was but a slight obstacle to his infantry, and that the fort could be entered from that side with but little delay." General Kershaw was one of the many thousands of southerners who knew otherwise. He told the court, simply, "I saw our column reach the northwest angle." Two officers of the 53rd Georgia were among the legions who knew by hard experience that the ditch on the west side of the fort was far more than "a slight obstacle": they described an "impassable barrier" "about sixteen feet high from the bottom of the ditch, and almost perpendicular . . . on the west side of the Fort."[51]

Captain John S. Norris, commanding the Phillips Legion, knew that his unit had not only arrived "at the North West angle of the Fort" but had actually straddled the apex; "part of our line was on the right and part of the line on the left of the angle." The wall there, despite Longstreet's wishful allegations, was "very high and steep [and] very smooth and slick . . . as if it had been smoothed over with a trowel." Trying to climb it in the aftermath of the rain was "very much like treading on ice." General Humphreys declared concisely that "the assaulting column moved . . . directly against the N. W. Salient." The prosecution's own witness, Lieutenant Thomas Adams of the 10th Georgia, answered a defense question about the focus of the attack: "Yes, Sir. I could see the point. It was made on the N. W. bastion." Another prosecution witness, Major Joseph Hamilton, described how four of his companies went right of "the N. W. corner" and five went to its left. General Bryan, also called by Longstreet's side, testified that "the assault was made on the N. W. Angle of the fort."[52]

Poor McLaws could only add, in his own defense, what everyone else knew: "I did assault at the North West Angle, & there it was the ditch was found impassable." "If there was no ditch . . . that offered any obstacle," the general wrote to the War Department in January, "I have been most egregiously misinformed." In fact, he had of course *not* been misinformed. The allegation reminded McLaws "of the fable of the lamb & the wolf. There is a

51. Gilchrist, comp., *General Orders*, 90; Kershaw deposition, McLaws Papers, PLD; joint deposition of Lieutenant Colonel W[iley] F. Hartsfield and Captain J[ames] W. Vandigriff, McLaws Papers, PLD.

52. Norris deposition, McLaws Papers, PLD; Humphreys letter, February 16, 1864, McLaws Papers, SHC; Adams, Hamilton, and Bryan testimony, McLaws Papers, SHC.

determination to get me into a difficulty, no matter whether I am in fault or the Corps commander is to blame."[53]

The *fifth* charge, a corollary to the fourth, was that McLaws "did make his attack upon a point where the ditch was impassable." The unmistakable implication, of course, was that some points *were* readily passable, had McLaws not disobeyed the orders to attack where Longstreet knew, by a sort of ex cathedra divination, that the ditch was shallow on the west and north-west. Before the trial, McLaws told a colleague that he had "the written certificates of fifteen or twenty officers who were at & in the ditch that the ditch & obstacles were greater there than any where else."[54]

In a document that offers wonderful immediacy, fourteen commissioned officers of the 13th and 17th Mississippi—every one of them survivors of the deadly twenty-ninth—summarized the nature of the ditch just two days after the frightful battle. Those two regiments had been at the forefront of the attack and had suffered dreadfully. The ditch was "continuous," they knew from hard experience; it varied from four and a half to six feet in depth and from eight to twelve feet in width; and the parapet above the ditch loomed "from 11 to 12 feet" above the surface. The fourteen officers had interviewed their noncommissioned officers and enlisted men to be sure of the facts and found that "all concur with us in the above statement." General Humphreys wrote a decidedly irreverent summary that can only have been a sardonic slap at Longstreet. After describing his brave men clawing their way up the vertical, slippery parapet, only to be shot in the head and fall back, Humphreys suggested pointedly: "Any one that doubts the existence of the ditch can satisfy themselves by making the same experiment made by the 13th and 17th regiments."[55]

Finally, *sixth*, with the proceeding's first bit of objective truth—albeit twisted harshly—Longstreet charged that McLaws "did fail to provide any of his assaulting column with ladders or other means of entering the enemy's works." No matter that the previous specifications showed Longstreet himself

53. McLaws deposition, McLaws Papers, PLD; McLaws to Samuel Cooper, January 17, 1864, McLaws Papers, SHC.

54. Gilchrist, comp., *General Orders*, 90; McLaws to D. H. Hill, January 23, 1864, D. H. Hill Papers, NCDAH.

55. The statement of the fourteen officers is covered by a note of concurrence by General B. G. Humphreys, the whole being dated December 1, 1863, in the McLaws Papers, SHC. An equally compelling summary came from survivors of Wofford's Brigade. Their undated statement (McLaws Papers, SHC) reported the views of twenty-one veterans of the charge, nine of them enlisted men.

insisting in official fashion that the ditch "was but a slight obstacle," McLaws had in fact *not* built ladders (nor birdhouses nor gallows nor choir lofts) in the few hours of Tennessee darkness between the orders and the assault. The obvious reason, McLaws wrote before the trial, was because "I had neither time nor material, nor means to make any, and for the reason that Longstreet & his staff had reconnoitered the work, and had impressed me with the assertion that there was no ditch that offered any material obstacle."[56]

Although the fragmentary surviving court transcripts do not include Longstreet's testimony, McLaws insisted that Longstreet "*himself* testified that he did not expect me to have ladders." In fact, the division commander was "assured" by both Longstreet and his staff, indeed "pertinaceously pressed with the fact that there would be but little difficulty so far as the ditch was concerned." Artillerist Porter Alexander testified emphatically to the prevalence of the notion that the ditch was insignificant. General Bryan reported that the preassault conference between McLaws and his brigadiers included no discussion of scaling ladders. "I was of the opinion," Bryan said, "that there was no ditch and I believe that was the general impression." Major Goggin also testified that he "did not hear the subject of ladders mentioned . . . the impression was general that there was no ditch." General Humphreys echoed Bryan: no one mentioned ladders; even had they done so, he had had neither "the time or the means of providing any." In any case, the army command had "positively asserted that . . . the ditch . . . was too slight to offer any impediment." Another witness confirmed the testimony about the prevailing notion that ladders were not needed to cross a ditch "so shallow as to be a mere scratching."[57]

The most fractious exchange in the formal testimony concerned Longstreet's widely expressed opinion, before the assault, that the ditch would be simple to cross. Buckner sought to protect his friend by consistently refusing to allow testimony to that effect into the record. Because the army knew of it widely, and so did the War Department, Buckner's ploy accomplished little.[58]

56. Gilchrist, comp., *General Orders*, 90; McLaws to D. H. Hill, January 23, 1864, D. H. Hill Papers, NCDAH.
57. McLaws to Marcus J. Wright, June 7, 1882, copy in the author's possession; McLaws to Samuel Cooper, January 17, 1864, McLaws Papers, SHC; Bryan and Goggin depositions, McLaws Papers, PLD; Humphreys letter, February 16, 1864, McLaws Papers, SHC; Goggin letter of February 17, 1864, McLaws Papers, SHC; Alexander testimony, McLaws Papers, SHC.
58. Court testimony, McLaws Papers, SHC. The heart of Buckner's resistance to entering Longstreet's opinion is recorded during the period when Lieutenant Adams of the 10th Georgia was on the stand.

Longstreet's after-the-fact awareness (universally shared, of course) that ladders would have been decidedly useful bore little relevance to the hurried preparations late on November 28. As McLaws pointed out, Longstreet's favorite, General Micah Jenkins, had for some time been slated to make the attack and no one suggested ladders to Jenkins either. When the attack shifted to McLaws's front, it was far too late to take on a construction job, and there were no materials for the purpose anywhere near. "Certainly it could not have been intended for me to make ladders that night," McLaws testified accurately, if plaintively; and in any event, such orders never came. Confederates in front of Knoxville had been reduced to the cold chore of fishing the corpses of horses out of the river to retrieve the shoes and nails from their stiff, dead feet: building ladders, or much of anything else, was beyond the army quartermasters' ability. McLaws summarized the situation: "It would have required fifty or one hundred ladders from fifteen to twenty feet long, and my Qmaster had . . . no nails, no axes, hatchets &c. The truth is no one thought of ladders."[59]

The whole army knew that the tenor of the testimony made Longstreet look foolish. One of the army's cavalry generals thought that the whole business at Knoxville "was utterly unworthy of a leader of any independent army." An aide to the same officer wrote that "we believed" McLaws's arrest was "for carrying out General Longstreet's own orders." General Evander M. Law, another target of Longstreet's ire, wrote to McLaws on April 29 that talk in Richmond was that the charges had been rejected. The order "for your release and restoration to command has been issued," Law reported. The War Department word was that Richmond was disgusted with the court's quiet acceptance of Buckner's attempts to railroad the proceedings. Only General Nicholls had resisted Buckner's machinations, but Nicholls was enough. "You," Law assured McLaws, "are the only man that comes off unscathed." Efforts by the corps commander to disobey orders restoring Law and McLaws to command "will inflict more injury upon him" than on the intended victims. "Longstreet is most certainly on the wane both in and out of the army," Law crowed.[60] As by far the best, most seasoned corps commander in Lee's army, Longstreet was invaluable. Driving him "on the wane" was a dreadful idea for

59. McLaws deposition, PLD; Krick, *Parker's Virginia Battery*, 252. The division's acting quartermaster, Captain J. J. Middleton, confirmed in his testimony (McLaws Papers, SHC) the complete unavailability of tools and materials necessary for constructing ladders.

60. Nathaniel E. Harris, *Autobiography* (Macon: J. W. Burke, 1925), 60–61; Law to McLaws, April 29, 1864, McLaws Papers, SHC.

the security of the Army of Northern Virginia, but it is easy to see why the victims of the general's dishonest manipulations would have taken pleasure in the notion.

Law's sources were impeccable. The "Findings and Sentence of the Court" appeared in official, printed form on May 4. The court found McLaws not guilty, not guilty, not guilty, and sort of guilty—the latter for not making the ladders that Longstreet had declared unnecessary. After mature deliberation, even though under the guidance of Longstreet's friend Buckner, the court could not avoid stating that the order about sharpshooters "was substantially complied with," and organizations had been selected to perform as "select bodies of men." Perhaps in embarrassment for Longstreet, the court did not even comment with a single word on the fantastic misstatements about a lack of specific directions, or that McLaws had not attacked at the northwest corner, where he obviously had, or that he had missed the nonexistent spot where the ditch was shallow—this despite taking much testimony on the subjects. He had not built ladders, that was clear: the court found him guilty in that regard and sentenced him to sixty days of suspension. Even then, the court expended a lengthy paragraph mitigating the one mildly pejorative result, saying that McLaws was not culpable to "any high degree," having been "encouraged" to think he would not need them by "those officers . . . whose opinion should have had the most weight with him"—that is, Longstreet.[61]

The extensive vindication of McLaws, and the resultant embarrassment to Longstreet, was not thorough enough to satisfy the War Department. Adjutant and Inspector General Samuel Cooper crisply rebuked the court for its one mild "guilty," saying that it was "not sustained by the evidence." Cooper also lashed Buckner and his colleagues for ignoring the most foolish of the specifications and making no finding on them—a finding that "was easy to be determined" from the testimony. Ignoring those fantastic fables was too easy on the accuser. Accordingly, the A&IGO announced, "the proceedings, finding, and sentence of the Court are disapproved. Major-General McLaws will at once return to duty with his command."[62]

The War Department bureaucracy reacted promptly with the necessary paperwork. On May 7, 1864, a Special Orders announced simply that "Major-General Lafayette McLaws will immediately rejoin his command." Lee, however, needed Longstreet far more than he needed McLaws. Even though

61. Gilchrist, comp., *General Orders*, 90–91.
62. Ibid., 91–92.

Longstreet had gone down gravely wounded two days after the General Orders announcing McLaws's vindication, Lee hoped for his return. Lee also had been uncertain of McLaws for some time. Accordingly, by May 18, a reshuffling had taken effect. Now the exonerated McLaws would assume "the command of the defenses of Savannah, Ga."[63]

Ironically, as a consequence of the Longstreet vendetta and the resultant reassignment, McLaws would be away from the Army of Northern Virginia

precisely when his range of talents would have been the most useful. The veteran division commander had done a solid job during that army's glory days, full though they were of the kind of maneuver and rapid marching that was not really his forte. Now that the army was heading into a less frenetic kind of warfare, much of the time on the defensive, he would have been in his element. The man described by Porter Alexander as "the best general in the army" for defensive alignments, "being very painstaking in details," would have been a useful adjunct to Lee on the Jerusalem Plank Road, near Hatcher's Run, and

Lafayette McLaws in old age.

around Fort Harrison. Instead, McLaws served the war's final year in exile in Georgia.

Neither James Longstreet nor Lafayette McLaws found either joy or comfort in large doses after the war. The bizarre events around Knoxville in November 1863, and even more the peculiar trial that ensued, surely contributed to the postwar bitterness that made Longstreet his own worst enemy through nearly four decades of quarreling with his fellow Confederate veterans and with himself.[64]

---

63. Special Orders No. 107/16, A&IGO, May 7, 1864; Special Orders No. 115/23, A&IGO, May 18, 1864. For other evidence about Lee's attitude toward McLaws at Salem Church, cited above, see Richard Rollins, " 'The Ruling Ideas' of the Pennsylvania Campaign: James Longstreet's 1873 Letter to Lafayette McLaws," *Gettysburg Magazine* 17 (1997): 16.

64. Late in life McLaws, impoverished and desperate, beseeched his mortal enemy from 1864 for a job under the political patronage available to Longstreet, who by then had embraced northern Republicanism. McLaws continued in his writings and his other correspondence to bewail his mistreatment but pathetically accepted favors from his onetime bête noir.

5

"We Have Never Suffered a Greater Loss Save in the Great Jackson": Was Robert E. Rodes the Army's Best Division Commander?

"I like him so much," James Power Smith wrote of Robert Rodes after a visit to the general's headquarters early in 1863. "He is very much admired by all and very popular."[1]

Every Confederate general officer—even such egregious failures as Roswell S. Ripley, Louis T. Wigfall, Beverly H. Robertson, and Robert A. Toombs—could boast an eager acolyte or two who cheerfully would have attested to their hero's popularity. The admiration of troops, furthermore, hardly constitutes the full gauge by which military leaders must be measured, or George B. McClellan and Joseph E. Johnston would loom far larger than their meager deeds warrant. The extent and fervor and near-unanimity of the gaudy high opinions of Robert E. Rodes, however, suggest an approval level among contemporary observers that deserves thoughtful consideration.

Scores of men commanded divisions in the Army of Northern Virginia and its antecedent organizations. A few of them were colonels, or even only captains, briefly succeeding to command under the exigencies of battle, notably in the dreadfully thinned army at Sharpsburg. Many more were brigadier generals in temporary authority as the senior officer present with a division, such as Raleigh E. Colston at Chancellorsville and William B. Taliaferro at Fredericksburg—both destined to be exiled soon after those battles. A small class of generals commanded divisions for a time then moved on to larger responsibility and greater fame at higher rank. That group, including such men as Jubal A. Early and John B. Hood, also belongs to a somewhat different category.[2]

---

1. James Power Smith to "My dearest sister," January 21, 1863, FSNMP.
2. A tribute to Hood's prowess is in a letter by the highly competent Frank Huger to his

Rodes's peers were the men who commanded infantry divisions in Lee's army for a considerable period of time, bore commissions at the commensurate rank of major general, and never permanently advanced to higher command. That group, with an asterisk or two of my own autocratic devising

General Robert E. Rodes

(what is "a considerable period?" what constitutes "permanently advanced?" etc.), includes twenty-three names: Richard H. Anderson, Charles W. Field, John B. Gordon, Bryan Grimes, Henry Heth, D. H. Hill, Robert F. Hoke, Benjamin Huger, Bushrod R. Johnson, Edward Johnson, D. R. Jones, Joseph B. Kershaw, Lafayette McLaws, John B. Magruder, William Mahone, John Pegram, W. Dorsey Pender, George E. Pickett, S. Dodson Ramseur, Gustavus W. Smith, Isaac R. Trimble, W. H. C. Whiting, and Cadmus M. Wilcox. Attractive reasons might be forwarded for excising a handful of names from the list and for adding a few others; but this roster affords a reasonable field of contemporaries for comparison.

Arranging the two dozen division commanders in a precise ranking of relative merit would require a fabulously subjective set of judgments. Such a list, dogmatically defended and with meticulously mitered joints and corners, might well be ridiculed as a foolish undertaking. Analyzing a major general's profile requires, however, contemplating the pool of peers and comparing them with one another. It would be hard to damn savagely proponents of awarding to Ramseur or Gordon or Kershaw the palm for "best division commander." Several other division commanders fall into a category fairly close to the top grouping. Most of the rest are relatively easy to dismiss. Even so broad, vague, and superficial an analysis as those few lines above brings into focus a revealing fact about the major generals in the Army of Northern Virginia: a handful stood out; several others performed capably at the next level; and one-half or more of the group cannot challenge for real distinction.

General Rodes has attracted far less popular attention than his record war-

---

mother, September 30, 1864, typescript in the author's possession. Hood, Huger said, had been "the first Major General in the country and next to Jackson the man best calculated to lead our troops."

rants for a simple reason having nothing to do with his performance. He is a victim of a familiar and entirely apt historical mot: the pen really *is* mightier than the sword. The players in some of the most riveting acts in the great drama of the Civil War come down to us either larger than life, if their writings survive; or, contrarily, only through a glass darkly if their writings do not survive.

A striking example of this phenomenon from the Federal perspective is the case of Joshua Lawrence Chamberlain, a hero of the fighting on Little Round Top at Gettysburg. Chamberlain's superior officer, Strong Vincent, and a fellow regimental commander, Patrick H. O'Rorke, gave their lives valiantly defending that key terrain. Chamberlain had the good fortune to live for many decades and describe his own prowess in dozens of autobiographical bouquets. Some fatuous pseudo-historical modern fiction has focused on Chamberlain and magnified his role. So has a good bit of hagiographical biography. In contrast, Brigadier General Ellis Spear, who fought beside Chamberlain much of the war, described Chamberlain and his writings in a markedly different vein: "a tissue of lies"; "inability to tell the truth"; "absolutely unable to tell the truth"; "inordinate vanity"; "egotism . . . colossal"; and "robbing the dead." Spear was particularly outraged at the mistreatment of Vincent's memory.[3] It is entirely possible (though hardly certain) that Spear was more wrong than right in his fulminations. What is inarguable, however, is that Chamberlain's visage looms infinitely larger than it otherwise would have done because he survived the war and because his writings survive today. Had Chamberlain died bravely at Gettysburg and Vincent and O'Rorke lived out the century, writing gracefully the while, they would be famous and Chamberlain would be virtually unknown—this without changing by one iota the actual character of any of the men or of their performances on July 2, 1863. The sword really is virtually powerless, postbellum, vis-à-vis the pen.

Robert Rodes is a victim of the same syndrome. Official reports and records amply cover his steady, sometimes brilliant, battlefield performance. The absence of a body of his own contemporary writings, however, dictates the obscurity of the essence of the man. That defect in the documentary record also precludes a major biography of satisfying depth and extent. By contrast, General S. Dodson Ramseur stands revealed as a fully dimensional

3. William B. Styple, ed., *With a Flash of His Sword: The Writings of Major Holman S. Melcher, 20th Maine Infantry* (Kearney, N.J.: Belle Grove, 1994), 297–301.

figure by a first-rate modern biography, a work stoutly buttressed by a flood of Ramseur letters to his wife and his brother-in-law.[4] Ramseur unquestionably deserves the attention: but by any reasonable yardstick, Rodes was somewhat more important since he not only outranked Ramseur throughout the war but also actually was the junior officer's immediate superior during some of the most important campaigns. To reiterate yet again: the pen and the sword inevitably switch places when the shooting stops.

During more than three decades at work in Confederate manuscripts, I repeatedly have heard rumblings that murmured of a cache of Rodes manuscripts surviving in some arcane corner. Three times those hints have come close to paying off. In the best instance, the widow of a Rodes descendant living in Virginia's Valley brought down from her attic in November 1987 one of the proverbial shoe boxes full of family papers. For some reason such family archives always repose in shoe boxes—never in hat boxes or pretzel tins (and most assuredly not in archivally designed Hollinger boxes). This batch of manuscripts did indeed prove to be the right stuff but in unfortunately slender volume. The only war-dated document in Robert Rodes's hand covered only a few lines. The stack also included a nice prewar letter home to his father. The rest of the box contained correspondence from Rodes women to other women, some of war date and some not, most of it interesting and worthwhile for historical purposes but none of it useful for shedding even a glimmer of light on the general.

This essay limns Robert E. Rodes the soldier on the basis of surviving evidence. Barring some happy discovery of a lode of his war letters, it is likely that Rodes the man will remain forever indistinct. Unless the general's widow was dissembling in 1900, the chance for such a bonanza simply does not exist. "His private correspondence," she boasted with misplaced pride, "save a (precious) few letters, I burned . . . and also his correspondence with [his] brother of which I kept a few mementoes only."[5]

---

4. Gary W. Gallagher, *Stephen Dodson Ramseur, Lee's Gallant General* (Chapel Hill: University of North Carolina Press, 1985).

5. Mrs. Rodes in Thomas M. Owen, ed., *Report of the Alabama History Commission to the Governor* (Montgomery: Brown, 1901), 184. I have lived in the South for more than three decades, bewildered intermittently during that time by the regional insistence on viewing anything written by a dead relative as secret and sacred and worth burning—even if the material had been carefully gathered, arranged, indexed, and even subjected to professional archival conservation by the ancestor. The advent of good photocopy processes has solved some of the problem: get copies from the reasonable folks while yet they live.

Long before anyone cared about anything he might write, Robert Emmett Rodes grew up in Piedmont Virginia. He was born in Lynchburg on March 29, 1829, into a family of means and standing. General David Rodes (the military title dated from Virginia militia service) served as clerk of the court in Lynchburg. By 1860 he reported his occupation to the census enumerator as "Gentleman," with the considerable net worth of $32,000.[6]

The decision to send young Robert to Virginia Military Institute no doubt grew in part from the success there that his older brother had enjoyed. Virginius Hudson Rodes (1824–79), who would serve on his brother-general's staff during the war, graduated eighth in the Institute's class of 1843. Two years later Robert stood in the matriculation line at Lexington.[7]

The VMI experience apparently took hold of Robert Rodes in much the same fashion that it has thousands of other young men over the decades. In 1859 he spent considerable effort attempting to aid a classmate, Charles A. Derby, a clergyman who was struggling with alcoholism. In 1863 Rodes wrote an exceedingly strong recommendation for Matthew R. Cullen, with whom he had attended the Institute fifteen years earlier. There is no evidence that Rodes and Cullen had had any dealings, nor even that they had met, during the intervening time; no old school ties bind more tenaciously than those forged in Lexington.[8]

Cadet Rodes thrived at the Institute in every way. Stern Francis H. Smith, the superintendent, wrote a few years later that "my heart has always turned with peculiar affection and interest" toward the young Virginian. At graduation, Robert stood tenth in general merit, being dragged down by demerits and by ratings of sixth in French and thirteenth in Latin. He ranked second

---

6. Charles D. Walker, *Memorial, Virginia Military Institute* (Philadelphia: J. B. Lippincott, 1875), 440; Population Schedules of the Seventh (1850) and Eighth (1860) Censuses of the United States, Campbell County, Virginia, RG 29, NA. The Rodes home still stood, though in wretched condition, at 1008 Harrison Street in Lynchburg in the mid-1990s. For the family's background, see Shelley Rodes Patterson, *A Short History and Genealogy of the English Family Rodes* (New York: Ferris, 1929).

7. V. H. Rodes's file at VMI. I have a copy of an interesting letter from V. H. Rodes to his father, January 20, 1842, voicing the immemorial disgust of cadets with studies and especially with food—"dry bread and *beef beef beef*" (original in possession of Mrs. Harold Brown, Winchester, Va).

8. Francis H. Smith to Rodes, September 30, 1859, VMI; Rodes to Smith, October 8, 1859, VMI; Rodes to Hon. J. A. Seddon, December 13, 1863, in CSR of M. R. Cullen, M331, "Compiled Service Records of Confederate General and Staff Officers and Nonregimental Enlisted Men," RG109, NA.

in tactics and third in most other subjects. Robert also was near the top in the coveted tactical offices, being first lieutenant—behind, of all people, John R. Jones, who would be spectacularly awful as a Confederate officer. David Rodes had hoped to send Robert to the University of Virginia for graduate school, but financial straits made that impossible.[9]

The high marks that Rodes earned at the Institute in engineering and mathematics and natural philosophy stood him in good stead as he launched a career. On the same day that he graduated, VMI gave him a post in the "Department of Tactics, Phil [Natural Philosophy—or Physics] and Mathematics." The next day he assumed duties as adjutant of the Institute. For two years the newly graduated young man served on the faculty of his alma mater. Then Rodes accepted a post as civil engineer on the Southside Railroad, which was connecting Lynchburg and Petersburg with a line that a decade later would be of paramount military importance. The pioneering work demanded energy and creativity. In 1851, Rodes declared that he had "no instruments worth a penny" to aid him as he coped with dreadful temporary quarters and an ever-changing right-of-way plan.[10]

Engineer Rodes moved to the nascent Texas Pacific at Marshall, Texas, in 1854; to the N.E. and S.W. Alabama Rail Road Company (sometimes called the Alabama and Chattanooga) in 1855; to the Western North Carolina Rail Road later in 1855; to Missouri for a time with the North Missouri Rail Road; and finally back to the Alabama line in October 1856 for a long stint as chief engineer. Rodes was making a success of the Alabama project until the state of the nation impinged on the business climate. Five days after South Carolina seceded, Rodes wrote that he was discharging assistant engineers (including a VMI graduate he had imported from Lexington) because "hard times, and gloomy political prospects of our country, have almost entirely put an end to our operations here."[11]

9. Smith to R. E. Rodes, October 17, 1856; rankings sheet of 1848 graduating class; David Rodes to Superintendent, May 25, 1848, all at VMI.

10. Orders No. 42–43, July 4–5, 1848, VMI; *Register of Former Cadets, Memorial Edition, Virginia Military Institute* (Lexington: Virginia Military Institute, 1957), 376; Walker, *Memorial*, 440–41; R. E. Rodes to "My Dear Father," Farmville, November 17, 1851, copy in the author's possession. Rodes family tradition holds that he left his post at VMI when he lost the professorship to Thomas J. Jackson by one vote (letter of Rodes's granddaughter, April 3, 1985, in the author's possession). There is good material about Rodes's years on the VMI staff in his jacket at VMI, including correspondence between Rodes and the superintendent in 1850 about the open professorship—in which Jackson is not mentioned.

11. Willis Brewer, *Alabama, Her History, Resources, War Record and Public Men* (Montgomery: Barrett & Brown, 1872), 567; Walker, *Memorial*, 441; R. E. Rodes to Col. F. H. Smith, August 5,

During his relatively brief career in Virginia, Robert Rodes had been married twice—apparently briefly—to a Mary Jones of Lexington and then a Jane F. Baxter of Lexington. Nothing is known of either Mary or Jane, or of the unions, except newspaper announcements that the marriages took place on December 12, 1848, and October 2, 1849. Rodes was twenty at the time of his *second* marriage. Who Mary and Jane were, and what became of them, is not of record. Eight years later, without mentioning having been married, Rodes admitted to having "been so long suspicious of praise of matrimony." On September 10, 1857, Rodes married Virginia Hortense Woodruff of Tuscaloosa. Hortense, as she identified herself to the census taker in 1850, was the daughter of a Tuscaloosa bookseller and was four years younger than the groom.[12] Rodes first met her in April 1855 and "since then" had been seeking her hand. Two weeks before the marriage, Robert remained uncertain of the event, presumably on the basis of his experiences in Virginia, and quaintly called his fiancée "the noblest and poorest woman in Alabama." Virginia H. survived Robert by several decades—long enough, unfortunately, to destroy wilfully her husband's letters and thereby constrict his place in history. Family legend says that Rodes's brother always had been in love with the widow and supported her financially for the rest of his life. The same lore declares that Mrs. Rodes was a stunning beauty. A Charlottesville matron concurred: "I've seldom seen a more attractive woman."[13]

1856, VMI, giving his residence as Mexico, Missouri; R. E. Rodes to the Trustees of the Lowndesboro Male Academy, December 25, 1860, in CSR of William G. Williamson, "Compiled Service Records of Confederate Soldiers Who Served in Organizations from the State of Virginia," M324, Roll 303, NA. Judging from several Rodes letters during this period at VMI, he was based in Eutaw.

12. For biographical sketches of Rodes's family and of his father-in-law and relatives, see Thomas M. Owen, *History of Alabama and Dictionary of Alabama Biography*, 4 vols. (Chicago: S. J. Clarke, 1921), 4:1456, 1802.

13. *Richmond Whig and Public Advertiser*, December 19, 1848; *Richmond Examiner*, December 22, 1848; *Rockingham Register and Valley Advertiser*, October 13, 1849; Walker, *Memorial*, 441; Seventh and Eighth Censuses of the United States for Tuscaloosa County, Alabama, pp. 160 and 449 respectively, RG29, NA; *Richmond Whig and Advertiser*, October 16, 1857; letter by Rodes's granddaughter, April 3, 1985, copy in the author's possession; Rodes to Francis H. Smith, August 28, 1857, VMI; Frances Courtenay Baylor Pollard to her brother, September 23, 1864, Baylor Family Papers, VHS. The few letters from Rodes to his subsequently pyromaniacal wife exude unmistakable devotion to her and also fervent religious expression. There is much evidence in staff diaries and letters (especially in the Jedediah Hotchkiss Papers, LC) that Virginia went to great lengths to be as close to her husband as military circumstances allowed. Mrs. Rodes's dates were November 11, 1833–August 21, 1907 (granddaughter's DAR application, copy at VMI). A letter from Francis H. Smith to Rodes, December 9, 1856 (VMI), refers to him as "an incorrigible Old Batchelor,"

During the late 1850s, Superintendent Francis H. Smith worked on Rodes's behalf for teaching posts at several southern schools. Although each of them did not suit for one reason or another, Rodes admitted that "I have always known that I would be happier and more useful as a teacher, than in my present profession." Just as war began to engulf the land, Rodes received an appointment as professor of Applied Mechanics at VMI. He held the post nominally until his death but never actually stood before a class. Instead he answered the military tocsin in his adopted Alabama by raising a volunteer company with a bellicose name: the "Warrior Guard." After drilling in Tuscaloosa and an excursion to Fort Morgan, the company reported to Montgomery for amalgamation into one of the regiments forming there. Rodes's military education and martial bearing, combined with respect he had earned during his Alabama sojourn, led to his election as colonel commanding the 5th Alabama Infantry. He made the most of the opportunity.[14]

Hostilities on the military frontier were drawing troops from the Deep South, the 5th Alabama among them, to Virginia. Before he left, Robert Rodes sat down and wrote a long, sober, meticulous will. It revealed that he owned five slaves (four of them children of the fifth) and that he had owed his brother $1,700 for two years. Perhaps the impetus to write a will came in part from the fact that Mrs. Rodes nearly died just as Robert prepared to leave for Virginia. As late as April 29, 1861, Virginia was "not past hope, but is *so* ill."[15]

---

which raises further question about the 1848–49 marriages. Comment in Rodes's 1857 letter about uncertainty whether the marriage actually would take place prompts wonder whether the 1848 and/ or 1849 nuptials fell apart at the last moment, despite being reported as a fact several days later. The mystery weddings, and their brides, remain obscure despite diligent searches in census, cemetery, marriage, death, and other records.

14. Walker, *Memorial*, 441; Rodes's CSR in M311, "Compiled Service Records of Confederate Soldiers Who Served in Organizations from the State of Alabama," Roll 146, RG109, NA. The correspondence between Smith and Rodes about various posts is at VMI. The quote in the text is from Rodes's letter of August 17, 1859, which also supplies his reasons for turning down several offers. A fine letter about his experiences early in the war is Rodes to Smith, January 13, 1860[61], VMI.

15. Robert E. Rodes Will, Tuscaloosa, April 30, 1861, in Tuscaloosa County, Alabama, Probate Court Records, Will Book 3 (1855–67), 180–84; Rodes to Peyton Randolph, April 29, 1861, John T. Harris Papers, Carrier Library, James Madison University, Harrisonburg, Va. Letters to Randolph on March 15, 19, and 29 and April 18 afford interesting sidelights on Rodes's early war career. That of March 19 includes Rodes's drawings of an improved design for casemates in seacoast forts. That of the twenty-ninth rails against political jockeying, which required "sweet and odorous . . . influence." I have Dale Harter of the Virginia State Archives to thank for finding the obscure Rodes-Randolph correspondence.

Although Colonel Rodes did not have an opportunity for marked distinction during the war's first major battle at Manassas in July 1861, he steadily demonstrated a sturdy competence that caught the eye of his superiors. General Richard S. Ewell, a doughty old campaigner, noticed the young Virginian and adjudged him a rising star. That August an aide of Ewell's wrote that his chief "thinks very highly of" Rodes "as an able man & efficient officer." Shortly thereafter, Ewell and others "much commended [Rodes] for his conduct" during a withdrawal north of Manassas. It was at Ewell's "repeated recommendations" that Rodes received advancement to brigadier general and command of the troops from whom Ewell recently had been transferred. P. G. T. Beauregard also had been active in favor of the promotion. Rodes's commission as brigadier bore date of October 21, 1861, and took rank from the same day. He accepted the appointment five days later, and it was confirmed on the last day of 1861.[16]

Rodes already had been commanding Ewell's Brigade intermittently, as its senior colonel, during the summer and fall of 1861. Ewell's growing responsibilities, which soon would turn him into a major general, often kept him away from the brigade. In early October Rodes had superintended the repulse of an enemy foray near historic Pohick Church, not far from George Washington's Mount Vernon. His military education in this acting role included responsibility for surveys, mapping, and work parties sent across the northern Virginia countryside on an olio of missions. Already the Rodes charm had worked its way on many of his subordinates. A young Virginian wrote home requesting a shipment of oysters to give to the new general and especially "all kinds of cakes sweetmeats &c," of which Rodes was "particularly fond."[17]

Thomas J. "Stonewall" Jackson also had his eye on the young officer. When Jackson needed a replacement to command his own old Stonewall Brigade, he

16. G. Campbell Brown to Rebecca Hubbard, August 20, 1861, Polk-Ewell-Brown Papers, SHC; G. Campbell Brown memoir, Brown-Ewell Papers, Tennessee State Library and Archives, Nashville; Percy G. Hamlin, "*Old Bald Head*" (Strasburg, Va.: Shenandoah, 1940), 134; Rodes's CSR in M331, NA. The time lapse between acceptance of the commission and its final confirmation was entirely typical. A fine example of Rodes's loyalty to Ewell is Rodes to Ewell, March 22, 1863, Polk-Brown-Ewell Papers, SHC.

17. Rodes to G. T. Beauregard, October 5, 1861, in Rodes's CSR, M331, NA; Eugene Blackford to mother, November 28, 1861, Gordon-Blackford Papers, Maryland Historical Society, Baltimore. The Blackford letters are full of unpublished insights about Rodes's habits and behavior. For a superb look at Ewell's activities during this period—and every other phase of his life as well—see Donald C. Pfanz, *Richard S. Ewell: A Soldier's Life* (Chapel Hill: University of North Carolina Press, 1998).

recommended A. P. Hill for the billet (an amazing and amusing choice, in light of subsequent events). If Hill was not available, Rodes was Jackson's next preference. Rodes, the exacting Stonewall said, was "known to be a good officer."[18]

Rodes's connection with Jackson remained some distance in the future. The brigade that Rodes commanded late in 1861 included his own 5th Alabama with the 6th and 12th Alabama and the 12th Mississippi. A few months later, in keeping with Jefferson Davis's notions about homogeneity, the brigade would become all Alabamian with the addition of the 3rd and 26th. Rodes's Brigade remained in reserve during the Battle of Williamsburg on May 5, 1862, but on the last day of that month it found action in daunting volume near Richmond at Seven Pines. In the midst of General Joseph E. Johnston's utterly mismanaged battle, Rodes boldly led his troops into the thickest of the fray. They suffered heavy losses—Rodes himself took a painful arm wound—but contributed substantially to what Confederate success emerged from the chaos. A black man called "Archie" rode through intense fire to fetch bandages and treatment for Rodes, enabling the general to remain on the front line. Writing to the secretary of war just after Seven Pines, D. H. Hill, a crusty officer and Rodes's immediate superior, called his subordinate "a capital Brigadier."[19]

Seven Pines thrust Rodes's name onto the army's lips, and the country's too. A purple poem, "Rodes' Brigade Charge at Seven Pines," appeared in papers on both sides of the lines. The piece ran for forty lines in five stanzas in the turgid vein then popular: "Down by the deep crimsoned valley of Richmond / Marched the bold warriors of Rodes' brigade. . . . And know ye that victory, the shrine of the mighty / Stands forth on the banners of Rodes' Brigade. . . . Come to the deep crimsoned valley of Richmond, And crown the young chieftan who led his brigade."[20] Questions of poetic merit aside,

18. T. J. Jackson to Maj. T. G. Rhett, Hd Qrs. Dept of N. Va., November 11, 1861, in possession of Jack Milne, Orlando, Fla. Jackson misspelled Rodes as Rhodes.

19. [Thomas E. Caffey], *Battle-Fields of the South, from Bull Run to Fredericksburgh* (New York: John Bradburn, 1864), 252; D. H. Hill to G. W. Randolph, June 6, 1862, in CSR of George B. Anderson, M331, NA. In a letter to Francis H. Smith from Lynchburg on June 17, 1862 (VMI), Rodes expressed misplaced optimism about the state of his wound. "Archie" was not among the slaves enumerated in Rodes's 1861 will.

20. Poem printed in an unidentified southern newspaper, which credited the *New York News*, in the scrapbook of Bella Little, Fredericksburg Area Museum and Cultural Center, Fredericksburg, Va.

the verse clearly reveals "the young chiefta[i]n" emerging into his country's consciousness.

Rodes fought again with distinction at Gaines's Mill during the Seven Days Battles a month after Seven Pines. His unhealed wound and a raging fever kept him out of the latter part of that week of desperate action, however, and away from his brigade for the next two months. As he marshaled the Alabamians for action at Gaines's Mill, Rodes played on his popularity and the unit's pride in a speech delivered in a ringing voice: "Men you fought like hell at Seven Pines, but did not get the credit you deserved. I want you to do so again and I shall see that your gallantry is acknowledged."[21]

The young general's two greatest days as a brigade commander unfolded in the arms of South Mountain, just north of Turner's Gap, on September 14, 1862, and then three days later in Sharpsburg's famous Bloody Lane, where he was wounded again. The stand at Turner's Gap may well have saved the army. The fight at Bloody Lane is one of the most famous of the entire war, on either side and in any theater.[22]

Rodes filled a relatively unimportant role at the Battle of Fredericksburg in December 1862, but the record he had compiled through the hectic summer marked him for advancement. During the winter after Fredericksburg, while Rodes occupied Grace Episcopal Church northeast of Guiney Station, the Alabama delegation in the Confederate Congress launched an ardent effort to secure his promotion to major general. Congressman J. L. M. Curry and six of his colleagues wrote to Jefferson Davis in February urging Rodes's credentials as the best candidate to take over D. H. Hill's division, in which he already was the ranking brigadier. Rodes "has distinguished himself by cool courage, high soldierly qualities, and rare skill and intelligence," the politician-memoirists declared. Because politicians inevitably declaim thus about constituents, a far more impressive testimonial was a petition seeking Rodes's promotion that was forwarded to the War Department bearing the signatures of every officer of the 3rd, 5th, 6th, 12th, and 26th Alabama, page after page of them. In an army of civilians, writhing under discipline imposed by professional soldiers, such a tribute bore considerable significance. Governor John Gill Shorter added his voice to the chorus in a letter to Davis dated March 6.

21. Thomas Catesby Jones reminiscence, Parry Family Papers, USAMHI.

22. *Richmond Daily Whig*, October 1, 1862. For a detailed tactical review of Rodes at the Bloody Lane, see Robert K. Krick, "It Appeared as Though Mutual Extermination Would Put a Stop to the Awful Carnage: Confederates in Sharpsburg's Bloody Lane," in Gary W. Gallagher, ed., *The Antietam Campaign* (Chapel Hill: University of North Carolina Press, 1999), 223–58.

"Alabama is proud of him," the governor wrote. A Montgomery newspaper echoed the refrain: "The glory of his deeds reflects upon this State."[23]

Chancellorsville may have been Robert Rodes's finest moment. As acting commander of the leading division in Jackson's flanking column on May 2, he adroitly pushed his troops on their long march and formed them into an irresistible tidal wave poised behind the enemy's flank. "Early" that morning the new division commander found a moment to scribble a note "In the field" to "My dearest wife." It echoed the calm certainty of a warrior. Operations on May 1 had produced "a little skirmishing. . . . Today we will whip them." When the division reached Jackson's goal, in the woods behind the unsuspecting Federal flank, Rodes and the corps commander personally aligned the units and then Rodes led them forward. Richard S. Ewell, convalescing in Richmond, heard that Rodes "seems after Jackson to be the hero" of Chancellorsville.[24]

When Jackson fell mortally wounded on the evening of May 2 and A. P. Hill went down soon thereafter, Rodes became the senior officer present with the Second Corps. Instead of taking charge personally, he collaborated with Hill in sending for cavalry chief J. E. B. Stuart to serve as interim corps commander. An aide who was present wrote later, "Rodes distrusted his ability to take command (I have always thought he threw away the opportunity of his life . . . modesty was a mistake in that crisis)." The vital importance of morale in the ranks, more than any lack of self-confidence, probably prompted Rodes to support using Stuart. It is hard to disagree with that judgment at that point in his career.[25]

Rodes's division, responding to Stuart's directions, played a crucial part in

23. Records of Grace Episcopal Church, Corbin, Va.; February 1863 (dated only as received, not when sent) memorial of seven members of Congress, led by J. L. M. Curry, to Jefferson Davis; two other notes from Curry to Davis of about the same period; petition signed by the officers submitted by Curry on March 9, 1863; and Shorter to Davis, March 6, 1863—all in Rodes's CSR, M331, NA; *Huntsville Daily Confederate*, May 20, 1863. Despite Alabama's claim to its adopted son, Rodes's native Virginia continued to pay him tribute: the people of Lynchburg bought their local hero a bay gelding (*Richmond Daily Whig*, November 24, 1863).

24. Charles Timothy Furlow journal, Yale University, New Haven, Conn.; Hamlin, "*Old Bald Head*," 134; Rodes to wife, May 2, 1863, Gratz Collection, Historical Society of Pennsylvania, Philadelphia. In the note, Rodes complained of being "very hungry indeed—nothing to eat and all day ahead of us."

25. Randolph Barton to A. C. Hamlin, August 31, 1892, Hamlin Papers, Harvard University, Cambridge, Mass. The loquacious and opinionated Henry Kyd Douglas agreed with the notion that Rodes was not yet "the man for the emergency" at Chancellorsville (Douglas to A. C. Hamlin, April 21, 1893, same collection).

Jackson attacking the right wing at Chancellorsville. Leading the front division in Jackson's right-flank attack was the brightest moment in Rodes's military career.

the army's victory on May 3. At a critical moment, Rodes pulled his pistol, "presented the muzzle" to the head of a cowardly officer, "and, with an epithet of odium, told him to forward his men, or he would blow his brains out." An exploding shell then wounded Rodes, but not enough to drive him from the field.[26]

The promotion to major general, long sought and well deserved, came to Rodes in direct tribute to his prowess at Chancellorsville. It was dated May 7, 1863, but—hardly by coincidence—took rank from May 2. On the seventh Rodes and J. E. B. Stuart rode through the Confederate camps amid a cacophony of cheers and applause. A tale that sounds fanciful but bears solid documentation insists that Rodes declined a promotion dated May 10, saying "that if he earned promotion . . . for gallant services, they were rendered on the 2nd of May." Lee endorsed Rodes's notion, according to the story, and arranged to have the commission revised. A knowledgeable Confederate staff officer who rode over the May 2 battlefield a few weeks later commented that this was where Rodes "won his reputation and promotion." Some contemporary sources also reported that the dying Stonewall Jackson urged Lee to promote Rodes. A longtime subordinate and friend insisted that it was actually what Rodes did on May 3 that "won the commission of a Maj. Gen. for Rodes . . . . which he well deserved." Jackson of course could have had no real knowledge of events on the third. Promotion in hand, whatever had triggered it, Rodes unfurled a distinctive blue flag crossed by white stars as his divisional ensign and set about to make the command his own special implement.[27]

The Gettysburg campaign followed so quickly after Rodes's promotion that he had no real opportunity to prepare for division command. Probably as

26. Pulaski Cowper, comp., *Extracts of Letters of Major-Gen'l Bryan Grimes to His Wife* (Raleigh, N.C.: Edwards, Broughton, 1883), 34–35; *Huntsville Daily Confederate*, May 20, 1863.

27. Rodes's CSR, M331, NA (the date of acceptance was May 28, but the confirmation did not occur until January 25, 1864); W. E. Ardrey diary, May 7, 1863, as printed in the *Matthews (N.C.) News*, September 1991–January 1992; Clement D. Fishburne memoir, 81, Alderman Library, University of Virginia, Charlottesville; Launcelot M. Blackford to his father, August 16, 1863, Blackford Papers, ibid.; Lee on Jackson's wishes as printed by the *Mobile Advertiser* and quoted in the *Richmond Whig*, February 15, 1864; William J. Seymour memoir, Schoff Collection, Clements Library, University of Michigan, Ann Arbor; Eugene Blackford to "My dear Mary," May 8, 21, 1863, Gordon-Blackford Papers, Maryland Historical Society, Baltimore; Newton N. Davis letter to sister, from near Orange C. H., August 28, 1863, Alabama Department of Archives and History, Montgomery. A member of Rodes's staff reported that when his general visited the dying Jackson, Stonewall "asked him why he did not push on" in the darkness on May 2 (Thomas Catesby Jones reminiscences, USAMHI).

a result, his performance there was disappointing. Dreadful failures by two weak brigade commanders on the first day delayed the division's ultimate triumph, and thereafter Rodes disappeared from center stage. His supporters were disappointed. Modern observers remain uncertain about what happened. Even so, in the aftermath of the Pennsylvania venture, an antiadministration southern newspaper, in an article that worried about corps command in Lee's army, took comfort in the "excellent judgment" of Early and Rodes. Eager to rectify the defects in leadership that Gettysburg had revealed, Rodes set about bypassing Alfred Iverson in favor of Robert D. Johnston, a salutary adjustment that he eventually effected. The division commander also evicted the inept Edward A. O'Neal from brigade command with similarly good results, although the exorcism took more effort and time than did the Iverson case.[28]

En route to Gettysburg, Rodes displayed a sternly intransigent attitude toward depredations against northern civilians. The brand-new major general issued a divisional general orders announcing draconian proceedings against anyone caught interfering with private property. Rodes declared that he was suspending the established court-martial mechanism and instituting summary punishment of any offenders. The system surely would not have survived even the most rudimentary legal challenge in civilian courts, probably not even a complaint up to army headquarters, but it displayed Rodes's determination to mold his division into the disciplined military implement he wanted.[29]

The lack of impact that Rodes had on the Battle of Gettysburg on July 2 and 3 in part resulted from his location on the army's left center, away from the decisive flanks. It also quite likely was a product of an aspect of Rodes's military personality. Although he was famous for his daring and aggression when engaged, the general was noticeably careful about first committing his troops to action. A major in the brigade noted that Rodes was known for his "extreme caution," and a Georgia captain described the general as "cautious, though brave." A German immigrant staff officer commented on the marked dichotomy between opening an engagement and finishing it. Rodes was "one

28. *Charleston Mercury*, November 21, 1863; R. E. Rodes to W. H. Taylor at Lee's headquarters, August 19, 1863, in the CSR of Wade Hampton, M331, NA. For details on the tactical experiences of Rodes's division on July 1 and the Iverson and O'Neal cases, see Robert K. Krick, "Three Confederate Disasters on Oak Ridge," in Gary W. Gallagher, ed., *The First Day at Gettysburg* (Kent, Ohio: Kent State University Press, 1992), 92–139. Grumbling about his fate by O'Neal is in Jerry Frey, ed., *In the Woods Before Dawn* (Gettysburg: Thomas Publications, 1994), 93–96.

29. Junius Daniel's Brigade Order Book, Ms. #NCC-3, SHC. The brigade order book also copied most of the division orders, which do not seem to have survived anywhere else.

of the best Division Commanders of the whole army," Oscar Hinrichs observed. "He is . . . always . . . very careful about fighting and never [has] been taken by surprise. . . . And during the fight he was efficient, careful and strong, besides quick in his movements and therefore hard to defeat." That military trait of engaging cautiously at first before exploding into action no doubt was especially pronounced in his first campaign as a novice major general. It may well account for Rodes's one low-profile battle at the head of a division.[30]

Health considerations probably also affected Rodes's performance in Pennsylvania. A nephew of General Early's who was present wrote that Rodes was "so sick that he was compelled to ride in an ambulance whenever practicable." The youthful Early also witnessed a close call at Gettysburg for both his uncle and General Rodes, when a shell went off within a yard of the group but did no harm.[31]

After considering all of those things about Gettysburg, it must be admitted that no comprehensive explanation of Rodes's low profile there can be constructed. That battle remains the salient quandary in assessing Rodes's otherwise seamless career as major general.

Once he established himself in division command, Rodes quickly spread an aura of competence, reinforced by a pleasant personal demeanor, that made him one of the most popular generals in the army. The flood of kudos to him from officers and men, uninterrupted by any notable negative reviews, makes a more impressive Festschrift than can be mustered for any other of the army's leaders below the rank of lieutenant general (and outstrips numbers of those officers too): "genial and courtly gentleman [with a] slow, genial smile" (10th Virginia private); "a generous . . . cordial and lovable disposition" (14th North Carolina corporal); "upright, truthful . . . soft and genial in his hours of ease and relaxation, he was universally beloved" (staff officer); "our beloved Maj. Genl." (4th Georgia); "a splendid fellow and an able officer" (member of General Paxton's staff); "Lion-hearted" (Virginia artillerist); "splendid division . . . greatest elan. . . . One of the best Division Commanders in the Army . . . an intrepid & accomplished soldier, and a gentleman of many noble qualities, &

30. Eugene Blackford to his mother, January 25, 1863, Lewis Leigh Collection, USAMHI; [Joseph B. Reese], "Letter from Capt. Reese," *(Putnam County, Ga.) Countryman*, October 25, 1864; Oscar Hinrichs journal, 28, copy in the author's possession. An article in the *Mobile Advertiser and Register*, June 30, 1863, declared that Rodes already had "disappointed the expectations of his friends" by excessive timidity around Winchester.

31. John Cabell Early, "A Southern Boy at Gettysburg," *Civil War Times Illustrated* 9 (June 1970): 40.

of unaffected & attractive manners" (Louisiana staff officer); "one of the bravest and best. . . . Gentlemanly and chivalrous" (General Bryan Grimes); "the best General officer [from] Alabama" (4th Alabama); "admirable. . . . There were never, anywhere, two better fighters than Rodes & Ramseur or two more attractive men" (General Porter Alexander); "very much attached to him. . . . A gallant soldier and splendid fighter. . . . A great man" (21st Virginia); "his composure was unsurpassed. . . . Good tactics, coolness, judgment" (Alabama soldier); "very cordial . . . stands as high as any . . . Genl in the service" (headquarters courier).[32]

Men who saw General Rodes thought that he looked like the very embodiment of a warrior. Many of them also underestimated his age. The resemblance to an imagined type of course had little to do with actual performance: after all, the wretchedly inept William Nelson Pendleton, of dignified mien and white beard, sometimes was mistaken for R. E. Lee. At the other end of the spectrum, there is no reason to believe that a wizened and disheveled fellow with his eyes too close together might not be a military genius: Bonaparte fell far short of godlike in appearance and stature. For what it may, or may not, be worth, Rodes *looked* like a military hero: "a commanding appearance. . . . A fearless brave soldier. Cool and collected . . . in battle" (14th North Carolina corporal); "one of the most pleasant looking men that I have seen for many a day" (Petersburg journalist); with Pender, "the most splendid looking soldiers of the war" (major on J. E. B. Stuart's staff); "one of the finest dashing young looking officers I ever saw . . . only about 26" (Ringgold Artillery); "a very young man . . . not more than 27 years old . . . a fine officer" (4th Georgia); "very striking appearance, of erect, fine figure and martial bearing" (Vir-

32. J. W. Minnich, "Incidents of the Peninsular Campaign," *Confederate Veteran* 30 (1922): 55; Preston L. Ledford, *Reminiscences of the Civil War* (Thomasville, N.C.: News Printing House, 1909), 79; Walker, *Memorial*, 457; John L. Johnson to "Dear Cousin, October 4, 1864, J. C. Bonner Collection, Georgia College, Milledgeville; Randolph Barton to A. C. Hamlin, August 31, 1892, Hamlin Papers, Houghton Library, Harvard University, Cambridge, Mass.; John Early Wood letter, September 19, 1864, in Margaret Williams Bayne, ed., *The Wood Family of Fluvanna County, Virginia* (Norfolk: Privately printed, 1984), 197–200; William J. Seymour memoir, Schoff Collection, Clements Library, University of Michigan, Ann Arbor; Cowper, comp., *Extracts of Letters of Major-Gen'l Bryan Grimes*, 23; Jeffrey D. Stocker, ed., *From Huntsville to Appomattox: R. T. Coles's History of 4th Regiment, Alabama Volunteer Infantry* (Knoxville: University of Tennessee Press, 1996), 101; Gary W. Gallagher, ed., *Fighting for the Confederacy: The Personal Recollections of General Edward Porter Alexander* (Chapel Hill: University of North Carolina Press, 1989), 373, 493; John H. Worsham, *One of Jackson's Foot Cavalry* (New York: Neale, 1912), 258; H. K., "Merited Promotion," *Richmond Sentinel*, May 27, 1863; George Thomas Rust to "Dear Beckie," May 1, 1863, Rust Papers, VHS.

ginian artillerist); "a splendid looking officer, had a fine voice" (King William
Artillery); "one of the finest looking & most excellent officers" (General Porter Alexander). A contemporary summarized Rodes's appearance: "He was
slender but of ordinary height, with a resolute expression, and a soldierly
bearing."[33]

The enthusiasm that Rodes elicited from his soldiery did not have its origins in a tranquil attitude toward their behavior. In an army that elected its
officers, evicting disciplinarians in favor of libertines, leaders faced a real challenge in imposing order and efficiency. By the spring of 1863, Rodes had long
been beyond the direct reach of a selfish electorate; but he still functioned in
an army of civilians that usually displayed scorn for officers who employed a
strict regimen. Rodes in fact was one of the most implacable proponents of
discipline in the Army of Northern Virginia, which makes his popularity the
more impressive. Capable officers such as General Charles S. Winder earned
such enmity by their sternness that they never recovered in the eyes of their
troops. An observer marveled at the phenomenon of Rodes's popularity despite his rigor: "The stern and military precision of Gen. Rodes were not such
as to render him a favorite with a citizen soldiery, but his troops always admired his ability . . . [and] the sight of him was sure to extort a cheer which
was rarely given to any besides save Gen. Jackson."[34]

Rodes apparently avoided Winder's fate by means of calm, evenhanded en-
forcement of his high standards, mitigating their implementation by his engaging, affable manner. "Although a strict disciplinarian," an Alabama general
said of Rodes, he was "when off duty, one of the most genial of men." Another Alabamian nicely captured the results of Rodes's style: "We fear him;
but at the same time we respect and love him." The leadership code promul-
gated by a prominent twentieth-century U.S. Marine reflects such a system.
Addressing young officers in a corps that has accomplished much with an attitude toward discipline infinitely more intense than any Confederate would

33. Ledford, *Reminiscences*, 79; [James D. McCabe], *The Grayjackets: And How They Lived,
Fought and Died* (Richmond: Jones Brothers, 1867), 230; Frank S. Robertson, "Reminiscences of
the Years 1861–1865," *Bulletin of the Washington County [Virginia] Historical Society* ser. 2, no. 23
(1986): 15; Michael A. Cavanaugh, *The Otey, Ringgold and Davidson Virginia Artillery* (Lynchburg:
H. E. Howard, 1993), 31–32; Davis Tinsley to "My dear Mother," May 18, 1863, UDC Bound
Typescripts, vol. 10, Georgia Archives, Atlanta; Robert A. Stiles, *Four Years Under Marse Robert*
(New York: Neale, 1903), 261; Thomas Catesby Jones reminiscence, USAMHI; Brewer, *Alabama*,
568; Gallagher, ed., *Fighting for the Confederacy*, 202.
34. Brewer, *Alabama*, 568.

have tolerated, General H. M. Smith suggested: "Avoid, as you would the plague, an uncontrolled temper. Shun favoritism. Treat every man with a similar firm kindness, and you will have mastered the rudiments in the art of command." One of Rodes's contemporaries described the general's system in similar terms: "firmness tempered with kindness. . . . Just, stern in the discharge of duty and in exacting it of others." A Pennsylvania girl—hardly a Confederate sympathizer—saw Rodes rein in some of his men who were indulging in mild looting in June 1863. She recalled how the general used "not a stern harsh command, but . . . in soft, gentle tones, and we saw a soldier's instant obedience in action." A colonel who fought under Rodes described his style fondly as "blunt" but "given to blarney."[35]

A letter from Rodes to the secretary of war early in 1864 supplies an invaluable glimpse of the general's emphasis on discipline. In recommending Colonel Edward A. O'Neal for an assignment to the mountains of northern Alabama, Rodes detailed the reasons that O'Neal did not suit him as a brigade commander. O'Neal might do well in that home front assignment, the general admitted, because of his "popular manners." Rodes had firmly opposed promoting O'Neal with the army because of that officer's dreadful failure on July 1 at Gettysburg but also "refering to discipline mainly, if not entirely." (Even John B. Gordon, whom Rodes described as "magnificent . . . in action," he had decried as "a horrible disciplinarian.") Both O'Neal and Cullen A. Battle had been suggested for brigade command but opposed by Rodes, who "would . . . do so again." The general acknowledged that "my requirements as to the qualifications of my brigade commanders . . . were much severer, and in accordance with a much higher standard than is usual in our armies." The problems with the brigadier candidates, Rodes reiterated in conclusion, centered upon each being "objectionable as a disciplinarian."[36]

A few days after Rodes wrote that firm manifesto, the men of his old brigade endorsed the general's leadership when they reenlisted "for the war, un-

35. General Cullen A. Battle, "The Third Alabama Regiment," 115, typescript in the author's possession; H. K., "Merited Promotion," *Richmond Sentinel*, May 27, 1863; General Holland M. Smith to graduating class at Quantico, August 22, 1942, *Fortitudine* 19 (Fall 1989): 5–6; Walker, *Memorial*, 457; Sarah E. Motts, *Personal Experiences of a House That Stood on the Road* (Carlisle, Pa.: Hamilton Library Association, 1941), 8–9; Thomas H. Carter to D. H. Hill, July 1, 1885, Lee Family Papers, VHS.

36. Rodes to Hon. J. A. Seddon, January 21, 1864, Frederick Dearborn Collection, Houghton Library, Harvard University, Cambridge, Mass.; Rodes to Richard S. Ewell, March 22, 1863, Polk-Brown-Ewell Papers, SHC.

conditionally." Not surprisingly, "the movement was begun by the 5th Alabama"—Rodes's old original command. This unflinching proponent of discipline ("the best disciplinarian" in the army, said Early) then issued a stirring broadside that persuaded the rest of the division to warranty their devotion by reenlisting en bloc for the war. A physician who heard Rodes speak at a reenlistment rally described his style as "very modest and hesitating." The doctor seemed surprised that the troops responded to that modest style with the "greatest manifestations of delight . . . echoed and re-echoed by thousands of voices." Although the troops had no other really attractive alternative options, such group reenlistments were very far from universal. The division's reaction left Rodes "extremely gratified."[37]

Generals committed to strong discipline—Stonewall Jackson being a prime case in point—often proved virtually impossible to please. By contrast, disciplinarian Rodes attracted strong loyalty among subordinates and nurtured protégés who performed up to standard. Three months after his critical review of O'Neal and Battle, Rodes wrote to Richmond in enthusiastic support of two other regimental commanders. He endorsed William Ruffin Cox as "the highest class of regimental commander . . . eminently well qualified" for brigadier and "a thorough gentleman—well educated, sober, and energetic." Rodes touted Bryan Grimes "in terms perhaps more enthusiastic," admitting that he did not really know "in my own mind which of the two is the better officer—both of them are remarkable."[38] That ardent appreciation of able junior officers reveals Rodes to be not a martinet but rather an earnest general officer with high standards.

Earlier Rodes had complained bitterly of the lack of discipline resulting from Richmond's tendency to overturn court-martial proceedings. He blamed the desertion epidemic after Gettysburg on the "perfectly natural" reaction to Jefferson Davis's "pardoning all men who are condemned to be shot and fi-

37. *Houston Daily Telegraph*, February 29, 1864; *Mobile Advertiser and Register*, February 11, September 17, 1864; Louis Leon, *Diary of a Tar Heel Confederate Soldier* (Charlotte, N.C.: Stone, 1913), 58; Edward Warren, *A Doctor's Experiences on Three Continents* (Baltimore: Cushings & Bailey, 1885), 319; *Richmond Whig*, February 15, 1864; Rodes to Eugene Blackford, February 9, 1864, offered for sale in Joseph Rubenfine Autograph Catalogue No. 69. A few days after this report, Rodes outfitted himself at bargain-basement prices, in an era of violent inflation, by paying $36 to a quartermaster for shoes, a jacket, and a pair of pants ("Unfiled Papers and Slips Belonging to Confederate Compiled Service Records," M347, NA).

38. Rodes to Confederate Adjutant & Inspector General, April 23, 1864, in William Ruffin Cox's CSR, M331, NA.

nally releasing all deserters unconditionally."[39] Trifling with malfeasance was not part of Rodes's plan.

The few discordant notes amid the symphony of applause for General Rodes came from men offended by his unquestionable penchant for discipline. A Georgian captain, writing a few days after Rodes became division commander, thought the general "will make a good and efficient officer, though we think he will be very Strict with both men and officers, which is all wright in So large a crowd of men." Before Rodes's elevation to command, another Georgian expressed the hope that Edward "Allegheny" Johnson might get the command instead since he seemed more popular. A member of the Alabama brigade responded to murmurings late in 1862 of Rodes "punishing severely . . . for slight offences." Such reports came, he said, from one who "knows little of what he says." "While a strict and rigid disciplinarian, and a man who never disobeys an order himself, I have never met a more just, conscientious and impartial officer. . . . Since our dearly bought experience in Maryland, necessity has forced strict discipline upon the army. . . . The army then was little better than a mob. . . . Few officers in the army have done as much as he has in promoting its efficiency."[40]

Bryan Grimes, whom Rodes eventually would support so ardently for promotion in 1864, actually began his relationship with the general in 1862 in a markedly adversarial manner. The two proud, prickly southerners snapped and snarled over minutiae connected with the precise meaning of marching orders. Rodes spoke "in a sharp tone"; Grimes "reluctantly obeyed"; Rodes wound up "very cross." Grimes gradually came to recognize his superior's merits and called Rodes "gentlemanly and chivalrous."[41]

The discipline that Rodes exacted of others extended to his own demeanor. Displaying a remarkably punctilious manner, Rodes refused to add to his staff, even as a volunteer, a young man proposed by his long-time benefactor and mentor, Superintendent Frances H. Smith of VMI. In an army prone to imbibing at least as much strong drink as it should, if not appreciably more, Rodes was notoriously sober. A young Alabamian claimed that all of the generals at a December 1861 review, including Rodes, were "*drunk*." G. Campbell

39. Rodes to William M. Blackford, August 13, 1863, Lewis Leigh Collection, USAMHI.

40. William B. Haygood to Mrs. & Miss Jackson, May 18, 1863, Edward Harden Papers, PLD; Irby G. Scott letter, March 24, 1863, PLD; *Mobile Advertiser and Register*, December 14, 1862.

41. Cowper, comp., *Extracts of Letters of Major-Gen'l Bryan Grimes*, 23–25; T. Harrell Allen, *Lee's Last Major General* (Mason City, Iowa: Savas, 1999), 140.

Brown of Ewell's staff, however, who was much given to criticism, attested to Rodes's sobriety. At Carlisle Barracks en route to Gettysburg, when someone found a keg of "lager beer" that turned out to be unexpectedly potent, Trimble, Ewell, Rodes, and several staffers fell under its spell. "I never saw Rodes intoxicated before or since," Brown wrote, "& it was an accident this time."[42]

A droll encounter early in 1864 seems to demonstrate the wry good humor that made Rodes such a successful leader. By that time it had become apparent to many observers that General Ewell was not a reincarnation of Stonewall Jackson and that the newly minted Mrs. Ewell exerted powerful influence over matters military as well as domestic. One day during the winter hiatus in operations, Rodes arrived at headquarters and inquired cheerfully, "Who commanded the Second Corps, whether Mrs. Ewell, General Ewell, or Sandy Pendleton, hoping it was the last." That mild (or stronger) irreverence, cheerily delivered, acknowledged a serious problem without perseverating.[43]

Rodes displayed his creative approach to improving the division's effectiveness when he inaugurated an unusual cross-training system during the fall of 1863. Having seen batteries fall silent when their crews fell victims to enemy fire, Rodes ordered that select infantrymen be instructed in how to fill in as artillerists. He stationed a battery of four guns near his headquarters. Each brigade would have the use of the battery for one day (Rodes specified the date for each unit). "At least one company for each Regiment" was to be drilled in "the Manual of the Piece." Furthermore, since the practice battery contained only smoothbore weapons, Rodes arranged for visits to a nearby battalion that used rifled cannon, to ensure familiarity with those guns.[44]

Rodes and his division played key roles, invariably with distinction, during the bitter battles of the Overland Campaign in the spring of 1864. At the Wilderness, Rodes tenaciously held the line on the Orange Turnpike. At Spotsylvania, his division occupied the northwest face of the Mule Shoe Salient. At a critical moment he urged his old regiment forward with a fiery

42. R. E. Rodes to Francis H. Smith, July 15, 1862, VMI; J. H. Bayol to "Darling sister Joe," December [no day] 1861, Bayol Family Papers, VHS; G. Campbell Brown memoir, Brown-Ewell Family Papers, Tennessee State Library and Archives, Nashville.

43. Jedediah Hotchkiss memoir of conversation with the Rev. B. T. Lacy, folder headed "Jackson's Staff," Hotchkiss Papers, LC.

44. "Circular," September 8, 1863, Hd Qrs Rodes Division, Junius Daniel's Brigade Order Book, Ms. #NCC-3, SHC. I have seen no equivalent system in any other division. No evidence survives of the profitable use of this training by infantrymen-cum-artillerists on subsequent battlefields, although it may well have happened.

speech delivered from the back of his war horse, quaintly named "Old John": "Boys, you played hell the other evening; now . . . I want you to run over those Yankees in front." When Federals broke through the salient to the right of Rodes's position early on the twelfth of May, the general participated in the desperate rally. Two men who saw him that day said that Rodes "seemed much excited" and "earnest and animated." May 12 was that kind of day for Confederates.[45]

A Confederate artillerist described Rodes at Spotsylvania in vivid language that embodied much of the general's image in the army: "He constantly passed and repassed in rear of our guns, riding a black horse that champed his bit and tossed his head proudly, until his neck and shoulders were flecked with white froth, seeming to be conscious that he carried Caesar. Rodes' eyes were everywhere, and every now and then he would stop to attend to some detail of the arrangement of his line . . . and then ride on again, humming to himself and catching the ends of his long, tawny moustache between his lips."[46]

When Jubal A. Early led the army's Second Corps across the mountains in June to defend the Shenandoah Valley, Rodes and his division constituted the corps' most reliable element. Early and Rodes had been at odds over some matter, its nature not of record, but they resolved their differences. An officer with the army noticed that "when any tight job is on hand, Rodes is always called upon. Early . . . relies upon . . . his judgment . . . in the most decided manner." The bitter struggle in the Valley against staggering odds actually involved more maneuvering than fighting for its first three months. "It was the grandest campaign of the war, considering the forces engaged," Rodes said, and he "prided himself on being with Early more than any part of his career."[47]

In the first real toe-to-toe showdown of the campaign, Rodes's career ended in death. The stress of coping with General Philip Sheridan's hordes showed in Rodes's demeanor in the engagement near Winchester on September 19. One of his men who had seen the general in battle innumerable times noticed that, surprisingly, Rodes "seemed to be excited as [if] he had a premonition." A fatal "ball passed through [Rodes's] head," striking behind his ear,

45. J. W. Williams, "Battles Around 'The Bloody Angle,' " *Greensboro (Ala.) Record*, July 30, 1903; Alfred Lewis Scott memoir, VHS; William B. Newman recollections, typescript in the author's possession. The 1903 account is an excellent source on Rodes at Spotsylvania.

46. Stiles, *Four Years*, 261.

47. *Mobile Advertiser and Register*, September 17, 1864; [Alexander M. Garber], . . . *A Sketch of the Life and Services of Maj. John A. Harman* (Staunton, Va.: "Spectator" Job Print, 1876), 32.

The Battle of Winchester—Ricketts's advance against Rodes's division on the morning of September 19, 1864.

before the engagement had raged long. The general fell from his horse into the arms of an aide, Lieutenant Joseph S. Battle, and "never spoke but died without a struggle." A soldier in the 5th Alabama who had been detailed into Winchester on quartermaster duty heard of "the awful catastrophe" and was "thunderstruck." He managed to locate Rodes's corpse, "lying in state" at a private house, surrounded by tearful women, and paid his last respects just before the Confederate left gave way and came racing through the streets.[48]

When Rodes went down, the army's fortunes in the fields east of Winchester went down with him, or at least so it seemed in retrospect to Confederate participants in the battle. Artillery colonel Thomas H. Carter blamed the day's disaster on Rodes's loss. So did North Carolinian Thomas P. Devereux, who wrote wistfully: "We would have whipped them if he had lived." The capable Bryan Grimes insisted that, but for the death of Robert Rodes—who was "our chief loss . . . [he] cannot be replaced"—Early would have won the battle. A Georgian surgeon, writing the next day, declared that Rodes's fall "had a good deal to do with the stampede. He was the best Maj. Gen. in this Army, and probably in the C. S. A. and his death produced a tremendous impression on the minds of the men." An artilleryman from the western Virginia mountains simply called Rodes "one of the bravest and best."[49]

A North Carolina colonel wrote eleven days after Rodes's death that the event "has cast a gloom over the whole of this army" because Rodes "had few equals as a military man, in him I lose a friend." General Jubal Early also rued "a heavy blow to me" in the loss of "a personal friend whose counsels had been of great service." With his broader perspective, Early saw Rodes as, in addition to a friend and counselor, "a most accomplished, skilful, and gallant offi-

48. Ledford, *Reminiscences*, 79; Colonel H. A. Brown to "My Dear Mother," September 30, 1864, James B. Gordon Papers, NCDAH; *Mobile Advertiser and Register*, September 30, 1864; Thomas J. Watkins memoir, 14th North Carolina, copy in the author's possession; William R. Cox, *Address on the Life and Character of Maj. Gen. Stephen D. Ramseur* (Raleigh: E. M. Uzzell, 1891), 40; Henry Beck diary, September 19, 1864, Atlanta History Center. Contemporaries split about evenly over the nature of the missile, whether a shell fragment or a musket ball, that inflicted the mortal wound.

49. Walker, *Memorial*, 456; T. H. Carter to John Warwick Daniel, December 18, 1894, in 1890–99 folder, Daniel Papers, PLD; Thomas Pollock Devereux to "Dear Mom," September 30, 1864, NCDAH; Bryan Grimes to Francis Marion Parker, October 4, 1864, in Parker's CSR, "Compiled Service Records of Confederate Soldiers Serving in Organizations from the State of North Carolina," M270, NA; Abner E. McGarity to wife, September 20, 1864, *Georgia Historical Quarterly* 30 (1946): 41–43; A. S. Johnston, "Captain Beirne Chapman and Chapman's Battery," *Monroe Watchman*, May 21, 1903.

General Robert E. Rodes

cer, upon whom I placed great reliance." Early's high compliments to Rodes
deserve special weight because the lieutenant general was far more prone to
spreading invective than benignancy. The ordnance officer on General Philip
Cook's staff quoted Early as calling Rodes "the best Division commander in
Gen. Lee's army." General Cullen A. Battle insisted that "no single death—
save that of Jackson, caused such deep regret and bitter sorrow."[50]

Southern press reaction was predictable. "When the Confederacy makes
up her jewels," an Alabama newspaper mourned, "Gen. Rodes will be among
the brightest and most precious." When his body passed through en route to

50. H. A. Brown to mother, September 30, 1864, NCDAH; Jubal A. Early, *A Memoir of the
Last Year of the War for Independence in the Confederate States of America* (Toronto: Lovell & Gibson,
1866), 92, 96; [Thomas B. Cabaniss], "Battle Near Winchester," *Macon Telegraph and Confederate*,
October 6, 1864; Battle, "Third Alabama," 119; *Richmond Daily Whig*, October 5, November 8,
1864.

Lynchburg, the Staunton newspaper cried: "May we never again be called upon to chronicle the fall of such an able chieftain and noble defender of our cause." On November 1, the remaining fragment of Early's army spent a day of mourning for Rodes and his friend Dodson Ramseur, suspending military duties and holding somber religious observances.[51]

The dead general left an infant son—"a *fine boy!*" Rodes boasted—and namesake (the boy eventually fathered eight children), who was eleven days short of one year old, and a daughter yet unborn, Belle Yancey.[52]

As Jedediah Hotchkiss, the veteran of staff service with Jackson and Ewell and Early, rode down the Valley on September 20, he met near New Market "the body of our poor Gen Rodes, borne by his staff to his afflicted wife." Hotchkiss was an exacting observer, more inclined toward waspish dismissals than warm encomiums, but the loss of Rodes moved him deeply. "We have never suffered a greater loss save in the Great Jackson," Jed told his wife. "Rodes was the best Division Commander in the Army of N. Va. & was worthy of & capable for any position in it."[53] The record suggests that Jedediah Hotchkiss was exactly right.

---

51. *Mobile Advertiser and Register*, September 24, October 4, 1864; *Richmond Daily Whig*, November 8, 1864; *Staunton Vindicator*, September 23, 1864; John T. Gay to wife, New Market, November 1, 1864, Special Collections, University of Georgia, Athens; *Richmond Daily Whig*, October 5, November 8, 1864. See also lengthy tributes in the *Richmond Enquirer*, October 3, 1864, and the *Wilmington (N.C.) Daily Journal*, November 15, 1864.

52. Letter by Rodes's granddaughter, April 3, 1985, copy in the author's possession; Jedediah Hotchkiss to wife, quoting Rodes, October 7, 1863, Hotchkiss Papers, LC. Robert Emmett Rodes, Jr., died in Tuscaloosa on January 11, 1925 (DAR application of his daughter, copy at VMI). Frances C. B. Pollard to her brother, September 23, 1864, Baylor Family Papers, VHS, describes Rodes's body in a Charlottesville hotel, covered with "a large & beautiful wreath of evergreens & white roses & buds." The Surname Vertical File, Roll 481, Alabama State Archives, Montgomery, affords much detail about Rodes and his descendants, including an important four-page questionnaire about the general completed by his widow. Belle Yancey Rodes was born January 11, 1865, married R. J. Treanor in June 1884, and lived in Savannah.

53. Jedediah Hotchkiss to wife, September 21, 1864, Hotchkiss Papers, LC.

6

Maxcy Gregg: Political Extremist and Confederate General

In the midst of the Federal disaster at Fredericksburg the Confederacy suffered the loss of one of its best brigade commanders. Somehow, a gap had been left open along the line and Federal troops making an abortive drive into the opening had mortally wounded General Maxcy Gregg. The dying South Carolinian, in a deathbed message to the governor of his state, reflected the guiding spirit of his political and military life. "If I am to die at this time," he said, "I yield my life cheerfully, fighting for the independence of South Carolina."[1] Maxcy Gregg had started down the road to Fredericksburg many years before as one of the first ardent advocates of secession and one of the earliest volunteers in support of South Carolina when that state made secession more than a political principle.

Maxcy Gregg's ancestors were a strikingly unlikely group of forebears for a fire-eating southern politician. His maternal grandfather, Jonathan Maxcy of Massachusetts, resigned the presidency of Brown University to become the first president of the school that became the University of South Carolina. Jonathan Maxcy's wife came from a prominent Rhode Island family. Maxcy Gregg was born to a daughter of this New England couple on August 1, 1814, in Columbia, South Carolina.[2]

This article, the author's first writing to appear in print, was published in *Civil War History* 19 (December 1973): 293–313. It is reprinted here, heavily augmented with new data, by permission of Kent State University Press.

1. *Richmond Dispatch*, December 16, 1862; *Charleston Daily Courier*, December 17, 1862.
2. Dumas Malone, ed., *Dictionary of American Biography*, 20 vols. (New York: Charles Scrib-

The young man had enough intelligence to tie for top honors in his college graduating class and enough pride and stubbornness to refuse to share the prize. In 1839 Gregg won admittance to the bar and began to practice law

General Maxcy Gregg

in Columbia. For the next two decades the practice of law and an extensive involvement in state and regional politics occupied his interest. Gregg also became immersed in the study of botany, ornithology, astronomy, and Greek literature and philosophy. His library and observatory became well known. For a brief period he abandoned those satisfying pursuits to accept a major's commission in one of the volunteer regiments raised for the Mexican War. Although he saw no battles, Gregg gained valuable experience in organization and drilling of raw levies. The bloodless adventure of the Mexican War perhaps proved less exciting than a duel in Charleston in

which Gregg served as a second. A pistol ball struck him in the side but inflicted only a slight wound because portions of his clothing deflected and held the bullet. Many years later, in 1862, a similar freak deflection saved Gregg during the rather more serious mayhem along Antietam Creek.[3]

Gregg's early support of secession evolved into an even more extreme advocacy of disunion. In 1850 he wrote that "the exclusion of slavery from California would justify the South in seceding, seizing California, and closing the Mississippi." Furthermore, he added, "The Northern man who denounces this as treason, I would simply meet with defiance. The servile Southern sycophant who raises the cry, invokes inexpressible scorn." When the Compromise of 1850 received widespread acceptance and southern efforts at joint

ner's Sons, 1928–36), 12:433–34; Ezra J. Warner, *Generals in Gray* (Baton Rouge: Louisiana State University Press, 1959), 119.

3. Clement A. Evans, ed., *Confederate Military History*, 13 vols. (Atlanta: Confederate Publishing Company, 1899), 5:399; *Charleston Daily Courier*, December 15, 1862; *Yorkville Enquirer*, December 24, 1862; *SHSP*, 14:208–9; J. F. J. Caldwell, *The History of a Brigade of South Carolinians Known First as "Gregg's" and Subsequently as "McGowan's Brigade"* (Philadelphia: King & Baird, Printers, 1866), 62; Louise Haskell Daly, *Alexander Cheves Haskell: The Portrait of a Man* (Norwood, Mass.: Plimpton Press, 1934), 82–83. Documents illustrative of Gregg's legal business, concerning a charity case, are in the Charleston Diocesan Archives (item 2553).

action failed with the Nashville Convention, Gregg demanded that his state secede, without support from the rest of the South if necessary. In fact, he wrote that he regarded "consolidation with Georgia and Tennessee . . . as only not quite so great an evil as consolidation with New York and Ohio."[4]

Gregg soon found that his was a minority opinion even within his state, but compromise was not acceptable to a man of such firmly held convictions. At one convention he filed a minority report that none of the other twenty members of his committee would support. Among its measures was a call to guard against "the corrupting influence of the federal government." Later in the 1850s he actively led the radicals in promoting a separate Southern Democratic Party that would demand southern rights on pain of secession. At the same time he advocated a reopening of the slave trade. When conciliatory measures temporarily gave promise of cooling the sectional strife, he was openly alarmed. On repeated occasions the lawyer-gentleman-politician delivered fiery tirades that inflamed his listeners.[5]

As a member of South Carolina's secession convention in 1860, Gregg jubilantly helped to draft the ordinance dissolving the union between his state and the United States, then contributed his assenting vote in the historic roll call. When the convention published its famous declaration of the causes leading to secession, however, he opposed the declaration on the grounds that it was too heavily concerned with slavery and thus a dishonor to the memory of those—Maxcy Gregg included—who had fought the even more important fights against the odious tariff, internal improvements, and the bank.[6]

The convention authorized the raising of a regiment of six-month volunteers and gave the coveted command of the regiment and the accompanying

4. *Confederate Veteran* 8 (1900): 428–29; David Duncan Wallace, *The History of South Carolina*, 4 vols. (New York: American Historical Society, 1934), 3:119; Harold S. Schultz, *Nationalism and Sectionalism in South Carolina, 1852–1860* (Durham: Duke University Press), 29.

5. Schultz, *Nationalism*, 35, 40, 171, 174; Malone, ed., *Dictionary of American Biography*, 7:598–99.

6. John A. May and Joan R. Faunt, *South Carolina Secedes* (Columbia: University of South Carolina Press, 1950), 11; Charles E. Cauthen, *South Carolina Goes to War* (Chapel Hill: University of North Carolina Press, 1950), 74. Gregg was one of seven men on the committee that drafted the ordinance. Subsequently he voted against ratification of the constitution, apparently on the grounds that it did not specifically exclude nonslave states (ibid., 90n.). There is some evidence that Gregg collaborated with men from other states in the interest of southern cooperation. See Ulrich B. Phillips, ed., *The Correspondence of Robert Toombs, Alexander H. Stephens, and Howell Cobb* (Washington, D.C.: American Historical Association, 1913), 522. The Toombs-Stephens-Cobb book was the second volume of the association's annual report for 1913.

Banner of the South Carolina convention

commission as colonel to Gregg.[7] After breathing fire for more than twenty years, the untried warrior was to be thrust upon a stage of blood and iron to test his dearly held tenets. He accepted the challenge happily and without apparent feelings of inadequacy.

The new colonel who gathered his men around Charleston Harbor was an

7. The commission as colonel bore date of January 1, 1861 (Gregg's official CSR in M267, NA).

imposing sight in a proud new uniform. He was a large, thickset man with "dark hair well sprinkled with gray" and a ruddy complexion hidden behind generous whiskers and mustache of gray. The civilian Maxcy Gregg struck observers as a "reserved . . . grave and quiet," somewhat deaf bachelor who looked older than his age and went about standing very straight in a suit of black.[8] Another observer described Gregg behaving "in his usual quiet way" when in settings without political context. It soon became apparent, however, that the battlefield stirred the same passions that flared in the political arena. An officer who knew Gregg well described him as "rather small of stature, but he impressed me . . . quite to the contrary, and on horseback he presented a very soldierly appearance."[9]

Through the month of January 1861, a new nation was forming as southern states left the Union. At the same time, the Confederacy's first regiment took shape as Gregg's 1st South Carolina Volunteers. At least sixty physicians and attorneys shouldered muskets among the ten companies that hurried to Charleston. Another of the volunteers in the regiment was William Downes Farley, who later achieved fame as J. E. B. Stuart's peerless scout.[10]

On Sullivan's and Morris Islands, the enthusiastic volunteers made the adjustment to a soldier's life, although admittedly "not without some complaint." Despite the wind and sand and unaccustomed exertion, this period was, in retrospect, halcyon days for Gregg's men. The colonel drilled his recruits endlessly and eventually succeeded in raising them to a level of competence unusual in the rather loosely drilled Confederate armies. One of his aides proudly styled his chief "a gentleman and a soldier, as kind as can be and as stern as Brutus." Some of the young gentlemen-soldiers, bridling under

8. In a droll story about Gregg's deafness (*Richmond Daily Dispatch*, June 28, 1884), a veteran of the Crenshaw Battery described riding through a long day with Gregg and having to repeat most of his comments—until the artillerist suggested "in a moderate tone . . . that he had left in his canteen a few drinks of whiskey." That news evidently penetrated Gregg's deafness easily and quickly.

9. *SHSP* 43:34; An English Combatant [Thomas E. Caffey], *Battle-Fields of the South* (New York: John Bradburn, 1864), 333; United Daughters of the Confederacy (hereafter UDC), *Recollections and Reminiscences, 1861–1865*, 9 vols. (N.p.: South Carolina Division, UDC, 1990–98), 5:185; *Confederate Veteran* 8 (1900): 428–29; Caldwell, *History of a Brigade*, 59; *Columbia Guardian*, July 26, 1861; David Gregg McIntosh, "A Ride on Horseback . . . Over Some of the Battlefields of the Great Civil War," SHC.

10. *Richmond Dispatch*, July 13, 1861; Douglas Southall Freeman, *Lee's Lieutenants: A Study in Command*, 3 vols. (New York: Charles Scribner's Sons, 1942–44), 1:280.

Fort Sumter in 1860

army discipline and disgruntled over being forced to dig earthworks, agreed that "we don't like Gregg."[11]

Even less amenable to Gregg's discipline were the captains of the vessels that occasionally served as transport and supply to his command. On at least one occasion, the colonel achieved the desired results by arresting the recalcitrant sailor until he promised to act as directed.[12]

Along with supplies, the boats brought an unending stream of curious visitors. Gregg indiscreetly discussed his superiors with one rather chatty female among this group. He confided in the lady that W. H. C. Whiting was doing all the work and had all the brains but that P. G. T. Beauregard was reaping

11. *SHSP* 12:482, 486, and 14:208–9n.; Susan W. Benson, ed., *Berry Benson's Civil War Book* (Athens: University of Georgia Press, 1962), 1–2; Caldwell, *History of a Brigade*, 64; *OR* 1:302; (all references are to Series I unless otherwise specified); Daly, *Alexander Cheves Haskell*, 49; Richard L. Beach, ed., *Remember Me: The Civil War Letters of Lt. George Robinson* (Bowie, Md.: Heritage Books, 1991), 31.

12. *OR* 1:269–70.

the glory. Furthermore, the defenses of Morris Island were so inadequate that someone had surely erred in the matter.[13]

This friendly but unprofessional chat fortunately led to no embarrassing repercussions for Gregg. He faced embarrassment to spare, though, on the morning of March 8, 1861, when one of the cannon under his command suddenly belched out a solid shot that flew unerringly into a wall of Fort Sumter. It was ascertained that there had been no hostile intent and that the shot had been accidental. A quick apology to the Federal representatives at Sumter and a round of explanations to the Confederate command closed the incident at a total cost of a few bricks and some anxious moments.[14]

Before five more weeks had passed, shot and shell poured from southern cannon into Sumter with very hostile intent indeed. Gregg commanded about thirteen hundred men and several of the guns in the ring around the besieged fort. It is hard to imagine that Gregg could have been less than a leader in welcoming the first fire, after more than two decades of sowing the wind. It must also have been a welcome relief to have the reality of action after three months of alarm-filled nights, long hours in the saddle, and "rockets flying in a suspicious place." Gregg and his soldiers joined all of South Carolina in savoring their first taste of victory at arms on the night of April 13, 1861.[15]

Before the celebrations quieted, news came from Virginia on April 19 of the pressing need for troops to defend that newly seceded state. Governor Francis Pickens urged General Beauregard to offer the honor of answering Virginia's call to Maxcy Gregg and the 1st South Carolina. Gregg accepted the honor gladly; but to his bitter disappointment, some of his companies refused to go to Virginia on the grounds that they had enlisted for service in South Carolina. Even so, just eleven days after the surrender of Fort Sumter, Colonel Gregg arrived in Richmond with five hundred men. One of the local newspapers reported to the anxious citizens that "every man of them looked a hero." Richmond had not yet become accustomed to soldiers in the streets, and the days of late April and early May turned into one long ovation for the South Carolinians. Crowds of civilians cheered every dress parade; storekeepers refused to accept payment for anything the men fancied; every trip through the streets resulted in kind words and attentions. The long war had not gotten

13. Mary Boykin Chesnut, *A Diary from Dixie* (New York: D. Appleton, 1905), 31.

14. *OR* 1:192–93, 273. A Gregg letter from this period, discussing ordnance needs of his regiment, dated April 6, 1861, is at Western Reserve Historical Society, Cleveland, Ohio.

15. *Richmond Dispatch*, April 11, 1861, said precisely 1,356 men, including artillery. *OR* 1:302 reported 1,100 men, excluding artillery. Daly, *Alexander Cheves Haskell*, 49.

much older before a numbness set in among the populace, and eventually the city's defenders came to be viewed as a real burden.[16]

In late May, the regiment was ordered to the plains of Manassas, an area quickly becoming a focal point for the Confederate forces in northern Virginia. Gregg promptly established a camp under strict discipline near Centreville. Throughout the second day in the new camp, refugees streamed through the area, driven to flight by the Federal invasion of Alexandria. One couple passed thousands of Confederate soldiers without being detained for more than cursory questioning. Near the end of their journey the pair ran into Maxcy Gregg's pickets, who sternly ordered the teenaged boy and girl into the imposing presence of the bushy-bearded colonel. Only after an exhaustive interrogation did Gregg decide that the youngsters represented no threat to the national security.[17]

One of the first skirmishes of the war in Virginia nearly included Gregg and his men, who were positioned in support of R. S. Ewell and J. Q. Marr when both of those officers were casualties of a Union raid on Fairfax Court House on June 1. A Virginia woman who saw Gregg at this juncture described him as "in fine spirits, and very sanguine." Two weeks later Gregg led a small force in a reconnaissance toward the Potomac. On the evening of the seventeenth he attempted to ambush a trainload of Federal troops at Vienna. Gregg had decided to abandon the effort after some fruitless waiting, and his column actually had started to move off when an approaching train whistle turned them around. As the train rolled into view the Carolinians greeted it with a surprise fire that sent its occupants racing for the woods. Gregg overcautiously sent skirmishers to feel out the woods where the enemy had fled: by the time it was clear that the Yankees were in rout it was too late for the small Confederate cavalry detachment to make an effective pursuit. After destroying six cars and some railroad equipment Gregg returned to his own lines.[18]

Brigadier General Robert C. Schenck, who commanded the Union troops at Vienna, decided that he had been attacked by 2,000 Confederates, including "a body of 150 armed picked negroes, who were posted nearest us in a grain field on our left flank, but not observed by us, as they lay flat in the grain

16. *OR* 51(2):17; Daly, *Alexander Cheves Haskell*, 51; *SHSP* 14:191; Benson, *Berry Benson*, 4–5.

17. Joseph M. Hanson, *Bull Run Remembers* (Manassas: National Capitol Publishers, 1953), 84–85.

18. *OR* 2:62, 128–30; [Judith W. McGuire], *Diary of a Southern Refugee During the War* (New York: E. J. Hall & Son, 1867), 25; Susan Leigh Blackford, comp., *Letters from Lee's Army* (New York: Charles Scribner's Sons, 1947), 15–16.

and did not fire a gun." This curious statement typified the sensational public reaction on both sides. Washington papers announced a "terrible rebel ambush," and spoke of 200 casualties. A private in one of the other South Carolina regiments wrote home proudly that Gregg's men had succeeded in "killing and wounding over three hundred without the loss of a man." The final official Federal report admitted loss of only a dozen men. Colonel Gregg himself gained quite a reputation in the affair, but he soon disappeared in the wake of new heroes when serious fighting began. A more lasting impact of the skirmish was its contribution to the burgeoning folklore about "masked batteries" behind each hill—a popular topic for fearful rumor among green volunteers.[19]

A most trying and disappointing period swiftly overshadowed Gregg's moment of glory at Vienna. His regiment of six-months volunteers reached the end of its enlistment on July 1 and had to be conducted back to Richmond for discharge from service. Virginians were not aware of the conditions that made necessary this release of short-term volunteers, and as the 1st passed towns women would come to their windows and tearfully call the men cowards and renegades. Colonel Gregg quietly accepted the abuse and left its rebuttal to a friendly correspondent of the *Richmond Dispatch*. That paper pointed out that the 1st had been mustered on a moment's notice from a civilian populace with the express goal of holding Forts Moultrie and Pinckney, a job long since done. Now that the strength of Virginia's defenses had increased somewhat, they must go back to South Carolina to make business and family arrangements before returning. Volunteers unhappy with discipline predicted that absolutely no one would come back to Gregg's regiment. That many did return, however, and promptly, is evident from the fact that six weeks later the regiment again stood at full strength in a camp on Richmond's Chimborazo Heights, with the arms, equipment, name, and banner—and many of the men—of the old regiment. In fact, several companies hoping to be included in Gregg's force had to be turned away because of the regulation that no regiment could exceed ten companies.[20]

19. *OR* 2:127; Blackford, comp., *Letters*, 16–17; *South Carolina Historical Magazine* 53 (1962): 3; Daly, *Alexander Cheves Haskell*, 51; Edward Porter Alexander, *Military Memoirs of a Confederate* (New York: Charles Scribner's Sons, 1907), 21.

20. Daly, *Alexander Cheves Haskell*, 52; Beach, *Remember Me*, 33; UDC, *Recollections and Reminiscences*, 2:343; *Richmond Dispatch*, July 13, 1861; *Yorkville Enquirer*, December 24, 1862; *OR*, Ser. IV, 1:468; Gregg letter to G. T. Beauregard, July 9, 1861, Dearborn Collection, Harvard University, Cambridge, Mass. Gregg received a new commission as colonel with the reorganized regiment, to take rank from July 25, although it was not confirmed until December—a typical bureaucratic

Gregg remained in Richmond during the brief period during which there was no 1st South Carolina for him to command. An incident concerning one of the returning companies of South Carolinians involved Gregg in a brief tangle with President Davis. Charles H. Axson, a thirty-five-year-old captain, commanded the company as it rode the trains north toward Richmond. Axson was something of a social lion and fond of parties and high living. He had also gained a reputation as a good officer. During the trip, a Georgian of Paul J. Semmes's Brigade murdered the captain in an unexplained altercation. As soon as the train stopped, Axson's company found the Georgian and hanged him on the spot. General Semmes and fellow Georgian Robert Toombs reported the affair with some heat and color to President Davis, who in turn promptly denounced Gregg and declared that he should be cashiered. Some South Carolina politicians friendly to Maxcy Gregg brought the story to him as it had reached their ears. The colonel accepted the news with equanimity and proceeded to have dinner and a chat with an aide before he undertook to write Davis. After lengthy dictation and revisions, he signed the sixth draft and sent it to the executive mansion in care of a fully uniformed staff officer. Davis received the young officer graciously until it became known that the call was business rather than social. He finally agreed to accept the letter in his office, but after reading for a short time, the president became so angry that he threw down the paper and began to pace around the office denouncing Gregg. When the young officer objected, he was dismissed. The next day Davis expressed regrets and apologized to Gregg in a letter. Here the matter ended. As a peculiar anticlimax, it was discovered that the "lynched" Georgian murderer actually had escaped with his life when some comrades cut him down before he had been hanging long enough to suffocate.[21]

Soon after this incident Gregg was sent with his regiment to Suffolk. There he spent the fall months training and drilling the men for the rigorous campaigns bound to come in the spring. Some companies responded to the training more rapidly than others. When the colonel complimented Company H by calling it a model unit, the remainder of the regiment began referring to members of the company as "The Models," in a mixture of derision and jealousy. During the stay at Suffolk, Lieutenant Alexander Cheves Haskell be-

---

delay (Gregg's CSR, M267, NA). Incredibly, Gregg has no CSR in M331, NA, the general officers' file—he must be the only Confederate general of whom that can be said.

21. Daly, *Alexander Cheves Haskell*, 55–57. Axson's CSR (M267, NA) includes only two slips, both concerning his service before the July dissolution of the regiment.

came adjutant of the regiment after he received some special assistance from
the colonel. Young Haskell was intelligent, well-educated, and observant, but
he suffered from severe stammering attacks that would hardly be appropriate
when reading the evening orders at parades. Gregg escorted his prospective
adjutant deep into some nearby woods and had him read orders at the top of
his lungs until he overcame the impediment. Haskell became a key member
of Gregg's staff and a close friend during the remainder of his chief's life.
Later in the war he achieved considerable success on his own as a cavalry commander. To the end of his life Haskell spoke fondly of "my dear and noble old
Colonel," who had been "so wondrous kind."[22]

Gregg received orders in mid-December 1861 that took him away from his
beloved 1st South Carolina, but under the happiest of circumstances. Orders
had come down appointing him a brigadier general in the Provisional Army
of the Confederate States and posting him in his home state under the command of R. E. Lee. General Gregg's new brigade was composed of the 12th,
13th, and 14th South Carolina Regiments. These untried troops were apparently somewhat wanting in morale and training; their new brigade commander at once undertook to correct the shortages. The brigade spent the
winter in mundane garrison duty near Pocotaligo in the military district commanded by one of the less inspired Confederate generals, J. C. Pemberton.
After several months of nothing more interesting than a false invasion alarm,
there came exciting and very welcome orders. Gregg's Brigade was to go north
to Virginia—to the seat of the war![23]

The small South Carolina brigade was first stationed at Summit Point on
the railroad near Fredericksburg, under the command of the former and future
head of Richmond's Tredegar Iron Works, Joseph Reid Anderson. Late in
May the whole command retired toward Richmond under arduous conditions
imposed by rain and mud. During the march Maxcy Gregg found himself
exercising considerably more command than he could have expected. The brigade finally reached the outskirts of Richmond and went into camp on the
Smith Farm along the Nine Mile Road and near the Chickahominy. There
the general, who had his headquarters at the James B. Crenshaw house, and
his troops underwent an uncomfortable and unhealthy month of camp life
before the opening of the Seven Days campaign.[24]

22. Benson, *Berry Benson*, 7; Daly, *Alexander Cheves Haskell*, 60–62.

23. *Richmond Dispatch*, December 16, 1861; Daly, *Alexander Cheves Haskell*, 64–66; *OR* 6:349.

24. *Yorkville Enquirer*, December 24, 1862; Daly, *Alexander Cheves Haskell*, 68–69; Caldwell,
History of a Brigade, 11; James B. Crenshaw diary entry, May 31, 1862, in *Our Quaker Friends of Ye
Olden Time* (Lynchburg, Va.: J. P. Bell, 1905). Haskell declared (in Daly) that Anderson could not

Gregg's old regiment, the 1st South Carolina, had been transferred several times since he left it at Suffolk in December. After wintering in North Carolina the regiment had returned to Virginia in April and now it was rejoined with its old commander. At the same time Orr's Rifles added their strength to the brigade, making a total of five regiments. This latter unit was officially the 1st South Carolina Rifles, though the less formal name was used to avoid confusion with the three other regiments called "1st South Carolina." David Gregg McIntosh's Battery, the "Pee Dee Artillery," was attached to the brigade and Haskell headed a staff of alert young officers. Haskell's lucid and charming memoirs are an unfortunately scarce historical record. Thus came together the famous Gregg-McGowan Brigade that gave such stellar service for the duration of the war.

The new brigade was promptly attached to the "Light Division" of A. P. Hill which was being formed. That renowned division served the Confederacy brilliantly until the brigades were separated during the reorganization following the death of General T. J. "Stonewall" Jackson. In a division full of good brigades and good generals, Maxcy Gregg and his South Carolinians stood out. Gregg soon formed a deep friendship with Hill and became, with North Carolinian Dorsey Pender, part of the division commander's intimate official family.[25]

Lee's offensive in late June 1862 developed into a group of battles known as the Seven Days campaign. During the week of fierce fighting Lee managed to generate a marginally coordinated offensive operation only on June 27 at Gaines's Mill and on June 30 at Frayser's Farm. Hill's division bore a large share of the fighting. The unsuccessful and costly Confederate assaults on Fitz-John Porter near Mechanicsville during the evening of June 26 did not include Gregg, who had been held in reserve by Hill. A staff officer who met Gregg for the first time during the twenty-sixth called him "the politest officer I ever saw." When pursuit of the retreating Federals began on June 27 it was natural that the fresh and unhurt South Carolinians took the point. The abandoned enemy camps afforded ample access to food and other lootables, but

---

cope with the situation during the retirement and turned the command over to Gregg on a technicality concerning commission dates. The date-of-commission portion of the story is not accurate, so the rest of the circumstances accordingly are somewhat suspect. In a letter dated June 3 (Haskell Papers, SHC), Haskell grumbled about "an impractical General who runs us about without transportation, and we starve"—referring evidently to Anderson.

25. *OR* 11(3):554; *SHSP*, 27:159; Martin Schenck, *Up Came Hill* (Harrisburg, Pa.: Stackpole, 1958), 29; Clifford Dowdey, *The Seven Days* (Boston: Little, Brown, 1964), 181.

the eager men ignored the opportunity. Later one of the veterans remembered ruefully that "our ardor prevented us from pillaging as freely as we learned subsequently to do."[26]

After a short advance the head of the column came under artillery fire that wounded two men. Investigation showed that the fire was "friendly," coming from troops under Stonewall Jackson. In this melancholy fashion Lee's troops made contact with the long-awaited Jackson. About noon, Gregg found Lee near the road in company with Longstreet, A. P. Hill, and Jackson. The general officers shared some sandwiches as they conferred. Lee directed Gregg to push forward. The Carolinians soon took Gaines's Mill on Powhite Creek, together with a quantity of liquor with which the men rewarded themselves, apparently having lost in the heat of the day some of the ardor that had driven them past interesting pelf that morning. To clear the enemy resistance, Confederate batteries shelled the opposite woods, then skirmishers opened a way across the creek. After some desultory sniping Gregg formed the 1st and 12th Regiments and ordered them forward. They routed the enemy resistance so effectively that A. P. Hill enthusiastically called their advance "the handsomest charge in line I have seen during the war." Before Gregg could order a continued advance, many of his troops fell asleep as an aftermath of their heavy exertions in the moist Virginia heat.[27]

All of this skirmishing, in fact all of their previous military experience, was but a pale prelude to the inferno that faced Gregg and his soldiers as they moved on against the three-tiered enemy line beyond Boatswain's Swamp. For about an hour and a half they lay under artillery fire, awaiting the formation of a concerted line by Hill's Division. Here the men got their first taste of "bomb ague," a disease with which most became painfully familiar. Crenshaw's Virginia battery, attached to Gregg's command, performed so nobly that the general urged Captain Crenshaw to put his three guns into action after the remaining three had been disabled, saying, "Bring them along; they are as good as six of the enemy's."[28]

About four o'clock the artillery duel gave way to an infantry attack that soon dissolved into a bitter and disorganized melee. At least one of Gregg's regiments disintegrated as a unit and became demoralized. Orr's Rifles

26. John Hinsdale journal, June 16, 1862, Hinsdale Papers, PLD; Caldwell, *History of a Brigade*, 16.

27. English Combatant, *Battle-Fields*, 333–34; Caldwell, *History of a Brigade*, 16–17; *OR* 11(2):836.

28. *OR* 11(2): 854; *SHSP*, 27:162 and 31:277.

launched a gallant but fruitless charge of the sort all too common during the early battles of the Confederate armies; their goal was a troublesome enfilading battery that roared from beyond a broad, open field. Within a few minutes the regiment lost 315 of the 537 men carried into the battle, and the battery had limbered to the rear by the time the South Carolinians closed on the Federal lines. The other four regiments were hard-pressed to maintain their first positions and did not achieve even the temporary penetration made by Orr's Rifles.[29]

General Gregg himself rode through the thick of the battle, striving to preserve order and achieve some progress in the midst of the torrent of lead. A member of the brigade remembered the general's appearance as the "sublimest spectacle I ever saw." The same eyewitness rhapsodized about Gregg's performance at Gaines's Mill:

> In the midst of the most fatal fusilade I ever witnessed, he rode up to the line and drew his sword, calling to them in a voice that rose above the whole din of battle, to make a stand. His horse reared in an ecstacy of excitement and terror, and then was before us the noblest equestrian statue of the world. The horse poised himself upon his hind feet, beating the air with his fore legs, his nostrils distended, and his eyes rolling fire. The rider sat motionless as marble, and raised to his full height, his left hand grasping the reins like a vice, his right extended to arms-length, pointing forward with a sword that dazzled with its brilliancy, and his whole countenance lighted with a zeal and energy, a power that commanded and inspired all men's hearts.[30]

Even after discounting the florid nature of Victorian descriptions, it is apparent that Gregg posed an impressive figure under the transforming influence of the spirit of battle. A fifteen-year-old private in the 14th South Carolina called his brigadier "one of the bravest men I ever knew." A member of A. P. Hill's staff wrote of Gregg's performance: "Hill is brave to a fault; but as for Gregg, he really loves danger."[31]

As darkness began to fall, a desperate charge by the 4th Texas and other Confederate units pierced the enemy lines and opened the way for a great, though expensive, victory for Lee. Gregg and his men contributed little to the

---

29. Benson, *Berry Benson*, 10–11; *OR* 11(2):854–55; *SHSP*, 27:162–64; *Charleston Mercury*, July 26, 1862.

30. Caldwell, *History of a Brigade*, 64.

31. Manuscript reminiscence of John W. Alexander, 14th South Carolina, copy in the author's possession; *Charleston Mercury*, August 2, 1862.

pursuit of the routed foe, being content to regroup and count the dreadful losses they had suffered. About 140 South Carolinians had been killed and 714 wounded, nearly one-third of the force that had entered the battle a few hours earlier as untested novices. For the wounded the ordeal was far from over: some remained without any attention for several days. Those men now beyond help weighed heavily on the mind of their general, who wept bitterly over the graves of some of his dead soldiers after the fighting had ended. Orr's Rifles had suffered more casualties than any other Confederate regiment at Gaines's Mill, and their percentage of loss during the battle remained among the highest for four years of bitter warfare.[32]

For two days the only exertion demanded of the brigade was a strenuous but not dangerous march. On June 30 they arrived on the indecisive and disappointing battlefield of Frayser's Farm in time to play a minor role at the close of the contest. Two Confederate brigades under the questionable leadership of Brigadier Generals W. S. Featherston and Roger A. Pryor had become badly shaken and in danger of destruction. Gregg threw in the 14th South Carolina and restored the position with minimal loss to his men. When the smoke had cleared, however, not a few of the Confederate officers turned to fighting their associates. One problem was in Gregg's own brigade. Colonel D. H. Hamilton, commanding the 1st South Carolina, was convinced that Major Edward McCrady of his regiment had displayed cowardice by reporting sick just before the battle at Gaines's Mill and that he had compounded this misdeed by going home to recuperate without permission from the colonel. Hamilton took this grievance directly to Secretary of War George Wythe Randolph and the adjutant and inspector general of the Confederacy, Samuel Cooper, rather than going through Gregg. This quaint and nonmilitary avoidance of channels was frightfully common among many Confederate officers. When Gregg learned of the affair, he interceded on behalf of the major, citing his service to the brigade staff during the battle and declaring him guilty of no misconduct. An ironic aftermath of this quarrel was that Colonel Hamilton himself missed the ensuing battles of the Second Manassas campaign on sick leave and his regiment was commanded by the maligned Major McCrady, who led the men well until he was severely wounded.[33]

A much more consequential argument erupted between A. P. Hill and

32. *SHSP*, 27:164; Caldwell, *History of a Brigade*, 65; William F. Fox, *Regimental Losses in the American Civil War* (Albany, N.Y.: Albany Publishing Company, 1893), 556, 562.
33. *OR* 11(2):781, 786, 848, 858–59, 870; *OR* 12(2):683–90.

James Longstreet, which finally resulted in Hill's transfer to the command of General Jackson. Gregg became involved in a roundabout manner when the degree of Longstreet's supervision over him at Frayser's Farm came into question. The whole untidy affair was surely reason for both Hill and Gregg to welcome their transfer in late July to join Jackson, but before a fortnight passed both were to be at odds with their new chief.[34]

In early August Maxcy Gregg received news of the death of his mother in South Carolina. The pressure of operations before a powerful enemy army made it impossible for him to return home. Thus August 9 found Gregg at the head of his brigade and chafing to enter the battle raging around the northern end of Cedar Mountain. Despite repeated appeals to Hill to be committed to action, he was ordered to spend the day guarding the trains against enemy cavalry units, which never appeared. A few days later one of the general's field officers grumbled that Gregg was "infected with the idea" that "the post of danger is the post of honor." As an inglorious footnote to the battle, Gregg's men broke into a panicky rout when awakened from their sleep on August 11 by some noise variously reported as a rattling ambulance, some Confederate cavalry, or two small dogs.[35]

On August 25, operations unfolded with dramatic suddenness as Jackson flung his wing of the army around Pope's right flank in the vicinity of Manassas. In the fighting that followed, Gregg's Brigade experienced one of its most glorious days and the general himself the greatest day of his life. Along the route of the famous march around Pope, civilians expressed much goodwill; the cry "Hurrah for South Carolina" was often heard from the women along the road. Some of the women had apparently been indiscriminate with their cheers in the past, for at one point a toddler shouted, "Hurrah for Sout' Ca'liny Massachute" several times before he could be hushed. Gregg's men adopted the lad's indiscreet yell as a sardonic war cry of their own.[36]

At the end of the long march waited a veritable pot of gold—the Federal supply depot at Manassas Junction. One of Gregg's men left an oft-quoted account of the ensuing revelry of hungry and ragged Confederates: "Fine whiskey and segars circulated freely, elegant lawn and linen handkerchiefs

34. For a detailed look at the Hill-Longstreet controversy, including much that did not involve Maxcy Gregg, see William W. Hassler, *A. P. Hill, Lee's Forgotten General* (Richmond: Garrett & Massie, 1957), chap. 9.

35. *Charleston Mercury*, August 11, 1862; *South Carolina Historical Magazine* 57 (October 1956): 219; Benson, *Berry Benson*, 16; Caldwell, *History of a Brigade*, 26–28.

36. Benson, *Berry Benson*, 17–18.

were applied to noses hitherto blown with the thumb and forefinger, and sumptuous underclothing was fitted over limbs sunburnt, sore and vermin-splotched . . . we were invited to help ourselves to anything in the storehouses, from a dose of calomel to a McClellan saddle."[37] The immediate aftermath of the fun was a good night's sleep near Manassas Junction; a more serious after-math was the Battle of Second Manassas, which followed.

Near midday on August 28 Gregg led his men into a position on the left of the Confederate line behind the famous unfinished railroad, near Catharpin Run and overlooking the Sudley Springs Road. The brigade deployed over a small, rocky knoll, with protection afforded by the railroad excavation in front and on the left. The left flank of the brigade was refused to the rear to protect the far northeastern end of the army. The South Carolinians constituted, in effect, a wedge with the angle pointing at the enemy. The position was inher-ently strong and the men who held it were determined, but there was a weak-ness to the right. Somehow between Generals Jackson, Hill, Gregg, and Thomas a critical gap remained unprotected between the brigades of Thomas and Gregg.[38] The inexplicably undefended 150 yards would lead to the death of many southern boys. Before the war came to Maxcy Gregg's knoll a bitter fight swirled around Groveton, a mile or so to the right. Although the brigade was summoned to help, it did not arrive until the action was over. Early the next morning the men returned to the little knoll. Many of them never left it.

August 29 dawned clear and soon turned intensely hot. There seemed to be limitless numbers of Yankees willing to trot up the slope against Jackson's line, especially against the far left end where Gregg and his men lay waiting. The soldiers who fought there with Gregg and survived the war all remem-bered the day of tense drama and desperate struggle as one of the most impor-tant events in their lives. The assaults on the Confederate position, historians calculate, consisted of six different waves, stretching through the day. The men resisting the assaults saw only an endless red haze. The deadly gap on the right drew Federals like a magnet, and they were soon able to pour an enflad-ing fire across the tip of Gregg's protruding line. Time and again Federal as-saults bore in, only to recede under determined counterattack, leaving a wake of bleeding and dead behind.[39]

Gregg began the battle with his headquarters about fifty yards in rear of

37. Caldwell, *History of a Brigade*, 31.
38. *OR* 12(2):679–80.
39. *SHSP*, 13:3–40; *OR* 12(2):679–97; *Richmond Daily Whig*, April 21, 1864.

the center of his brigade. During the bloody battle his presence and spirit inspired his men to the terrible task they faced. On foot throughout the day, he strode up and down the line through the hail of lead. After the brigade had held on until it seemed impossible to do so again, and another attack was building, it suddenly became apparent that the troops badly needed ammunition. Gregg sent this message to A. P. Hill: "Tell General Hill that my ammunition is exhausted, but that I will hold my position with the bayonet." Hill responded: "He is the man for me." In this crucial moment the fire-eating secessionist-turned-general was aroused to a fever pitch. Drawing his old scimitar (handed down from a veteran of the Revolutionary War), Gregg paced among his surviving soldiers, saying: "Let us die here, my men, let us die here." As he strode among the men, the general absentmindedly lopped off with his heirloom sword the heads of daisies growing on the knoll.[40]

Support from Lane's Brigade arrived in time to save Gregg and his remnant for a time, but yet again they lay in the grass with fixed bayonets, ready to rise and meet the enemy with steel if he charged. Mercifully, the battle ended for the day and the brigade was spared further loss. It was as well, for 613 of them had been shot, including all but one of the field officers present. The general escaped with only a superficial leg wound. The reports of the great Confederate leaders who had watched Gregg in his death struggle were almost embarrassingly complimentary. Hill's report said: "The stubborn tenacity with which Gregg's brigade held its position this day is worthy of highest commendation." Lee himself wrote that "General Gregg, who was most exposed . . . successfully and gallantly resisted the attacks of the enemy." Fellow brigadier W. Dorsey Pender, whose troops helped salvage the position at one point, wrote simply that Gregg was "fighting nearly all day."[41]

Late on the evening of August 30, in a backwash of the great Confederate assault that routed the enemy, some of the skirmishers thrown out by Gregg to protect his line had a moment of confusion during which they exchanged fire with some elements of Jubal Early's brigade. Fortunately there was no harm at either end from the "friendly" fire, but the memory of this potential

40. Hassler, *A. P. Hill*, 91; *OR* 12(2):671; *SHSP*, 13:34–35; marginalia by a brigade veteran in a copy of Edward McCrady's published speech about the battle, in possession of John "Stumpy" Bass of Spring Hope, N.C. Gregg's sword, with silver grips and brass scabbard, engraved with the state's palmetto tree, survived in 1988 in the hands of descendants of Alexander Cheves Haskell.

41. *OR* 12(2):556, 672; *Yorkville Enquirer*, December 24, 1862; W. Dorsey Pender to Louis G. Young, September 30, 1862, Robert Gourdin Papers, Emory University Special Collections, Atlanta.

tragedy may have flickered across Gregg's mind a few months later at Fredericksburg. If so, the harmless brush near Bull Run had far-reaching consequences.[42]

The desperate struggle of the Confederacy for a national existence did not allow the army to recuperate from its losses. Just three days after their heroic day on the rocky knoll, the men who fought for Maxcy Gregg were again thrown into battle. This fight came to be known as the Battle of Ox Hill, a rather small affair in a pouring rain. It added another 104 of Gregg's men to the lengthening list of casualties.[43] Again, no respite. On to Maryland!

The march north began under conditions of poor supply that were difficult even by the sparse standards of the lean and mean Confederates. About one-third of Gregg's men marched without any shoes at all, and the whole army was so dependent on the country for food that the soldiers remembered the ensuing march and battle as "the green corn campaign." One side product of the necessary foraging was a series of disciplinary incidents involving the uncompromising Jackson and the less rigid Gregg. In one of the imbroglios the core of the problem was an apple orchard located much too close to a roadside stop. Orders against foraging of course proved far from effective in keeping famished soldiers and ripening fruit apart. When Frank Paxton, of Jackson's staff, saw men in the orchard he immediately arrested the colonel of the nearest identifiable regiment. That happened to be Dixon Barnes of the 12th South Carolina. Brigade tradition records that the South Carolinians were innocent, indeed pure as the driven snow, and that the true offenders were actually members of the Stonewall Brigade. In any case, Colonel Barnes was marched at the rear of his regiment, while Maxcy Gregg sorrowfully bowed to the order that put him there. When the regiment subsequently became engaged, Barnes approached Gregg brimming with emotion and begged to be allowed to go in with his men as a private. The unavoidable orders of the corps commander made even that impossible, said Gregg. At that juncture A. P. Hill rode into the painful tableau and asked the source of the problem. Hill was a veteran of almost as many conflicts with Jackson as with the Yankees and he did not hesitate to order, with pale and stern face, "General Gregg, I order you to give Colonel Barnes his sword and put him in command of his Regiment."[44]

42. Jubal A. Early, *Autobiographical Sketch and Narrative of the War Between the States* (Philadelphia: J. B. Lippincott, 1912), 127–28.
43. Caldwell, *History of a Brigade*, 39.
44. *SHSP*, 14:205; Daly, *Alexander Cheves Haskell*, 77–78.

Another roadside halt set the stage for a further problem. This time the coveted commodity was firewood in the form of a farmer's fence. Against both standing and specific orders the South Carolina boys proceeded to turn organic matter into heat energy until the dawn's early light revealed bare fields and no fences. In short order all five of the brigade's regimental commanders were under arrest and perhaps Maxcy Gregg himself. A financial arrangement with the owner of the farm was quickly worked out and the Confederate officers went back to their posts.[45] An interesting contrast is illustrated by the vast spiritual gulf yawning between this stern protection of private property and the consciously incendiary policies of George Custer, Philip Sheridan, et al. later in the war.

A third point of conflict arose between Jackson and Gregg during the operations of late August and early September. Jackson's displeasure erupted over the failure of Hill's division to march at the very early hour that had been designated. Jackson approached General Gregg directly to ascertain reasons for the delay and Gregg responded with some shortness in defending his men's need for certain creature comforts in advance of the march. The exchange left a bitterness between the two that did not abate during the three months that remained before Gregg received his mortal wound. One of the men of the 1st South Carolina who had marched ahead of the army noticed Gregg and Jackson coming up behind him, riding side by side. The soldier overheard the corps commander say, "There are but few commanders who appreciate the value of celerity." Celerity was surely one of Jackson's many military virtues and apparently one that he thought Gregg did not appreciate adequately.[46]

The culmination of the intramural conflict came when Gregg filed charges of maladministration against Jackson. After he had heard nothing for some time, Gregg sent an aide to Lee to ascertain reasons for the delay. Lee had by then become accustomed to turning aside adroitly the wrath of his irascible lieutenants. He dismissed the matter by saying, "Take these papers to General Gregg and tell him that at such a time as this the country cannot afford quarrels."[47]

While the Confederates sorted out (or nurtured, in some instances) their internal problems, the common enemy remained. Jackson and Lee conspired

45. *SHSP*, 14:209–10.
46. Freeman, *Lee's Lieutenants*, 2:147–48; Benson, *Berry Benson*, 25.
47. Wallace, *History of South Carolina*, 3:179n.

to gobble up better than twelve thousand of them in and near Harpers Ferry after a grueling circuitous march that converged three columns on that place. Gregg and his men made up the leading element of the main column as it liberated Martinsburg, just west of Harpers Ferry. The enthusiastic greeting from the town included thrilling thanks and encouragement from the maidens of Martinsburg, but one of the somewhat jaded men of the brigade hoped that "a soldier may be pardoned for dwelling on the more substantial comforts of bread and meat."[48]

Almost immediately after the capture of Harpers Ferry, Hill's division set out on a forced march to the banks of Antietam Creek, where Lee confronted a huge Federal army. Gregg had been detailed to help in the paroling of the captured Federals and thus marched near the end of the column rushing toward the sound of the guns. The twenty-mile march was among the most trying of the war, since the intense heat and a road several inches deep in dust compounded the desperate nature of the hour. The time was near four o'clock when Hill's division reached the field to find Lee's army in danger of imminent destruction. Gregg led his own and two other brigades into the breach on the right flank of Lee's position and found a situation so serious that he ignored the approved tactics for shaking a column into line. He merely shouted to his four-abreast column, "Commence firing, men, and form the line as you fight." For a time, Confederates mistook Gregg's men for northern troops because they had taken the opportunity to appropriate some of the blue clothing recently captured. The enemy had no trouble recognizing them when the volleys began pouring into their ranks. On one portion of the field, Gregg's troops used converging fire to herd the Federals into a hollow and there lashed them with repeated volleys fired as though on a drill field.[49]

During a brief lull between assaults, Gregg and two of his aides rode through some thick corn in front of their men. A sudden volley from a Union line about forty yards distant ripped among them. Several balls hit the officers' mounts, and one struck the general near his right hip with such force that he was nearly unhorsed. An aide held him on the horse long enough to scamper back to the lines and then helped him down. Gregg ignored the pain long enough to send staff members off to rearrange the brigade's command structure. When the stretcher bearers arrived and prepared to tend the wound, the

48. Caldwell, *History of a Brigade*, 41–43.
49. Daly, *Alexander Cheves Haskell*, 79–80; Alexander, *Military Memoirs*, 268; Benson, *Berry Benson*, 27–28.

examining sergeant exclaimed: "General, you aren't wounded, you are only bruised." Gregg leaped to his feet to enjoy the pleasant surprise and soon dashed back into action after mounting himself on one of the horses that had been drawing the ambulance intended for his body. The next morning at breakfast, as Gregg opened his large silk handkerchief for a napkin, out dropped a flattened rifle ball. The only damage was a great black bruise on his right hip. Within two weeks he was reported to be "well and quite recovered." Gregg was fortunate to have escaped so lightly, for the volley that hit him was apparently the same fire that had inflicted a mortal wound on Gregg's fellow brigadier L. O'Bryan Branch.[50]

When Lee's tattered remnants retreated back across the Potomac, it was Gregg and his battle-hardened men who guarded the rear of the Army of Northern Virginia. General McClellan mounted only a feeble pursuit by some cavalry units, and a firm volley from the South Carolinians dispersed them. Gregg and his staff remained north of the river until the very end, to assure the passage of all the trains. As Gregg and his last hundred men abandoned the Maryland shore, they came upon an ambulance full of wounded who had been deserted by a cowardly driver. The injured Confederates begged to be taken along, a cry the chivalrous Gregg would not ignore. He shouted to his nearest soldiers: "My men, it is a shame to leave these poor fellows here in the water! Can't you take them over the river?" Willing hands pulled the ambulance through to safety, while onlookers contributed a loud rendition of "Carry me back to Old Virginia." When the enemy followed across the river, Gregg took command of a portion of A. P. Hill's Division, with which he drove the pursuers into the water in short order.[51]

The dreadful trial by fire in Maryland was followed by a period of calm days that remained forever in the minds of some Confederate soldiers as the happiest days of their army. A glowing fall in the Shenandoah Valley soothed some of the scars of hard civil war. The harvest season and the beautiful scenery provided food for body and soul, and nothing more wearing was asked of the men than an occasional raid to tear up the Baltimore & Ohio Railroad or an enforced mass bathing in the Opequon. Discussion around the fires centered on the various favored methods for destroying some of the lice that in-

50. Daly, *Alexander Cheves Haskell*, 81–86. A fine account of this episode is in A. C. Haskell to Ezra A. Carman, June 16, 1896, Box 3, Carman Papers, Antietam Studies, NA.

51. Varina Davis Brown, *A Colonel at Gettysburg and Spotsylvania* (Columbia, S.C.: State Company, 1931), 43; Henry B. McClellan, *The Life and Campaigns of Major-General J. E. B. Stuart* (Boston: Houghton Mifflin, 1885), 133; *OR* 19(1):957.

habited everyone, it being an accepted conclusion that one would never get them all.[52] In late November the marches of the brigade became earnest and steadily eastward. During the first days of December Maxcy Gregg made his last bivouac, in the hills south of Fredericksburg.

Another battle was brewing up around the once lovely old town, now suffering the ravages of repeated enemy occupation. Another On-to-Richmond drive was gathering steam under the direction of another Union commander, Ambrose E. Burnside. On December 11 the mighty Federal army lunged ponderously across the river after some angry fighting with William Barksdale's Mississippians and a heavy shelling of the town. The shelling did little to enhance the city's colonial charm.

The Confederate line forming west of the town ran for seven miles. Within a few hundred yards north of the southern end of the line a boggy piece of woodland extended out into the otherwise open plain running from the Confederates to the river. When A. P. Hill laid out his positions, presumably under Jackson's directions, he left the boggy wood undefended. The grim and costly lesson about gaps in the defensive line that should have been learned at Second Manassas already had been forgotten. On the plains of Manassas, the gap had been to the right of Gregg's men and had been only about 150 yards wide. Here the gap extended fully 500 yards, perhaps more, and here Gregg was posted 500 yards behind the gap rather than across it or on one of its flanks.[53]

To compound the confusion, the woods between the gap and the brigade were so very dense that events to the front were completely invisible, to the point that some of the privates who fought for Gregg never did learn that there had not been a friendly line in front of them. One of the brigadiers posted obliquely to Gregg's front informed the South Carolinians of the gap's existence. The Confederate high command's acceptance of the fatal gap in the line usually is explained by assuming that enfilading artillery fire would effectually seal the space from hostile occupation. One of Jackson's aides said that someone had theorized that Gregg's Brigade had been thrown back "with a view to supporting the front line on either the right or left, as might be needed," a decidedly unsound premise. D. H. Hill and others reported (while marveling at Jackson's prescience rather than questioning the preparations) that Stonewall himself commented when he saw the gap: "The enemy will

52. Caldwell, *History of a Brigade*, 52–55.
53. Alexander, *Military Memoirs*, 298–99.

attack here." In retrospect, a few observers in the army thought that Gregg was culpable, including the captain of an Alabama company who wrote home that "he is censured by some for being too careless." General James H. Lane, however—commanding the brigade just left of the gap—declared definitively that the alignment was "A. P. Hill's great mistake & cost the gallant Gregg his life." General James J. Archer, who commanded the other shoulder of the gap, opposite Lane, agreed emphatically. "Hill himself," Archer wrote a week later, "told me that Gregg was close enough to the 'interval' to prevent my being flanked."[54]

When battle was joined on the morning of December 13, a grim panoply of war unfolded below the Confederate ridge. Shiny ranks of soldiers and bright muskets rolled across open fields toward the southern lines. Far to the right a brilliant young horse artillerist earned the nom de guerre "The Gallant Pelham" for his daring exploits. None of this was visible to the South Carolinians, who were well out of visual range of the battle. When northern infantry finally steeled themselves and walked into the teeth of the Confederate artillery fire, then ran through the heavy musketry, they were almost automatically deflected into the boggy wood from which no fire was coming against them. A shallow draw further contributed to steering them into the area where they could do the most harm. Soon masses of Yankees were pouring through the hole in the Confederate line while the brigades on either side of the breach turned back their flanks to keep the hole from widening. One of the brigadiers near the irruption sent an aide through the woods to General Gregg to ask for help; at least one courier fell dead from enemy fire as he reached the vicinity of the South Carolinians.[55]

At some point during the day, Gregg had been near the farther front line, for young Sandie Pendleton of Jackson's staff had had occasion to shout through Gregg's deafness that the Yankees were shooting at him. The general replied: "Yes, sir; thank you, they have been doing so all day." When the un-

54. *SHSP*, 10:446 and 43:30; Benson, *Berry Benson*, 32–33; D. H. Hill to R. L. Dabney, July 21, 1864, Dabney Collection, Union Theological Seminary, Richmond; *Richmond Examiner*, May 10, 1866; *OR* 21:654; *Alabama Review* 10 (1957): 135; James H. Lane to A. C. Hamlin, November 30, 1892, Hamlin Papers, Houghton Library, Harvard University, Cambridge, Mass.; Archer letter to "Bob," December 21, 1862, in C. A. Porter Hopkins, ed., "The James J. Archer Letters," *Maryland Historical Magazine* 56 (1961): 138–39.

55. *OR* 21:654, 657; Joseph J. Norton notes for an 1886 speech, in the Norton Papers, South Caroliniana Library, University of South Carolina, Columbia (repository cited hereafter as SCL/USC).

checked advance of the Union assault broke over the brigade, however, he had apparently not received the tardy warnings sent from in front. Most of the men had stacked their arms, as ordered, and were taking such shelter as they could find from the occasional artillery round that managed to penetrate the heavy woods to their position. Their first warning was a spattering of small arms fire coming against them and steadily increasing in volume. Some companies grabbed their weapons and returned the fire, but others obeyed their officers and waited. The unhappy experience of past woods fights in which friends had been shot weighed on the officers' minds: surely there must be some Confederates out there in front who would have to fall back over them before the enemy could close in! The lead was sleeting in very heavily by then, most of it fortunately aimed a little too high.[56]

The veteran South Carolina brigade stood along an informal military road that followed the crest of an irregular ridge. The road curved in such a fashion that no one part of the line could see all of the rest. As the crisis neared, General Gregg was positioned between Orr's Rifles, the farthest right of his five regiments, and the old 1st South Carolina, next left from Orr's.[57]

Gregg, perhaps remembering the nearly disastrous brush with Early's men at Manassas, wanted to be sure he did not fire on friends. The general's chronic deafness no doubt contributed to his uncertainty. Riding rapidly in front of his men, he knocked up their muskets with his hands and vainly shouted to cease firing: "You are firing on our friends." Most of the men had seen visible enemies by now and were beginning to fight in earnest. The high fire that was missing most of the infantrymen poured in on the level of a man on horseback. Almost at once Gregg was hurled from his horse by a ball that went "right through the small of the back" and into his spine, causing a wound both serious and extremely painful.[58]

56. Hunter H. McGuire, *Stonewall Jackson* (Richmond: R. E. Lee Camp No. 1, C. V., 1897), 19; Caldwell, *History of a Brigade*, 59; Benson, *Berry Benson*, 31–33; Joseph B. Kershaw to illegible correspondent, May 12, 1888, Gregg Papers, SCL/USC.

57. Norton 1886 speech notes, SCL/USC. Norton accumulated certificates from veterans attesting that Gregg fell near the left of Orr's Rifles and that the general's behavior was clearly focused on keeping his men from firing on what he thought to be friends. Confirmation of Gregg's location at the mortal moment is in the diary of John M. Phillips in Georgia Division, UDC, *Confederate Reminiscences and Letters, 1861–1865*, 13 vols. (Atlanta: Georgia Division, UDC, 1990–2000): 7:107.

58. *Charleston Daily Courier*, December 17, 1862; letter of J. A. Wren to mother, December 26, 1862, copy in possession of the author; statement of Lt. W. A. Miles, Orr's Rifles, in Norton Papers, SCL/USC. A survey prepared in the 1890s, well within living memory of veterans, placed the general's wounding site precisely where the exhibit cluster is now situated, discussing the event

The impressive Union assault actually was doomed to failure because of inadequate support. The flanks of the breach held, Gregg's men were supported by many comrades, and together they hurled their enemy back through the boggy wood and beyond into the open plain. As the counterattack swept through the forest, some of the advancing Confederates noticed a badly wounded man who dragged himself painfully up by holding to a little tree and, cap in hand, waved them on after the routed Federals. Thus Maxcy Gregg watched his last charge, cheering painfully from the sidelines rather than riding in front with drawn sword.[59]

The friendly hands of staff members carried Gregg off the field, to the rear, then finally to the Yerby house, "Belvoir," several miles south.[60] There he was placed in a bed in the center of a large room where several surgeons and officers gathered. The general "was in great pain, and seemed very much exhausted." Among the visitors who came in during the evening was James Power Smith of Jackson's staff, who conveyed regards and sympathy from the corps commander. Another welcome visitor from Jackson's staff was the medical director of the corps, Dr. Hunter Holmes McGuire. The doctor reluctantly concurred in the hopeless prognosis of his colleagues.[61]

Shortly after McGuire returned to headquarters, Jackson asked him to go back to see Gregg again. McGuire consented but explained that the South Carolinian was beyond medical help. After arriving at the Yerby house and speaking again with Gregg, the doctor was surprised to meet Jackson in the hall. Gregg had asked for an interview with Jackson himself, so the corps commander had ridden through the night to the dying man's side.[62] Gregg was

---

(copy at FSNMP, filed at the Chancellorsville Visitor Center). A late-life claim (such things are virtually inevitable) that a disgruntled Confederate killed Gregg appeared in the *Anderson (S.C.) Independent*, February 25, 1988. A. P. Hill blamed Gregg's deafness for part of the confusion (Hopkins, ed., "James J. Archer Letters," 139).

59. William C. Oates, *The War Between the Union and the Confederacy* (New York: Neale, 1905), 166.

60. Among his bearers probably was his "faithful servant, William Rose," a slave who had accompanied Gregg to the Indian and Mexican Wars as well as through his Confederate service. A pocket watch inscribed as "the dying gift of Gen. Maxcy Gregg" to Rose is in the McKissick Museum, University of South Carolina, Columbia.

61. *SHSP*, 43:32; James Monroe Anderson to Gregg's sisters, January 9, 1863, Gregg Papers, SCL/USC.

62. The initial appearance of this article in 1973 described Jackson as riding to Gregg's bedside through a night streaked with the Northern Lights. That presumed that the visit (and those of Hill, McGuire, and McIntosh) came on the night of December 13–14—and that the Aurora Borealis display also occurred that night. The best evidence still suggests that the visits occurred that night

suffering intensely and obviously mortally wounded. In this condition he had become concerned about the hard feelings between himself and Jackson not long before. In particular he expressed regret for a harsh endorsement that he had added to some official document. Jackson had either forgotten the incident—an unlikely lapse for the exacting disciplinarian—or he found some acceptable way to gloss over the matter. Far more important to Deacon Jackson was his lieutenant's spiritual health. The pious Jackson, much moved, steered the painful conversation toward heavenly topics: "Let me ask you to dismiss this matter from your mind and turn your thoughts to God and to the world to which you go." The dying brigadier responded tearfully, "I thank you very much."[63]

When Jackson returned to his bivouac from the visit to the Yerby house, he discussed Gregg with a visiting congressman "in emphatic terms of praise, affection and regret."[64]

A. P. Hill also visited his maimed brigadier and found him on a couch in the center of a large room, "unconscious . . . dying . . . beyond all assistance." Gregg's "mind was wandering and his speech inarticulate." General Hill bade his friend and subordinate farewell with a kiss on the forehead. Coping with the continued Federal threat kept R. E. Lee from visiting Gregg's deathbed, but the army commander wrote of how he "deeply lamented" the loss of an officer of such "disinterested patriotism . . . unselfish devotion [and] high integrity and commanding intellect."[65]

Three neighborhood women ministered to the dying general. Gregg stirred at one point, for a lucid moment, and commented, "Twas pleasant to feel the soft touch of woman." When Chaplain James Monroe Anderson of the 12th

---

after the battle (though they may conceivably have been split over both nights), rather than the night during which Gregg died (early on the fifteenth). There is now ample evidence, however, that the Aurora Borealis streaked the horizon on December 14–15. The almost invariably reliable Freeman, *Lee's Lieutenants* (2:373–74 and n.) placed the phenomenon on the earlier night, based on evidence in Jedediah Hotchkiss's contemporary diary. The Hotchkiss note, however, is at the end of a day's entry and evidently should have been dropped a line. Many firsthand witnesses, several of them writing at the time, make it clear that the skies lit up on the evening of the fourteenth.

63. McGuire, *Stonewall Jackson*, 19–20; *SHSP*, 43:34.

64. A. R. Boteler, "A Night with Jackson," *Columbus (Ga.) Enquirer*, August 10, 1881, and *Shepherdstown Register*, August 20, 1881.

65. *Charleston Mercury*, December 30, 1862; *Charleston Daily Courier*, January 9, 1863. Captain David Gregg McIntosh of Gregg's artillery observed Hill's visit and Gregg's condition (McIntosh, "A Ride on Horseback," SHC).

South Carolina knelt to pray by the bed, Gregg motioned him closer and whispered, "Mr. Anderson, I would kneel if I could."[66]

Another scene, as death closed in, served as an index of both the man and the times. Gregg, the South Carolinian even more than the Confederate, dictated a wire to his governor: "If I am to die at this time, I yield my life cheerfully, fighting for the independence of South Carolina." At 5 A.M. on December 15, the bullet finished its work and Maxcy Gregg cashed in the pledge made to his governor. He had been a brigadier general for one year and one day. Five days later marked another anniversary, the second anniversary of a day most dear to Maxcy Gregg. On December 20, 1860, he had signed the longed-for document that declared South Carolina separate from the Union. On December 20, 1862, he was buried with the aid of a sermon that would have warmed his heart: "We meet this day in the house of God to mourn—to mourn for ourselves, and for the State, the mother that has borne us all!"[67]

66. Matilda Hamilton diary, December 14, 1862, typescript in the author's possession, courtesy of the late, great George H. S. King; J. M. Anderson letter to Gregg's sisters, January 9, 1863, Gregg Papers, SCL/USC.

67. *South Carolina Historical and Genealogical Magazine* 6 (October 1905): 180–81; Matilda Hamilton diary, December 15, 1862; *Richmond Dispatch*, December 16, 1862; *Staunton Spectator*, December 23, 1862; Benjamin M. Palmer, *Address Delivered at the Funeral of General Maxcy Gregg in the Presbyterian Church, Columbia, S.C.* (Columbia: Southern Guardian Steam-Power Press, 1863), 3, 11; *Charleston Daily Courier*, December 16, 1862; *Columbia Daily Southern Guardian*, December 22, 1862; *Southern Churchman*, March 13, 1863.

7

The Coward Who Followed J. E. B. Stuart

The Civil War's most famous cavalryman began the war as colonel of the 1st Virginia Cavalry. After J. E. B. Stuart's promotion out of the regiment, Colonel Fitzhugh Lee assumed command. Lee amassed an imposing record and rose to the rank of major general. William E. "Grumble" Jones followed Fitz Lee as colonel commanding the 1st. Jones, an intimate of Thomas J. "Stonewall" Jackson and a very skilled officer despite the personality that amply warranted his nom de guerre, became a general officer and fell at the head of a small army at Piedmont in 1864.[1]

James H. Drake and William A. Morgan served later in the war as colonels of the 1st Virginia Cavalry. Although neither Morgan nor Drake achieved the lasting fame of the regiment's first three commanders, they won the intense affection and respect of the regiment. One trooper said of Morgan, "a braver and better man never drew sword in the defence of any cause." Colonel Drake, a profane man in his fifties who bore a striking resemblance to Lieutenant General Richard S. Ewell, performed in a manner that made him "much beloved by his men." At a public meeting convened after Drake's death, veterans of the 1st Virginia Cavalry called him one of Virginia's "bravest, most gallant

---

1. The cordial relationship between Jones and Jackson is not widely recognized. Perhaps the best source on Jackson at West Point is a very long letter by Jones to R. L. Dabney, September 10, 1863 (copy at WVU). Jackson's emotional letter to Jones of March 24, 1855 (copy at the Stonewall Jackson House, Lexington, Virginia), concerning the death of Elinor Junkin Jackson, is probably the most intensely personal correspondence extant by Jackson to someone outside his family. Considerable war-date correspondence of warm tenor between the two survives as well.

and devoted sons," talked of his "sublime courage," and hymned the "dashing and fearless" performance of "a friend" noted for "courtesy and uniform kindness."[2] No Confederate regiment spawned a pantheon of colonels-turned-generals as prominent as Stuart, Lee, and Jones, and Drake and Morgan carried on the tradition in fine form.

Then there was Colonel Welby Carter.

Richard Welby Carter was born near Rectortown in Fauquier County on March 11, 1837, scion of one of Virginia's most distinguished families. He attended Hollowell's School at Alexandria in preparation for the Virginia Military Institute. The Hollowell's staff evidently succeeded in instilling neither discipline nor academic ardor in their well-bred pupil because he had an extremely difficult time at the Institute.[3]

Young Carter started his college education as a member of the class of 1859 at VMI, finishing his "rat" term ranked next to last among the cadets who survived the year. Mathematics, French, geography, and composition all thwarted Carter thoroughly, leaving him near the bottom of the class in each discipline. Only Declamation suited him: he ranked fourth in that undertaking. Carter's conduct was even worse than his palsied attempts at scholarship. He teetered on the brink of expulsion at the end of his first year with precisely two hundred demerits, one short of automatic dismissal.[4]

Carter's second year progressed worse than his first. Midway through the term the Institute expelled Carter for misbehavior, and he was obliged to have recourse to influential relatives to seek readmission. In January, his kinsman Richard Henry Carter wrote to Superintendent Francis Henney Smith (heading his correspondence "House of Delegates"—whence Smith and the Institute received their funding) announcing that the Carters had been able to persuade the VMI Board of Visitors to reinstate Welby. R. H. Carter enclosed a communication from the chairman of that board but mitigated his political intervention by admitting the "correctness" of the Institute's original action.

---

2. B. J. Haden, *Reminiscences of J. E. B. Stuart's Cavalry* (Charlottesville: Progress Publishing Co., 190–), 19, 26–27; *Richmond Sentinel*, August 17, 1863. For a lengthy article by Morgan, see the *Shepherdstown Register*, December 8, 1871, and for an obituary, the *Baltimore Sun*, February 16, 1899. Drake's photograph, with an excellent story about him, is in the *Winchester Star*, July 7, 1993. Another fine article about Drake appeared in the *Winchester Times*, September 13, 1882.

3. American Historical Society, *History of Virginia . . . Virginia Biography*, 6 vols. (Chicago: American Historical Society, 1924), 6:97.

4. Final standings for 1855–56 year, VMI.

Colonel R. Welby Carter

The political Carter also wrote: "I have talked plainly to Welby and he appears determined to endeavor to give entire satisfaction."[5]

Welby fell very far short of giving entire satisfaction when he returned to Lexington on his political visa. Six months after R. H. Carter's optimistic pronouncement, his young relative faced a court of inquiry into "maltreatment of new cadets." Thomas H. Williamson, later a colonel on Stonewall Jackson's staff during the Confederate war, presided. The other member of the court was Raleigh E. Colston, destined to be a Confederate general officer. Colston and Williamson concluded "that the presumption is very strong that" Cadet Carter was involved in malfeasance. On August 19, 1856, General Orders No. 72 dismissed Carter from VMI to protect "the honor, good faith, and reputa-

5. Richard H. Carter to Col. Francis H. Smith, January 25, 1856, VMI. I have found no indication of the nature of Carter's behavior that resulted in this first expulsion from VMI.

tion of the Institute." The document afforded the privilege of resigning to avoid dismissal. Carter resigned.[6]

Perhaps on the basis of his slender military education, but more likely because of his family's local prominence, the twenty-two-year-old Carter became captain of a volunteer cavalry company organized in 1859. The "Loudoun Light Horse" galloped off to Harpers Ferry when John Brown launched his moral revolution there and remained in the vicinity until the hanging of that northern hero. Captain Carter retained command of the Light Horse and entered Confederate service with the company in April 1861. In keeping with prevailing antebellum notions of chivalry, he declared his civilian occupation to be "Farmer and Horseman."[7]

The Loudoun Light Horse spent a month detached to serve with the famed Shenandoah Valley cavalryman Turner Ashby, then was assigned as Company H of J. E. B. Stuart's 1st Virginia Cavalry. In the famous charge by Stuart's horsemen up the Sudley Road at First Manassas, Carter's company rode in the forefront, losing six men killed—a tremendous toll by cavalry standards for a small unit. Through the succeeding fall and winter, Company H performed duty as a headquarters detachment for Gustavus W. Smith. General Smith mentioned Carter and the company in passing at the end of his long report of the Battle of Seven Pines, as "courier guards at headquarters." Despite his steady ascension in rank on the basis of seniority, that is the only time Carter elicited so much as passing mention in a report or dispatch published in the *Official Records* during the war's first two and one half years.[8]

Welby Carter earned as venomous a set of reviews from his contemporaries as any Confederate officer in the eastern theater—but he also received steady

6. Manuscript General Orders at VMI: No. 60, July 29, 1856; No. 63, August 5, 1856; and No. 72, August 19, 1856. The official register of VMI alumni and matriculates simply ignores Carter's second stint in Lexington, specifying his enrollment as "1 yr." See *Register of Former Cadets, Memorial Edition, Virginia Military Institute* (Lexington: Virginia Military Institute, 1957), 25.

7. Robert J. Driver, Jr., *1st Virginia Cavalry* (Lynchburg: H. E. Howard, Inc., 1991), 159; American Historical Society, *History of Virginia*, 6:97; Eighth Census of the United States, M653, Loudoun County, 564, NA. The family next to the Carters in the census was a big crop of Dulanys. The Carter enumeration shows neither occupation nor worth for Richard W., age twenty-three.

8. Lee A. Wallace, Jr., *A Guide to Virginia Military Organizations, 1861–1865* (Richmond: Virginia Civil War Commission, 1964), 47; Driver, *1st Virginia Cavalry*, 14–16; OR 11(1):993; (all references are to Series I). The utter absence of Carter's name in so many volumes of official reports and correspondence is extremely surprising for an officer of his rank and in a unit so distinguished. There is in OR 51(2):211 a routine note written by Carter to Joseph E. Johnston dated August 3, 1861.

promotions throughout the war. He became major with rank from July 24, 1862; lieutenant colonel sometime in 1862; and colonel upon the death of the 1st's beloved Colonel Drake on July 16, 1863.[9]

As the senior officer present, Lieutenant Colonel Carter commanded the regiment at Chancellorsville and Brandy Station. As full colonel and permanent commander, Carter led the 1st in the Bristoe and Mine Run campaigns. Somehow he gained during this period the fiery enmity of several Confederates, of ranks ranging from sergeant to major general. It is a popular modern pastime to belittle southern primary sources as the work of silly sycophants blindly adhering to "The Myth of the Lost Cause." The casual deconstruction of contemporaries' statements and viewpoints does not reflect well on those who wield such an ax; nevertheless, it is a simple fact that harsh and bitter public criticism of officers was not in keeping with early Victorian habits, either during or after the war, whether North or South. Despite that tendency, a number of Confederates spoke very unkindly about Colonel Carter. A strong body of critical comment from several Civil War observers usually carries more significance than a similar modern outpouring because of the different attitudes prevalent in the mid-nineteenth century.

Sergeant B. J. "Jerry" Haden of Fluvanna County absolutely loathed Carter and declared emphatically that his comrades felt the same way. Carter's service record describes him as a strapping, soldierly man, two inches taller than six feet in height, with hazel eyes, dark complexion, and dark hair. The carefully uniformed officer gazing steadily out of a war-date photograph displays a reasonably martial mien. Haden's take on Carter's appearance, however—no doubt molded by unhappiness with the colonel's demeanor—was nothing short of vicious: "Carter, of whom I shall have but little to say. . . . Notwithstanding [that] he was always fat and looked greasy, I never knew of any member of the regiment to possess enough of cannibalism to ever wish to eat him."[10]

Jerry Haden reported favorably on the three early colonels who became generals, and he heaped unstinting praise on both Carter's predecessor (Drake) and successor (Morgan). The latter, as lieutenant colonel, saved the regiment from doom, Haden thought: "While he had no love for Colonel

---

9. Robert K. Krick, *Lee's Colonels* (Dayton, Ohio: Morningside, 1992), 85; Carter's jacket in "Complied Service Records of Confederate Soldiers Who Served in Organizations from the State of Virginia" (M324, Roll 2), Record Group 109, NA. The chain of promotions to vacant commissions for the 1st Virginia Cavalry during 1862 is unaccountably vague about dates.

10. Carter's CSR, NA; Haden, *Reminiscences*, 27.

Carter, for the sake of the men, [Morgan] would always, upon approaching the enemy, ride up and say 'Follow me boys, I will see you through.'" The inarguable valor of Carter's Loudoun company at First Manassas presumably had included its captain (a family narrative asserts that he came out with bullet holes in his hat and in a sleeve). If Captain Carter was in fact at the forefront of that charge in May 1861, it may have wrought a change in his notions of optimal military deportment. In 1864 the whole army would hear charges in that vein.[11]

The unsupported word of an enlisted man, conceivably disgruntled by some slight or by the friction of military hierarchy, would not suffice to launch much in the way of conclusions—even though Haden represented his opinion as being very widely shared. Officers far removed from Carter's control, however, spoke as harshly as Haden. Captain James Keith Boswell of Stonewall Jackson's staff, an extraordinarily popular and proficient officer, called Carter "white livered" and "a coward and denounc[ed] him about as vigorously as a good and consistent christian . . . could well do." The perspicacious and historically invaluable Jedediah Hotchkiss, also an aide to Jackson, referred to Carter as being known for "cowardice."[12]

Keith Boswell and Welby Carter came together early in 1863 as part of a remarkable, and ultimately tragic, love quadrangle. Boswell was so woefully smitten by a Virginia girl that his friends contrived to find a way to end "his lamentations" over being unable to see her. They persuaded the romantically inclined General J. E. B. Stuart to send the lovelorn staff officer to scout in the vicinity of the home of the object of his obsession. On January 20, 1863, Boswell surveyed the road network around Paris, Virginia, and went that evening to "Glen Welby," a Carter home place in Fauquier County. Boswell's friend and kinsman James Keith was present. So too were a young Methodist preacher ("J.S.") and R. Welby Carter. All of the men but James Keith were suitors of Sophia deButts Carter (R. Welby's cousin), who was present. Boswell and Welby Carter "got into a heated discussion" about, of all things, "the propriety of allowing children to play cards at home." Their intense dislike for each other was evident.[13]

---

11. Haden, *Reminiscences*, 27; American Historical Society, *History of Virginia*, 6:97. The latter source is a biographical compendium almost entirely made up of autobiographical narratives or family accounts of subjects dead by the time of publication.

12. Jedediah Hotchkiss memorandum at Frame 426, Roll 49, Hotchkiss Papers, LC.

13. I have not unearthed the identity of "J. S." James Keith does not supply it in *Addresses on Several Occasions* (Richmond: Appeals Press, 1917) or in his contemporary letters at the Virginia Historical Society. The account of the suicide at "Glen Welby" in this and the next paragraph is

Bad weather the next day kept everyone indoors. The young people gathered in the parlor and Miss Carter sang songs requested by her admirers, who sang along if in favor and boycotted the music if it had been selected by a competitor. Her demeanor made it apparent that the preacher had fallen out of contention. The shunned admirer seemed "calm but somewhat dejected" and soon went upstairs. At 7:30 in the evening, as Boswell was pressing his suit earnestly, the party was stunned by a loud report from the upper story followed by a heavy thud on the floor. The rejected suitor had killed himself with a pistol ball to the brain—using Boswell's pistol that he had picked up while passing through the hall. Boswell concealed a suicide note that would have dismayed Miss Carter. Before he left Glen Welby, Boswell expressed himself directly and unmistakably to Sophia: "Can you learn to love me?" "It can never be." "Great God, then farewell forever!" Captain Boswell had three months to live. During that short span he won the distinction of promotion to chief engineer on Stonewall Jackson's staff, then fell dead in the same volley that mortally wounded his general. The captain's final weeks of life surely were much affected by the deadly January events at Glen Welby; in fact, he returned to Jackson's headquarters "in a mentally distracted condition . . . almost like a lunatic." Boswell spoke most bitterly of the behavior of Colonel Carter, who returned to the 1st Virginia Cavalry, but there is no record of complaints about the adored Sophia, other than the suggestion that she must have been rank-conscious in choosing against a mere staff captain.[14]

Welby Carter evidently fought with the 1st Cavalry as executive officer at Chancellorsville and Gettysburg, including the regiment's major role in the cavalry battles in northern Virginia en route to Pennsylvania. Whatever Car-

---

from Boswell's diary in Thomas K. Skinker, *Samuel Skinker and His Descendants* ([St. Louis]: Published by the Author, 1923), 260–65, and collateral references throughout the Hotchkiss Papers, LC. A Hotchkiss memorandum (Roll 34, 198–99) describes the conspiracy with Stuart to send Boswell to Fauquier County as a sort of "flank movement on 'Old Jack.'" The preacher's Methodist affiliation is from a description of the episode in the G. Campbell Brown memoir, Brown-Ewell Papers, Tennessee State Library and Archives, Nashville. Much of Brown's version is at odds with Boswell's own account. For instance, Brown omitted Carter's role and concluded that at the time of his death, Boswell was "betrothed" to Miss Carter.

14. Skinker, *Samuel Skinker*, 265; Marcus J. Wright, *List of Staff Officers of the Confederate States Army* (Washington, D.C.: GPO, 1891), 17; Hotchkiss memorandum, Hotchkiss Papers, LC; Brown memoir, Brown-Ewell Papers. In his diary entry for January 30, Boswell admitted that R. W. Carter "treated me with more kindness than usual" when the two met back in the Confederate camps that day. Boswell was delivering a letter to Carter, apparently from Sophia, which must have been an odious chore under the circumstances.

ter's participation, he did not earn so much as passing mention in any report or dispatch in the *Official Records*. Upon the death of the regiment's beloved Colonel Drake in mid-July 1863, Carter automatically inherited the colonelcy by seniority and acceded to regimental command. The report of another colonel concerning a cavalry fight near Raccoon Ford on October 11 included cursory mention of Carter, literally in parentheses. The *Official Records* again do not mention the colonel in connection with the intense cavalry actions during the Bristoe and Mine Run campaigns that fall.[15]

In December 1863, Welby Carter made an appearance in the official records of the Union—not the Confederate—army. On the seventeenth the 1st Virginia Cavalry was following General Fitzhugh Lee south from Staunton, through dreadful winter weather ("sleeting very fast"), toward Lexington. Despite the sleet, the men exhibited "fine spirits," cheering "vociferously" at the ladies along the route. Colonel Carter, meanwhile, spent the day a hundred miles from his regiment, presumably on leave of some sort. A Federal patrol took Carter prisoner at Upperville, near his home (and near Sophia Carter), and sent him on a tour of northern prison camps. For nearly eight months the colonel remained a prisoner of war, first at Camp Chase, Ohio, then at Fort Delaware in the middle of the eponymous river, and eventually at Hilton Head, South Carolina. Finally on August 4, 1864, Carter returned to Confederate lines by exchange.[16]

Welby Carter's Confederate tenure had only two months to run when he returned from captivity. No doubt some time passed between the August 4 exchange and Carter's actual return to the head of the 1st Virginia Cavalry, but he had assumed the regimental command by September 21, when the regiment fought ably near Front Royal. Captain Charles F. Jordan described Carter's role as ineffectual, if not downright pusillanimous, in this engagement. Jordan "deliberately disobeyed" Carter's orders, the captain wrote, "knowing that if I obeyed it would be . . . ruinous to my command." Later, "Colonel Carter moved off to the rear without assisting us in the charge."[17]

15. *OR* 29(1):471.

16. Driver, *1st Virginia Cavalry*, 75–76; Carter's CSR, NA; Mary Dulany diary, December 17–18, 1863, in *The Dulanys of Welbourne* (Berryville, Va.: Rockbridge Publishing Company, 1995), 119–20. For an account of the return to the family of a spur taken from Carter when he was captured, see American Historical Society, *History of Virginia*, 6:98. This family sketch of Carter simply extends his captivity from December 1863 to the end of the war, thereby avoiding the whole unhappy story of Tom's Brook and 1864–65.

17. Charles F. Jordan to Thomas T. Munford, October 11, 1872, Munford-Ellis Family Papers, PLD.

General Jubal A. Early

On October 9, 1864, Carter's military career foundered dismally and for the last time. At the Battle of Tom's Brook the Confederate cavalry suffered its worst defeat of the war in Virginia, and Colonel Carter attracted a substantial share of the blame. Perhaps expecting the colonel of the 1st Virginia Cavalry to be a reincarnation of Stuart, Lee, Jones, and Drake would be unreasonable: but incontinent flight from the battlefield really fell short of any acceptable standard.

Southern fortunes in the Shenandoah Valley were distinctly on the wane by October 1864. Union general Philip H. Sheridan outnumbered Confederate general Jubal A. Early by a staggering margin, especially in mounted men. Sheridan often could field as many cavalry as Early mustered in all arms combined. Furthermore, much of the Confederate cavalry was poorly organized, ill-armed, uncertainly led, and utterly devoid of discipline. The 1st Virginia, however, belonged to a fine brigade on loan to the Valley from the Army of Northern Virginia and had every reason to expect a continuation of the success it had known so often before. General Thomas L. Rosser had come to the Valley to straighten out the cavalry problems in that sector, but the task proved to be beyond his powers to effect. When Sheridan turned loose his army on October 6 to burn and savage the Shenandoah Valley—an ugly interval still known as "The Burning" in that region—an enraged Rosser chased the arsonists far beyond the reach of protection from southern infantry. Sheridan stopped his retreat, turned about, and easily overwhelmed the sparse Confederate force. Rosser's foolish movement too far north triggered the defeat, but the day turned into a disaster when the Virginia cavalrymen succumbed to their fears and allowed their retirement to dissolve into incontinent flight.[18]

The Confederate cavalry available on October 9 could not have won the Battle of Tom's Brook, but the utter rout of the gray-clad horsemen did them no credit. They had never before been so panic-stricken, nor would they ever be again. On the evening before Appomattox many of these same men would be firing and falling back, calmly and methodically doing their best in the face of even more overwhelming odds. What went wrong at Tom's Brook? An infectious panic took hold of enough men that even the proudest and most seasoned veteran eventually had to turn his horse's head south and scamper for safety. The officers whose duty it was to forestall such results came under review, and R. Welby Carter's behavior could not stand the scrutiny.

Jerry Haden found no reason to change his harshly negative opinions about Carter based on events at Tom's Brook—in fact, a good bit of the sergeant's attitude may well have been based on that battle. "Our beloved Colonel Carter," Haden wrote sarcastically, "run twenty five miles, never stopping until he got inside our infantry line at New Market." In his contemporary journal, Major James DuGué Ferguson, a seasoned member of Fitzhugh Lee's staff, assigned blame to Rosser's rashness but placed the tactical onus on Welby Carter and noted that the colonel was relieved of command on the spot. Ferguson spent most of October 15 writing up formal charges and specifications against Carter.[19]

18. No definitive history of the Battle of Tom's Brook exists. A study of Sheridan's rampage against civilians, full of local oral tradition as well as more traditional sources, is John L. Heatwole, *The Burning* (Charlottesville, Va.: Rockbridge Publishing Co., 1998).

19. Haden, *Reminiscences*, 41; J. D. Ferguson, "Memoranda of the itinerary and operations of Major General Fitz. Lee's Cavalry . . . May 4th to October 15th 1864 . . . ," Roll 49, Frame 387 et seq., entries for October 9 and 15, Hotchkiss Papers, LC. For the possibility of an earlier court-martial of Carter, which cannot be traced in fragmentary Confederate records, see *Dulanys of Welbourne*, 87.

General Rosser bluntly ascribed responsibility for the rout at Tom's Brook to Carter, "the misbehaving colonel," and to General Jubal A. Early, neither of whom deserved all of the blame. The assault on Early was nothing but a characteristic Rosser quest for a scapegoat to cover his own deficiencies. Early was more than equal to the task of fending off Rosser's animadversions, in one sally calling the cavalryman "a most consummate ass," comparing him to Judas Iscariot, and suggesting that like Judas, "the most creditable act" left for Rosser would be to "go and hang himself." Carter made a far better target for Rosser's charges. The uncontested abandonment of a key stone wall by the 1st Virginia Cavalry unraveled the whole line, Rosser asserted. Since the regiment was "one of the best in the service," it might have stemmed the Federal tide and changed the complexion of the day. Carter's offense, Rosser wrote, was "disobedience of orders and . . . leaving the field and his regiment during the battle and remaining absent from his command for twenty-four hours."[20]

Word spread in the army that General Early, for once agreeing with Rosser, had declared that Welby Carter ought to be shot for desertion in the face of the enemy. Within a few days a court-martial convened to try Carter for cowardice. Although the Carter wealth and connections came into play as they had done to mend bridges at VMI and the colonel was "ably defended," the court promptly found him guilty and "cashiered" him from the service. The court sustained charges of "Misbehavior in the face of the Enemy" and "Neglect of duty." An appeal to President Jefferson Davis to intervene and reinstate Carter went unheeded. After the war, while embroiled in a savage quarrel with Rosser, Early professed to wonder whether Rosser had not used Colonel Carter as a scapegoat; in 1864, he had had no doubts at all.[21]

The Carter family did not give up on finding relief for their son's trouble,

20. Unidentified Baltimore newspaper, Roll 58, Frame 438, Hotchkiss Papers, LC; Thomas L. Rosser, *Riding with Rosser*, ed. S. Roger Keller (Shippensburg, Pa.: Burd Street Press, 1997), 48–49; "Battle at Tom's Brook," *Philadelphia Weekly Times*, March 22, 1884.

21. Driver, *1st Virginia Cavalry*, 103; Rosser, *Riding with Rosser*, 49; Early in *Philadelphia Weekly Times*, June 14, 1884. Because official copies of Confederate courts-martial do not survive, the handful of transcripts extant are from private papers of involved individuals. None is known to exist for this court. Sketchy outlines of the results of courts usually appeared in the general orders of the Army of Northern Virginia, but general orders for the Valley District are fragmentary. Valley District General Orders No. 57, November 21, 1864, survives only in a manuscript copy in the Jubal A. Early Papers, Huntington Library, San Marino, Calif. The court found Carter not guilty of the second charge, "Disobedience of orders." An untitled ledger book at NA includes an entry dated November 24, 1864, that says "Cashiered" and notes that the president had declined to intervene.

attacking Rosser as an "unprincipled villain." On March 22, 1865, with the Confederacy's life span down to a matter of hours, Virginia governor William "Extra Billy" Smith wrote to Jefferson Davis beseeching the president to over-turn the ruling against Welby Carter. Smith knew the family well, he said, and could attest that it was inconceivable for a Carter to be a coward. In any case, the family's name must be protected against stain. Smith claimed to know that the whole problem was based on Rosser's personal hatred for Carter.[22]

Meanwhile, Welby Carter had fallen into Federal hands again. On the eve of George Washington's birthday, a detachment of the 8th Illinois Cavalry descended on the countryside around Middleburg, where Carter was living at home as a cashiered colonel and private citizen. Lieutenant William C. Ha-zelton of Company D led the party that climbed the front steps of the Carter house. While the Yankees hammered at the front door, a sergeant galloped around back and found "a large portly man in his drawers and stocking feet" hiding "behind an old chimney." A black youngster identified the captive as his father, Colonel Carter. The erstwhile Confederate colonel soon found himself inside the familiar walls of Fort Delaware once again.[23]

Two months after Lee surrendered at Appomattox, Welby Carter remained a prisoner in the North. His father launched a letter to United States authority that offered the pathetic plea that his boy had not been a Confederate at all when captured and ought never to have been taken prisoner in the first place. The elder Carter adduced evidence that Welby had been cashiered by the Confederate army and therefore was not a colonel or even a private soldier— only a simple civilian, and extremely anxious to take the oath of allegiance. The humiliating plea did no good: the Federals did not release Carter until July 19, 1865, after most other Confederate prisoners of more orthodox back-ground and performance had gone home.[24]

The remaining two decades of Welby Carter's life unfolded more smoothly

22. *Dulanys of Welbourne*, 248, 260, 268; Governor Smith to Jefferson Davis, March 22, 1865, in Carter's CSR, NA.

23. William C. Hazelton to "My dear Mother," February 23, 1865, in "Life and Letters of William C. Hazelton, 1856 to 1865," typescript copy in the author's possession; Carter's CSR, NA; *OR* 46(2):627; *Dulanys of Welbourne*, 272–73; Abner Hard, *History of the Eighth Cavalry Regiment, Illinois Volunteers* (Aurora, Ill.: n.p., 1868), 318, 333, 335. Hazelton was promoted twice within a few weeks after Carter's capture, but the two things likely had nothing to do with each other.

24. John Armistead Carter letter of June 9, 1865, in "Unfiled Papers and Slips Belonging to Confederate Compiled Service Records," M347, Roll 64, NA.

than his early years. Away from the demands of VMI and out of the unforgiving spotlight focused on a military commander, Carter lived a comfortable existence. Sophia had broken their engagement "because he had been drunk," but she relented. Carter married Cousin Sophia on July 13, 1867, and had three daughters by her; the daughters produced fourteen grandchildren. The couple lived at "Crednal" in Loudoun County, where the colonel raised prize-winning horses and cattle and attended the Methodist church. He died December 18, 1888, at the age of fifty-three. Sophia outlived the colonel by more than a third of a century. In 1915 the United Daughters of the Confederacy named a chapter in honor of Colonel Carter.[25]

It is remotely conceivable that Captain Boswell, Sergeant Haden, Colonel Morgan, General Rosser, Lieutenant Hazelton, Captain Jordan, Jedediah Hotchkiss, Major Ferguson, the VMI faculty, and General Early all erred somehow in their reports on Colonel Carter—and that Governor Smith's blanket amnesty extended to all things Carter in fact was apt. Nothing, however, can refurbish Carter's record to such a degree that he can fill a niche adjacent to the other commanders of the 1st Virginia Cavalry. J. E. B. Stuart, Fitzhugh Lee, William E. Jones, James H. Drake, and William A. Morgan are a distinguished and famous fraternity. R. Welby Carter affords a fascinating comparison.

---

25. *Dulanys of Welbourne*, 240–41; Horace E. Hayden, *Virginia Genealogies* (Washington, D.C.: A. L. Sauls Planograph Co., 1931), 648–59; American Historical Society, *History of Virginia*, 6:98. Hayden misdated the marriage to 1865 or 1866. The family sketch reports Carter's death on December 18, but an obituary in the *Loudoun Mirror*, December 27, 1888, quoting an undated *Alexandria Gazette*, says that he died "early Friday morning" (the nearest Friday being December 21). Given the circuitous nature of the newspaper report and the tendency to confuse death dates and funeral dates, the December 18 report may be more credible.

8

"The Cause of All My Disasters": Jubal A. Early and the Undisciplined Valley Cavalry

Two and one-half millennia before the opening of the Shenandoah Valley campaign of 1864, Assyrian military men achieved temporary superiority over their neighbors when they perfected mounted tactics and inaugurated the cavalry arm. When Philip H. Sheridan's horsemen swarmed over Jubal A. Early's at Winchester and Cedar Creek in the fall of 1864, they were marking the end of a long era of mounted combat. Cavalry reached the apex of its importance and usefulness in American military history during the Civil War. Decades of mounted adventuring remained in the future of the western plains, but large-scale clashes on horseback faded from the American experience when the Confederacy died.

The importance of cavalry during the Civil War left many Confederate leaders fuming over what they perceived to be the ineptitude of the horsemen available to them. Cavalry baiting became virtually endemic throughout the southern armed forces. The unchallenged leaders in those verbal assaults were Early and D. H. Hill. It was apparently Hill who coined the satirical jibe that swept the armies: "Who ever saw a dead cavalryman?" Hill unleashed a particularly savage sally when he assumed a new command early in 1863. In a published proclamation, he declared that cavalry pickets "who permit themselves to be surprised, deserve to die, and the Commanding General will spare no

This chapter first appeared in Gary W. Gallagher, ed., *Struggle for the Shenandoah* (Kent, Ohio: Kent State University Press, 1991), 77–106, entirely without notes. It appears here, with notes added and otherwise extensively revised, by permission of Kent State University Press.

efforts to secure them their deserts." Mounted troops bringing in "sensational reports," Hill blustered, would be "court-martialed for cowardice."[1]

Jubal Early took command of Confederate affairs in Virginia's important granary, the Shenandoah Valley, in the summer of 1864 under the conviction that the cavalry he inherited in that district resembled those of D. H. Hill's caricature. From the start, Early had been scornful of inept cavalry. During the war's first year he had written darkly, "I have been bothered I think enough with inefficient cavalry companies." The topography of the Valley and the brutal numerical odds that Early faced during the next several months would focus even more attention than usual on his cavalry arm. A young Vermont soldier among the invaders of the Valley summarized the effect of geography on operations there in three droll sentences addressed to his home folks: "The Shenandoah Valley is a queer place, and it will not submit to the ordinary rules of military tactics. Operations are carried on here that Caesar or Napoleon never dreamed of. Either army can surround the other, and I believe they both can do it at the same time." Across and around that complex terrain Early's army moved 1,670 miles during four and one-half months and fought seventy-five engagements, according to the calculations of the careful staff diarist Jedediah Hotchkiss.[2]

By any gauge, Early was a curmudgeon. He hesitated not at all in allotting blame to subordinates at all levels. One of his young brigadiers boasted in a contemporary letter of an unaccustomed compliment from the army commander and noted that it was particularly noteworthy coming from "one of the most cross grained & faultfinding Gens. in the C.S. Army." Boundless nervous energy drove "Old Jubilee" to incessant prowling, both physically and spiritually. A young man who saw him in 1864 described the general as an "active nervous man, with a curious mixture of force of character and apparent volatilness. His most striking characteristic was unceasing restlessness." Early defended his renowned profanity as a salutary and cathartic trait. "If Gen.

1. The Hill manifesto appeared as a two-sided broadsheet from "Head Quarters, Goldsboro' N.C., February 25th, 1863." It bears no labeling as either General Orders or Special Orders. For readers familiar with Confederate-imprint nomenclature, this item is Parrish number 1186. The Parrish listing locates only a single copy recorded in any American library.

2. Early letter, September 19, 1861, in Early's CSR, M331, NA; Wilbur Fisk letters published in a Montpelier newspaper, from Laura V. Hale, *Four Valiant Years in the Lower Shenandoah Valley, 1861–1865* (Strasburg, Va.: Shenandoah Publishing House, 1968), 404–5; Jedediah Hotchkiss, *Make Me a Map of the Valley: The Civil War Journal of Stonewall Jackson's Topographer*, ed. Archie P. McDonald (Dallas: Southern Methodist University Press, 1973), 244.

[Robert E.] Lee had only taken it out now and then, as I do, in a good swear," someone claimed to have heard Early say years after the war, "he would be alive at this day!"[3]

In that crusty vein, three days after the largest battle of the campaign "Old Jube" ground out a lengthy broadside to his men in scathing indictment of their behavior. "I had hoped to have congratulated you," he began, "[but instead] I have the mortification of announcing to you, that, by your . . . misconduct, all the benefits of that victory were lost and a serious disaster incurred." In what must have been a wretchedly unsuccessful effort to stimulate the troops, Early compared them unfavorably to the "proudly defiant" men under Robert E. Lee in the Petersburg trenches. The only hope for the Valley men to "again claim them [the main army's soldiery] as comrades," Early announced, was "to erase from your escutcheons the blemishes which now obscure them."[4]

Early, however, displayed considerable skill under dreadful conditions in the 1864 Valley campaign. His loyalty and devotion to the cause and his eagerness to fulfill Lee's injunctions reveal a man doing his level best with what was at hand. The Buttermilk Rangers, as Early called his Valley cavalry—implying a fondness for foraging and domestic scenes far from the cannon's roar—clearly performed at inadequate levels on many occasions. When the general told Lee that the weakness and inefficiency of his cavalry "has been the cause of all my disasters," was he offering a valid judgment? Just how bad was the Valley cavalry in 1864?[5]

A first casual, almost reflexive, impression of cavalry operations might suggest the notion that discipline among Civil War cavalry units was not quite as important as among their counterparts in infantry and artillery service. Cavalry's role customarily involved smaller groups, in widely separate locations, requiring less of the shoulder-to-shoulder training and regimen so necessary to tactical evolutions of the other arms. In fact, of course, precisely that dispersal and lack of large-scale, visually controllable action made discipline absolutely

3. Zebulon York to B. R. Wellford, July 18, 1864, White-Wellford-Taliaferro-Marshall Papers, SHC; Thomas Hughes, *A Boy's Experiences in the Civil War* (Washington, D.C.: privately printed, 1904), 17; Henry M. Field, *Blood Is Thicker Than Water: A Few Days Among Our Southern Brethren* (New York: George Munro, 1886), 96.

4. Tall broadside signed in type "J. A. Early, Lt. Gen'l.," dated "Head Quarters Valley District, October 22d, 1864," and address to "Soldiers of the Army of the Valley." The broadside bears the Parrish Confederate-imprint number 1597.

5. *OR* 43(1):555, 558 (this and all references are to Series I).

essential to the successful functioning of cavalry. The disciplinary needs of cavalry units became magnified later in the war as cavalrymen more and more often fought dismounted as "Mounted Infantry," an outgrowth of one of the war's evolutionary tactical developments. A North Carolinian who admired Early admitted that the general's strengths did not include the imposition of discipline and that discipline was absolutely essential. "Genl Early is no disciplinarian," the Tar Heel wrote home with dismay twice within a few weeks during October 1864.[6]

The fabulously inefficient Confederate remount system contributed considerably to Early's cavalry woes. Southern cavalrymen supplied their own animals. If a horse died in service, the Confederate government paid the creature's appraised worth in badly inflated currency, but the dismounted trooper faced the chore of finding a new ride on his own. As the war progressed, that task passed beyond difficulty to the level of near impossibility. The appraisal system documents an average 1861 value for cavalry mounts of $150. Two years later, with the war only half over, it cost twice that much merely to board a horse in Richmond for one month.[7]

As the demands of an all-encompassing war made horseflesh valuable beyond measure, cavalrymen quickly learned that risking their private stock in battle made no sense. Personal courage aside, the nagging voice of common sense suggested that combat élan risked the horse and threatened to end the soldier's cavalry career. The same situation encouraged and stimulated emphasis on capturing horses and carrying them away from danger. That aspect of Confederate cavalry affairs figured prominently in the closing phases of the first Battle of Winchester on May 25, 1862. Two years later, operations in the Valley suffered dramatically from the same problem.[8]

Most of the cavalrymen with Early's army in the Valley in 1864 suffered also from the fact that their homes were situated behind enemy lines. Many of them came from counties that belonged to the recently proclaimed Union-

6. Samuel P. Collier to parents, October 22, 1864, and to "My Darling" (Sue), October 1864 (day illegible), Collier Papers, NCDAH. The second letter uses identical language but substitutes the pronoun "he" for Early's name.

7. In examining nearly two thousand Confederate CSRs (M324, NA) while preparing the roster for Robert K. Krick, *9th Virginia Cavalry* (Lynchburg: H. E. Howard, 1982), I saw massive evidence that the vast majority of horse appraisals in 1861 came in at exactly $150. For the dear cost of boarding horses by 1863, see Mary Elizabeth Massey, *Ersatz in the Confederacy* (Columbia: University of South Carolina Press, 1952), 71.

8. For a good summary of the remount problem, see Thomas T. Munford, "Reminiscences of Cavalry Operations," *SHSP*, 12:346–48.

ist state of West Virginia. Others lived in areas of the Valley itself and in southwestern Virginia where Federal columns were running amok, armed not only with muskets and commissary requisition forms but also with flaming torches. The effect of such circumstances on mounted men with the means to ride home can readily be imagined. Few other American fighting men in the nation's long history have faced the ordeal of standing to fight in a distant place while their home folks had to cope with destruction and want at the hands of a hostile, pillaging, invading force. Cavalry units from other parts of Virginia and the South that were considered to be more stalwart included relatively few men whose homes lay at the mercy of an enemy; and infantry from the subjugated counties had far less mobility to employ in heading for home. The mobility of mounted men lent wings to intentions probably shared by many envious soldiers of the other arms.

Cavalry morale cannot have been helped by the scorn in which the mounted men were held by their comrades of the other branches. "The Confederate foot soldier was not noted for his admiration or his respect for his compatriot who bestrode a horse," a North Carolinian wrote. "Early's footsoldiers' love for a cavalryman was even below the Confederate average." A member of the 21st Virginia Infantry called his mounted comrades "utterly worthless." Another infantryman expressed the hope that the Yankees would capture all of the southern cavalry. "They will never fight," he reasoned—perhaps hungrily—"so I think it useless to have them in the army eating rations from the government." A staff officer relished exactly that result when it happened. The Yankees "did little damage and much good," he wrote, "by taking the worthless horses of a still more worthless cavalry company."[9]

An independent inspector who plied his trade among the Valley cavalry just a few days before active campaigning began in the spring of 1864 came back from his travels distinctly discouraged: in one small brigade, three regimental commanders were under arrest; "drills very rare"; "officers and men seem unfamiliar with tactics"; absence without leave approached epidemic levels; "guns were all rusty"; many men without shoes; and most men armed only with rifles, not carbines or pistols. In summary of the condition of John C. Vaughn's command, the discouraged inspector concluded that "it should be dis-

9. Walter Clark, ed., *Histories of the Several Regiments and Battalions from North Carolina in the Great War*, 5 vols. (Goldsboro, N.C.: Nash Brothers, 1901), 2:257; John A. Craig letter, October 15, 1864, VHS; Samuel P. Collier letter, undated fragment, Collier Papers, NCDAH; diary of Oscar Hinrichs, engineer officer, typescript copy in possession of the author.

mounted, and he be sent to some disciplinarian or left out of assignment."[10] The dire assessment of Vaughn and his troops would prove to be entirely accurate in the months to come.

The officers who attempted to lead the Valley cavalry almost invariably recognized the existence of serious shortcomings in both men and units. The more sympathetic observers offered explanations and qualifiers, but even they virtually never pretended to deny the problems. Colonel Thomas T. Munford, who came from the "regular" cavalry service east of the mountains, explained that the Valley mounted units "were armed with miserable guns for the service exacted of them, and . . . never had a fair show . . . [and] could not do impossibilities." General John McCausland described his horsemen as "badly armed, badly mounted, and worse equipped—in fact, they were mostly mounted militia. The men would have made good soldiers if there had been time to discipline them, and arms and equipments to furnish them."[11]

McCausland was among those charged with instilling that requisite discipline. A story told about the general illustrates the independence traditional with civilian soldiers and especially pronounced in the Valley ranks. A private ordered to report to McCausland with an ax for fatigue duty in camp examined the task that his superior pointed out to him with some care. "Can *one man* do it?" inquired the reluctant lumberjack. McCausland assured him that one man could. "Well, then," said the detail, shouldering his ax, "I'll go back to camp," leaving McCausland bemused in his wake.[12]

General Basil W. Duke of Kentucky, who had some experience with cavalry operations in Virginia's secondary theaters, wrote a long and thoughtful description of the late-war plight of the irregular cavalryman:

> Almost destitute of hope that the cause for which he fought would triumph and fighting on from instinctive obstinate pride . . . is it surprising that he became wild and lawless, that he adopted a rude creed in which strict conformity to military regulations and a nice obedience to general orders held a not very prominent place? This condition obtained in a far greater degree with the cavalry employed in the "outpost" departments than with the infantry or the soldiery of the large armies. Many Confederate cavalry men so situated left their commands altogether and became guerrillas, salving their consciences with the thought that the desertion was not to the enemy.[13]

10. *OR* 32(3):842–44.
11. Munford, "Reminiscences," *SHSP*, 13:140; John McCausland, "The Burning of Chambersburg, Penn.," *SHSP*, 31:268.
12. *The Land We Love* 3 (May 1867): 81.
13. Basil W. Duke, *Morgan's Cavalry* (New York: Neale, 1906), 394.

Duke's apologia is notable not only for its sympathetic perspective but also for its calm acceptance of the basic fact that irregular cavalry suffered from shortcomings so pervasive as to be routine.

Marylander Bradley T. Johnson expressed mixed admiration and dismay over the Valley cavalry he commanded in 1864. He described his brigade as "about eight hundred half-armed and badly disciplined mountaineers from southwest Virginia, who would fight like veterans when they pleased, but had no idea of permitting their own sweet wills to be controlled by any orders, no matter from whom emanating." Johnson used three adjectives to describe his men that nicely define the situation: they were, he declared, "brave . . . fearless . . . [and] undisciplined." General W. H. F. Payne saw more thorns than roses in the mixture. Of his own command, Payne wrote, "The discipline of the Brigade is not near so good as it ought to be." He suggested—in vain, of course—that cumbersome court-martial procedures be streamlined so as to make discipline rapid and visible. Another Confederate officer wrote in similar spirit soon after the campaign that "want of discipline had greatly demoralized the men."[14]

When the Valley cavalry moved into northern North Carolina during one winter in search of forage for both man and beast, their demeanor quickly prompted outraged cries for relief from local civilians. In response to one cavalry officer's halfhearted attempts to deny the reports, Governor Zebulon B. Vance wrote to the secretary of war: "The concurrent testimony of the citizens of about twenty counties with at least fifty letters to that effect in my office would seem to be sufficient to establish a fact of general notoriety." During October 1864, at the height of Early's campaign in the Valley, Secretary of War James A. Seddon complained bitterly about the "most predatory and discreditable manner" in which supposedly friendly cavalry had "plundered and ravaged without discrimination or hindrance, often inflicting most serious losses on the families of men in the Confederate Army or now in Yankee prisons." To Seddon's understandable horror, "even women are said to have been plundered." The secretary's plaintive conclusion echoed the forlorn hope of everyone connected with the problem: "Some decisive means seems necessary to restrain the license of our irregular cavalry, and bring them into subordina-

14. Bradley T. Johnson, "My Ride Around Baltimore in Eighteen Hundred and Sixty-Four," *SHSP*, 30:217; J. L. Scott, *36th and 37th Battalions Virginia Cavalry* (Lynchburg: H. E. Howard, 1986), 23; letter of unidentified Confederate officer in William Swinton, *Campaigns of the Army of the Potomac* (New York: Charles B. Richardson, 1866), 558n.

tion and efficiency." No one ever managed to discover any such decisive means.[15]

Drinking contributed to the disarray in the Valley cavalry. An officer who led some of Early's mounted men to the outskirts of Washington in July 1864 responded to a question about why the command halted before penetrating into the streets of the Federal capital city: "He said that he was afraid if he carried his men into the town that he would never get them out. . . . They would have filled up the barrooms and saloons and that would have been the end of them." A member of the 14th Virginia Cavalry wrote late in 1864 in his diary: "It was a drunken spree. There has been a real Regimental drunk today." Not long thereafter he added: "There are few who don't indulge. I am sorry to see it." A Kentuckian new to the Valley saw Rosser's "celebrated Brigade" for the first time in late October and found "most of them drunk. . . . Good looking, well dressing boys, on good horses, but with too much liquor."[16]

General John D. Imboden reported on the incredible lengths to which one incurable drunkard went to feed his habit. When the sot returned drunk from a detail that had been slaughtering beef, Imboden personally locked him in a stout log smokehouse. After three ostensibly dry days the fellow remained intoxicated. Imboden had him searched to the skin and found that during the cattle detail "he had taken a piece of the entrails, cleaned it, filled it full of whiskey and wrapped it around his waist, using it like a hose."[17]

Allegations of drunkenness extended to Early himself—in fact, much talk in Richmond eventually attributed all of the troubles in the Valley to the general's indulgence in the Demon Rum (a popular bête noir in that era). Early angrily issued a strident demand to the Senate, where some of the talk had been circulating, for a formal hearing. "I utterly deny it," the general snapped. He probably had grounds for disgust. James Power Smith, a Presbyterian divinity student and staff officer handpicked by Stonewall Jackson, wrote at the

15. *OR*, 18:934 and 43(2):900.

16. George Q. Peyton, *A Civil War Record for 1864–1865* (Fredericksburg, Va.: Robert A. Hodge, 1981), 57; John Baxter Moseley diary, VHS; Edward O. Guerrant, *Bluegrass Confederate: The Headquarters Diary of Edward O. Guerrant*, ed. William C. Davis and Meredith L. Swentor (Baton Rouge: Louisiana State University Press, 1999), 565. For repeated references to drinking during this campaign in the relatively tightly administered 1st Virginia Cavalry, see DeWitt Clinton Gallaher, *A Diary Depicting the Experiences of DeWitt Clinton Gallaher . . . While Serving in the Confederate Army* (Charleston, W.Va.: Privately printed, 1945), 17, 19, 22, 28.

17. Oliver Taylor, "The War Story of a Confederate Soldier Boy," *Bristol (Va.-Tenn.) Herald-Courier*, February 27, 1921.

time: "There is less drunkeness in the army now than I have ever known. . . . General Early's orders have quite stopped the sale or importation of liquor." Jimmie Smith's relentless piety, demonstrated over several decades during and after the war, makes him an impeccable witness on such matters, at least as they concerned behavior at headquarters; there unquestionably was plenty of brandy elsewhere in the Valley.[18]

Shortages of supplies of every sort (always excepting brandy) exacerbated problems for the cavalry even more than for the infantry. Keeping a horse in operation required a considerable volume of forage—and as the campaign ground on, even the once fertile Valley could not supply it. Captain Richard E. Wilbourn of Early's staff kept a diary during three months of the 1864 campaign. In the back he copied orders that passed through headquarters. Wilbourn's documents paint a picture of logistical chaos even before the campaign's major battles began: the cavalry operated with "inexcusable carelessness"; "I can't find any one to stop these disorganized troops"; McCausland complained, incredibly, that even "Stragglers . . . are worn out"; "officers and men are entirely demoralized"; "I have no serviceable horses"; supplying guns to men returning from convalescence "is equivalent to throwing the arms away"; and, finally, wearily, "I have not a bushel of corn." Infantrymen began to " 'Caw' like ravens" when horses passed, suggesting that "our poor old horses would only make buzzard bait, and that we should turn them over to the buzzards and not be driving them." The South's granary was becoming a wasteland.[19]

In July, a member of the staff of General John C. Breckinridge added his vote to the worried official chorus when he wrote of Early's "wild cavalry," about "the inefficiency of which there was constant complaint and almost daily exhibition." When word reached Richmond during August of renewed cavalry problems in the Valley, General Braxton Bragg hurried a note to Early in solicitous language that did nothing to challenge Bragg's reputation as a master of equivocation. In endeavoring to rein in and reorganize the wild cav-

18. *Letter from Lieutenant-General J. A. Early, Asking Further Enquiry into the Causes of the Recent Reverses in the Valley of Virginia* [Richmond, 1865]; James Power Smith to sister, November 24, 1864, FSNMP. The Early letter is a four-page pamphlet published by the Confederate Senate by order dated January 9, 1865.

19. Each of the quotes is from a different communication copied by Wilbourn into his journal (typescript copy in the author's possession). They date from between August 8 and September 6, 1864. The buzzard quote is from the memoir of Andrew Nelson Campbell, West Virginia University, Morgantown.

alry, Bragg suggested, Early should do something, but not too much. "It is feared that too radical a change may produce dissatisfaction in those commands raised mostly in the country now held by the enemy and cause many desertions," the Richmond bureaucrat declared. "At the same time it is felt that some stringent measures are necessary to secure discipline and prevent disaster."[20] Early must have snarled when he read that fence-straddling exhortation, but in fact it presented nothing more than a truth already well known to everyone in a position of responsibility in the Valley.

Early's frank and earnest correspondence with R. E. Lee reviewed the options for revising the structure of his cavalry, without any need for Bragg's restatement of the patently obvious. The tactical verities militated against success for his horsemen, Early knew. Their equipment—with rifles, rather than pistols and carbines, and without sabers—left the cavalrymen unable to fight mounted, and they did not like to fight afoot. One Valley cavalry officer described long rifles as "useless things for mounted men. . . . I would rather

General Bradley T. Johnson

command a regiment armed with good oaken clubs." An independent inspector concluded that because of the troops' wretched armament, they "cannot properly be termed *Cavalry*." Federal troopers carried "from *seven* to *twenty two shots* to *each man* whilst our men have *but one long Rifle*, and that very unwieldy on horseback." The rifles provided an advantage if one were dismounted, but most of the Valley clashes involved fighting on horseback. Whether the men were firing mounted or afoot, efforts to use them came up firmly against the fact that "the command is and has been demoralized all the time." An obvious and much mooted solution was to attach the men to infantry commands. Early liked the idea but feared it would not work. "It would be better if they could all be put into the infantry," the Valley commander told Lee, "but, if that were tried, I am afraid they would all run off." Early continued to squirm on the horns of that unforgiving dilemma throughout the 1864 Valley campaign.[21]

20. *OR* 43(1):1008.
21. *OR* 43(1):557–59; Harry Gilmor, *Four Years in the Saddle* (New York: Harper & Brothers,

R. E. Lee's own conclusion blamed the officers, discipline, and training—not the men. "As soon as an opportunity offers I desire to reorganize the Cav in The Valley," Lee told the secretary of war. "The men in my opinion are as good as any in the service. The want of efficient officers & the absence of proper discipline & instruction has been its ruin."[22]

Perhaps the most telling indictment against the undisciplined Valley cavalry came in an official document submitted by General Bradley T. Johnson in August. In reporting on operations early in that month, Johnson chronicled a degree of misbehavior almost beyond fathoming. "Every crime in the catalogue of infamy has been committed," Johnson declared, most of it perpetrated upon southerners and the families of Confederate soldiers.

> Highway robbery of watches and pocket-books was of ordinary occurrence: the taking of breast-pins, finger-rings, and earrings frequently happened. Pillage and sack of private dwellings took place hourly. A soldier of an advance guard robbed of his gold watch the Catholic clergyman of Hancock on his way from church on Sunday . . . in the public streets. Another of a rear guard nearly brained a private of Company B, First Maryland Cavalry, for trying to prevent his sacking a woman's trunk and stealing her clothes and jewels. A lieutenant at Hancock exacted and received $1,000 . . . of a citizen; a soldier packed up a woman's and a child's clothing, which he had stolen in the presence of the highest officials, unrebuked. . . . Ransoms varied from $750 to $150, according to the size of habitation. . . . A lieutenant knocked down and kicked an aged woman who has two sons in the Confederate army, and after choking the sister locked her in a stable and set fire to it. This was because the two women would not give up horses he and his fellow thieves wished to steal.

The general concluded his ghastly report (from which the passage above is only an extract) with a bit of arrantly misplaced optimism when he suggested that some means might be found to inculcate "a higher tone of morals and discipline" in every southern soldier "which will restrain him from disgracing

---

1866), 245; inspection report 9-J-39, dated October 24, 1864, M935, NA. For confirmation that the more regularly managed cavalry from the Army of Northern Virginia employed much better armament, including supplies of pistols and carbines, see Thomas L. Rosser to Edward L. Wells, March 11, 1898, Wells Papers, Charleston Library Society, Charleston, S.C. That premise is substantiated by an inspection report dated January 30, 1865 (item 2-P-52) in M935, NA, which shows an ample armament of pistols and Sharps, Spencer, and Burnside carbines on hand.

22. Lee to Secretary of War, October 31, 1864, in CSR of T. L. Rosser, M331, NA. The entire letter, unlike most from army headquarters, is in Lee's own hand.

himself and his countrymen by such deeds."[23] The inevitable excesses of individuals in war aside, it is impossible to envision any large group of cavalry from the Army of Northern Virginia behaving in like fashion. Jubal Early's horror at the prospect of solving his cavalry needs with such a crew of highwaymen can readily be imagined, and perhaps understood, under the impact of evidence such as that presented by Johnson.

The deficiencies of the cavalry organizations and their constituent members make strikingly clear the importance of solid leadership. The lack of discipline early in the war made the task of later officers all but impossible. Any analysis of Valley cavalry leaders must begin with Turner Ashby, who shone brightly in the war's early days in that region and who remained in death the *beau sabreur* for a whole generation of Valley youth. Viewed in a larger military context, Ashby deserves laurels as perhaps the finest company commander of cavalry in American military history. At levels above that, however—and he rose through four ranks beyond captain—Ashby progressed steadily further out of his depth. The gaggle of mounted youngsters trailing in his wake in early 1862 would and could do anything he asked. Ashby eventually commanded twenty-seven companies unorganized into battalions or regiments, and at least twenty-six of them operated below par at any given time because they were beyond the reach of his personal magnetism. General Richard Taylor deftly summarized Ashby's strength and his great weakness and at the same time identified the role of a discipline that the Valley cavalry never would know. Ashby was, Taylor wrote,

> the most daring and accomplished rider in a region of horsemen. His courage was so brilliant as to elicit applause from friend and foe, but he was without capacity or disposition to enforce discipline on his men. I witnessed his deep chagrin at the conduct of our troopers after the enemy had been driven from Winchester in May. With proper organization and discipline, his bold riders under his lead might have accomplished all that [was possible] . . . for light cavalry. . . . Valor is as necessary now as ever in war, but disciplined, subordinated valor, admitting the courage and energies of all to be welded and directed to a common end.[24]

Ashby was the archetype against which the Valley cavalry measured all of his successors, without knowing that the yardstick was itself out of plumb.

23. *OR* 43(1):7–8.

24. Richard Taylor, *Destruction and Reconstruction* (Edinburgh: William Blackwood and Sons, 1879), 87.

During the early stages of the 1864 Valley campaign, a sterling but largely unheralded cavalry officer held the potential to lead the motley crew of horsemen there in the right direction. Brigadier General William E. Jones carried the nom de guerre "Grumble," which he had earned fairly and well in a succession of clashes that displayed an unlovely temperament. General J. E. B. Stuart and "Grumble" Jones thoroughly loathed each other, but Jones had given indications that he was nearly as skillful in military affairs as he was maladroit in human affairs. Unfortunately, on June 5, 1864, with the campaign almost a month old, Jones fell victim to the criminal indolence of two subordinates at the disastrous Battle of Piedmont. A Federal bullet struck him down after cavalry generals John C. Vaughn and John D. Imboden stolidly watched the enemy advance unhindered across their front at the crisis of the battle. In this fashion one of the brightest hopes for leadership for the Valley cavalry fell dead, having been put to death by that very same inept Valley cavalry as thoroughly as though by guillotine.

Two months and two days after the debacle at Piedmont, Generals John McCausland and Bradley T. Johnson collaborated on a mutual embarrassment at Moorefield that has received far less attention than it deserves. Between them, McCausland and Johnson distributed their troops in a manner so slovenly that they were surprised and routed in what must be adjudged the most thorough fiasco suffered by any Confederate cavalry force in the Virginia theater during the entire war. A Georgian newspaper correspondent described the event as the result of a "monstrous truth"—that the two units had become "utterly worthless" after falling into "the habit of robbing friend and foe."[25]

Into this unsettled picture rode Major General Fitzhugh Lee, a seasoned and successful divisional commander from the more regular cavalry units east of the mountains and a man of solid reputation. Fitz knew he faced a huge task. One of his staff described the Valley horsemen as "a dreadful organization" and "great stampeders." No better man for the job could be imagined. Fitz Lee's uncle General R. E. Lee and Jubal Early both must have expected great things from the young officer. Whether their expectations would have been fulfilled must remain a matter for conjecture because a bullet slammed into Fitz Lee's thigh during his first real action in the Valley, at the Third Battle of Winchester. Its effects put young Lee out of service throughout the

25. "Letter from P. W. A.," *Macon Daily Telegraph*, September 30, 1864. The same correspondent, Peter W. Alexander, used the "utterly worthless" phrase again in an article in the *Mobile Advertiser and Register*, October 4, 1864.

campaign. In ill omen, enemy fire also killed Lee's mare, "Nelly Gray," which had served him well since 1861 under all manner of enemy attention. Years later, Fitz took Jubal Early to task for using the expression "The fighting is beginning, the cavalry is going to the rear"; but he likely was defending the regular cavalry of the Army of Northern Virginia, not those under his command in the Valley so briefly.[26]

Eight general officers who struggled with cavalry command in the 1864 Valley deserve a summary review in order to grasp the scope of Early's resources. W. H. F. Payne attended Virginia Military Institute, practiced law, and was thirty-four years old at the height of the campaign. John C. Vaughn was an uneducated Tennessee merchant, aged forty. Bradley T. Johnson was a thirty-five-year-old Maryland lawyer, educated at Princeton. William L. Jackson, aged thirty-nine and another lawyer, was a second cousin to the infinitely more distinguished Thomas J. Jackson. John D. Imboden, aged forty-one, practiced law after an education at Washington College in Lexington. John McCausland graduated from VMI and taught there before the war; he was only twenty-eight during the 1864 Valley campaign. Lunsford Lindsay Lomax was also twenty-eight and a Virginian, educated at the U.S. Military Academy. Williams C. Wickham was a forty-four-year-old lawyer, educated at the University of Virginia.

A composite drawn from that group would be a lawyer slightly older than thirty-five years, with little or no military experience. Training at Virginia Military Institute helped to prepare Payne and McCausland for their tasks, but only West Point–educated L. L. Lomax actually had antebellum experience as a military officer. Of the eight, only Wickham and Lomax had held responsible commands in "regular" Confederate cavalry service. It probably was more than coincidence that Wickham and Lomax also proved to be the most solid officers, though neither won any notable laurels in the Valley. The other six, to one degree or another, simply were not up to their assigned tasks. Perhaps those tasks were more than could reasonably have been asked of anyone.

Imboden remains more familiar today to students of the war than many others of like rank and service because of the proverbial relative strengths of the pen and the sword. His writings, in the familiar *Battles and Leaders* set

26. Charles Minnigerode to mother, August 31, 1864, typescript copy in the author's possession; Fitz Lee to Early, May 12, 1890 [?—last two digits of the year are uncertain], copy in the files of Gettysburg National Military Park, Gettysburg, Pa.

among other forums, understandably throw favorable light on his accomplishments. In some instances Imboden found an opportunity to elbow his way into the reflected glow of the legendary Stonewall Jackson. During the 1864 operations, however, many superiors and colleagues held Imboden up as the symbol of Valley cavalry incompetence. General John C. Breckinridge telegraphed to Richmond in June: "The cavalry under Imboden doing less than nothing. If a good general officer cannot be sent for them at once they will go to ruin." When the cavalry flank at the Third Battle of Winchester collapsed, a Confederate staff officer identified the fastest of the fleeing men as being from Imboden's command. "When a number of Imboden's Cavalry rushed pell mell through the streets of Winchester, far in advance of all other fugitives from the battle-field," this witness testified, "a large number of the most respectable ladies joined hands & formed a line across the principal street, telling the cowardly Cavalrymen that they should not go any further unless they ran their horses over their bodies."[27]

General John D. Imboden

Bradley T. Johnson, himself outspoken on the lack of discipline, struck others as part of the problem. After the disaster at Moorefield, Jedediah Hotchkiss of Early's staff wrote home to his wife and described Johnson as "culpably negligent" and the affair as "extremely disgraceful." "There is but one opinion about Johnson," Hotchkiss said pointedly, "and the only wish is that he had been captured also. He . . . is a bold & dashing fellow, but has no discipline."[28]

Reports of John C. Vaughn's abysmal misbehavior at Piedmont attained such wide circulation that Jubal Early probably was not surprised to find Vaughn incompetent. Within hours after Early reached Lynchburg, he sent a panicked telegram back to Richmond. "It is of the utmost importance to have another commander than [Vaughn]," wrote the crisis-beset lieutenant general. "Answer at once."[29]

27. *OR* 40(2):658; memoir of William J. Seymour, Louisiana staff officer, University of Michigan Library, Ann Arbor.

28. Jedediah Hotchkiss to wife, August 10, 1864, Hotchkiss Papers, LC.

29. *OR* 51(2):1020.

The field-grade officers of the Valley cavalry doubtless varied as much as would any other cross section of humanity when elected by those intended for command; but there is little evidence that any men of high potential were waiting to fill the widening command breach. One Valley regiment (the 17th Virginia Cavalry) began the war with a colonel described as "a good hearted man but not much for emergencies" and also as "a very cautious man . . . anxious that no one should get hurt and more especially himself." To that same regiment belonged a major who sought to return to command during the 1864 Valley campaign, despite having misappropriated more than a thousand dollars to his own use earlier in the war by filing pay vouchers for nonexistent men and forging approval signatures on the documents. Some of the wildcat cavalry in the theater probably would have admired his imagination and style, but there seems little reason to believe that the embezzler could offer much of use to the faltering Confederate cause.[30]

Before the campaign wore on toward its painful end, Early entertained hopes of making something of the Valley troopers. He endeavored, for instance, to encourage that same 17th Virginia Cavalry and the other regiments in its brigade by applauding their efforts at Monocacy: "He told them that he was proud of their achievement—that he had never seen trained infantry fight any better . . . and he congratulated us on the success we had achieved and the honor we had gained by our gallant work."[31] Three months later, Early had given up on eliciting cavalry élan by use of such encomiums, and in any case they were far less apposite by then.

Some observers suggested the obvious expedient of combining the irresolute units with better-disciplined organizations that had been imported from Lee's army to reinforce Early. General Robert Ransom, who had struggled with the Valley cavalry problem earlier in the year before being transferred, wrote a very long proposal that shuffled units all around the organizational chart. To deal with Vaughn's brigade, Ransom suggested with startling simplicity: "Dismount at once the whole of it." Some of Imboden's units might be combined and then transferred intact into Wickham's regular brigade, "at the same time relieving Brigadier-General Imboden." The stray battalions, operating as permanently frail regiments, should be consolidated into genuine

30. Addison Austin Smith, "A Story of the Life and Trials of a Confederate Soldier . . . ," Jackson County, West Virginia, Historical Society; John Harper Dawson, *Wildcat Cavalry* (Dayton, Ohio: Morningside House, 1982), 15–16.

31. Nathaniel E. Harris, *Autobiography* (Macon: J. W. Burke, 1925), 87.

regimental organizations to be led by "meritorious officers from the cavalry of Northern Virginia." In that manner the men "will be taught to fight; and the indifferent officers gotten rid of." Ransom also suggested that "there should be at least three inspectors at each division headquarters." To a friend in Richmond, however, Ransom confided that the Valley cavalry had reached "such a point of lawlessness & disorganisation" that he knew nothing really would work.[32] Ransom's thoughtful proposals, and others like them, foundered on the twin shoals of bureaucratic indifference and hostility to change among the independent and disdainful units that were their targets.

Thomas Lafayette Rosser went to his grave convinced that he was the "Saviour of the Valley," as some hopeful and incautious journalists styled him during the early fall of 1864. Rosser's advent in the Valley raised hopes that he would indeed be its savior at a time when miracles clearly were needed. He was the last of the fresh hopes for the Valley cavalry, and he arrived just as the final chapter in the 1864 campaign opened.

Tom Rosser was born in Virginia but had resided in Texas since his early youth. Five days after his natal state seceded and two weeks before he was due to graduate, young Rosser resigned from West Point and offered his services

General Thomas L. Rosser

to the Confederacy. By the time of the Battle of Cedar Creek, the general was twenty-eight years old. Despite an enormous cache of Rosser manuscripts at the University of Virginia, no scholarly biography of the energetic but enigmatic man yet exists. The surviving letters reveal an enthusiastic man-child of mercurial bent, writing to a young wife in moods belligerent and pious and various other shades as well. Rosser labored under a deep suspicion of "Jeb" Stuart, whom he thought—without any justification— did not support him in his breathless quest for promotion. The young man's letters to his wife often speak harshly of his superior (Stuart "is now an open enemy of mine") in terms and on subjects that should interest Stuart biographers. They also show Rosser as querulous, complaining, and generally unlovely. Eventually Stuart began to grow weary of Rosser's liberties.

32. *OR* 43(1):1004; Mrs. Alexander R. Lawton letter, without salutation, September 29, 1864, with a continuation dated October 3, Alexander-Hillhouse Papers, SHC.

A fortnight before his death, the cavalry commander wrote patiently but sternly to his subordinate: "However great my personal regard for you [it cannot] be relied upon to the extent of justifying you in disobeying orders of the plainest and most unmistakeable import." Long after Stuart's death deprived him of that target, Rosser carried on an ardent quarrel with his wartime rival, Colonel T. T. Munford. "It tickled me to see what a fool he was," Munford wrote of Rosser to Senator John Warwick Daniel in 1905. The postbellum paper feud, which survives in gratifying volume, is amusing, entertaining, and informative by turns.[33]

The huge and athletic frame of Rosser contained a warrior's spirit that marked him as a leader of men in mounted battle. His vast store of personal bravery prompted otherwise unimpressed witnesses to use phrases such as "Brave as a Lion" about Rosser. Rather like Turner Ashby, though, Rosser's grasp apparently did not extend far enough beyond the reach of his eye and his sword arm.

In May 1864, a young officer in the 35th Virginia Cavalry Battalion ("the Comanches"), of Rosser's famous Laurel Brigade, concisely reported his dashed hopes that Rosser would prove to be a capable leader. "We have fought hard and faithfully and lost heavily," wrote Captain Franklin M. Myers, "but I can't see why we should have done so. My bright dream that Rosser was one of the first calvery Generals in our service is gone. He is no General at all." Myers praised Rosser's bravery in the same line that he damned his judgment: "As brave a man as ever drew breath, but knows no more about putting a command into a fight than a school boy." Deterioration of morale and efficiency in the Laurel Brigade followed with dreadful certainty. "We have lost confidence in him so fast that he can't get a good fight out of us any more," stated Myers, "unless we know positively what we are fighting."[34]

Given his observations on Rosser the brigade commander, Myers cannot have harbored many illusions about the general's prospects in even more complex and responsible roles. Other Confederates great and small echoed Myers's judgment after Rosser failed in the Valley. Virginian Mark T. Alexander wrote from Rosser's camp in the fall that, sycophants aside, the general "is

33. Rosser to wife, April 5, 1864, Thomas L. Rosser Papers, Alderman Library, University of Virginia, Charlottesville; J. E. B. Stuart to Rosser, April 25, 1864, ibid.; Munford to Daniel, 1905 Folder, John Warwick Daniel Papers, PLD. Stuart's letters urging Rosser's promotion, despite the latter's grousing to the contrary, are in Rosser's CSR, M331, NA. The collection of Rosser Papers at Alderman contains two thousand items.

34. Frank M. Myers to "Dear Home Folks," May 16, 1864, copy at USAMHI.

After the war, Jubal A. Early refought the 1864 Valley Campaign
in print, flinging aspersions at some of his former subordinates,
especially Rosser, "a consummate ass."

extremely unpopular with the Division, they having been whipped in every
fight since he has been with us, they say by his bad management." The coterie
around headquarters, Alexander thought, were "a set of men who would black
his boots if necessary." The rest of the mounted southerners in the Valley
longed for a rapid convalescence for Fitzhugh Lee and his prompt return to
command.[35]

After the war, Early's dissatisfaction with Rosser bubbled over in one of
those newspaper brawls that so attracted Early and that prompted him gleefully to dip his pen in vitriol. The "somewhat notorious" Rosser, Early declared, had, in describing events in the Valley, "shown his utter disregard for
the truth." One of Rosser's published sallies prompted his former commander
to write of the cavalryman: "Having previously figured extensively as a falsifier
of history, he has recently appeared in another role—that of a consummate

35. Mark T. Alexander to mother, November 15, 1864, Alexander Papers, Swem Library, College of William and Mary, Williamsburg, Va.

ass, and it must be confessed that he has proved himself an adept in that character." Warming to his task, Early eventually compared Rosser's apostasy from
the truth to that of Judas Iscariot, concluding that Christ's betrayer had much
the better of the comparison: Judas, after all, finally threw away his blood
money and hanged himself. Were Rosser to emulate that example, Early suggested, "we might regard the act as some atonement for [his] apostasy and the
most creditable act [he] could now perform."[36]

In 1889, Rosser suggested that the root of the problem with Confederate
cavalry in the 1864 Valley affairs was that "Early handled his army as infantry
against cavalry, while Sheridan handled both his cavalry and his infantry as
infantry." That analysis is not invalid, but it displayed a grasp that Rosser himself was missing during the fighting and about which he could do, or at least
did do, nothing during the war's last autumn. A Laurel Brigade colonel
agreed, referring to Early's "very foolish prejudice against cavalry and conse-
quent ignorance of its use on the field." Even though Rosser and Colonel
Thomas T. Munford engaged in a lifelong snarling contest, in this instance
Munford—unknowingly—agreed with Rosser about uneven handling of the
various arms. Munford wrote late during the 1864 campaign that the greatest
problem in the Valley was the lack of an army commander who could handle
all three branches, "who knows when to use each and all, & the value of each
and all." Early seemed to him to assign the cavalry routinely to the flanks to
do random chores, whatever the circumstances. Closer to the event, Rosser
knew better. A general orders that he issued to his division just three days
after the Battle of Cedar Creek bore as its title a simple admission: "The want
of discipline has been the cause of additional disaster to this army."[37]

Jubal Early the postwar controversialist was not necessarily the same man
struggling with harsh realities in the fall of 1864, but neither did his loathing
for Tom Rosser in the 1880s spring whole from the ground. Early probably
asked himself at the beginning of October 1864, without the priceless advantage of hindsight, the same question his army eagerly considered: Is Rosser as

---

36. Newspaper clippings, generally without provenance, reproducing the Early-Rosser vituper-
ation are in the Hotchkiss Papers, LC, Reel 58, Frames 436–39.

37. Thomas L. Rosser, *Address of Gen'l T. L. Rosser . . . February 22, 1889* (Baltimore: Sun
Book and Job Printing Office, 1889), 42; M. D. Ball, "Rosser and His Critics," *Philadelphia Weekly
Times,* July 12, 1884; T. T. Munford to father, November 17, 1864, Munford-Ellis Papers, Box 10,
PLD; *General Orders, no. The want of discipline has been the cause of additional disaster to this
army. . . .* (Charlottesville?, 1864). The general orders, which does not have a number filled in, is
signed in type by command of Rosser.

good as we hope he is and as good as he sometimes has looked? Is he another Grumble Jones or Fitz Lee? Or is Rosser another out of the Imboden/Vaughn mold? The answers would bring comfort only to men in blue in 1864. At the time, Early probably watched the results with more sorrow than venom, but what he saw did supply ample grist for his subsequent written squabbles with Rosser.

In a lively postscript to the campaign, played out in 1887, Tom Rosser found another opportunity to cast himself as the "Saviour of the Valley." By then the former Confederate had gained considerable prominence through association with George A. Custer, his West Point friend and 1870s hunting companion on the plains. In 1887, Phil Sheridan announced, with all of his considerable insensitivity, that he planned to visit the Shenandoah Valley to see whether it had yet recovered from his 1864 visit. Sheridan had trampled southern property and prerogatives with impunity during Reconstruction, but a decade later his remarks raised a publicity firestorm. Rosser, who not coincidentally was essaying a run at Virginia politics just then, led the outcry ("cold, cruel and brutal . . . barbarous . . . wanton") that ensued. He had more success in that endeavor than he had against Sheridan in 1864, when denouements were determined by access to big and well-armed battalions.[38]

The "regular" cavalry from east of the mountains that fought under Rosser in the Valley included some relatively new commanders whose performance is difficult to gauge. Williams C. Wickham seems to have performed solidly, with potential for good results given an opportunity, but he could not take hold against the racing ebb tide. During the fall Wickham went off to Richmond to occupy the seat he held in the Confederate States Congress. Lunsford Lindsay Lomax fell into the same category. He was well trained and apt, with successes to his credit in northern Virginia, but he arrived at his opportunities late in the war. The twenty-eight-year-old professional soldier had performed creditably in the thrashing of Sheridan at Trevilian Station in mid-June 1864, coming away with George Custer's mess chest and wagon, among other trophies. A few days later Lomax took out an advertisement in the *Richmond Examiner* enumerating the stolen southern silverware in Custer's gear and offering its return to the lawful owners.[39] Lomax's performance in the Valley seems in retrospect similar to that of Wickham—solid and apparently

38. "Rosser on Sheridan," *Richmond Whig*, May 5, 1887, and *Martinsburg Statesman*, May 12, 1887.

39. "A Major-General Who Steals Spoons!," *Richmond Examiner*, June 29, 1864.

hopeful but in fact hopeless. Had his chance at important command come early in the war, Lomax might today be part of the Confederate cavalier legend with an equestrian bronze reminder gracing some Virginia roadside.

That the poverty of cavalry command in the 1864 Valley operations would in many instances extend to field-grade officers was inevitable. The immutable arithmetic of war had subtracted some of the best leaders by way of casualty lists. Others had been promoted out of regimental command—many of them to positions beyond their capacity, as we have seen. The famous 1st Virginia Cavalry will serve as a vivid case study. A succession of notable cavalrymen had commanded this regiment during the war, beginning with J. E. B. Stuart himself. Later Fitz Lee was colonel of the regiment. So was Grumble Jones. Colonel James Henry Drake followed those able men. Although Drake never shared the fame of the other three, his men loved and respected him. The forty-year-old prewar plasterer, mechanic, and militia officer typified a class of men who blossomed to competence under the demands of warfare. By late 1864, however, all of those men were gone from the regiment; three of them were dead. That left an aristocratic Virginian named Richard Welby Carter as colonel of the illustrious command, and Carter was an unmitigated disaster. A complete separate chapter of this book discusses his difficulties.

After examining the litany of horrors Early faced from both cavalry troops and cavalry leaders, the battlefield developments themselves hardly hold any major surprise. Repeatedly during the late summer and fall of 1864, Confederate cavalry fell victim to Federal mounted forces that outnumbered them by large proportions. In the process, momentum built for the northern squadrons and drained away from their southern counterparts. It is not a glaring exaggeration to suggest that when infantry forces clashed in the three largest battles of the campaign, Early's veterans fought with amazing fortitude against Sheridan's corps until their lines were compromised by collapse of their mounted colleagues on a flank.

At the Third Battle of Winchester on September 19, Gordon and Ramseur and Rodes stood stalwart against swarming Federals for hours, and Rodes died in the process. They blistered each Federal infantry effort and inflicted thousands of casualties (although Sheridan finally won the field, he lost in one day more men than Stonewall Jackson killed and wounded during the course of his entire fabled 1862 campaign in this same Valley). It is hard to imagine how any infantry could have done more than Early's achieved that day east of Winchester. In fact, few performances on other battlefields of the war equal it. The rupture on his left that doomed Early's army came through ground held primarily by his cavalry. Whether any available force could have held under the circumstances may be argued, but the familiar result left the Confederate army in rout. Significantly, most of the substantive rear-guard efforts that can be discerned today, from accounts of that chaotic evening, came from infantry units. At Winchester and elsewhere in the Valley, the cavalry betrayed its ineptitude by failing to discharge its traditional screening function during retreats. Colonel George H. Smith, acting brigade commander (vice the mortally wounded George S. Patton I), wrote a few days after the battle that the cavalry "constituted the principal part of the crowd that stampeded through Winchester."[40]

Three days after driving Early from Winchester, Sheridan closed with the Confederates again a few miles south of Strasburg at Fisher's Hill. The position there to which Early had retreated seemed to have enough natural strength to offer the southerners a bulwark of some consequence. On its right (eastern) flank, Fisher's Hill—really a succession of hills perpendicular to the Valley Pike—dropped precipitously into the North Fork of the Shenandoah River. Across the front of Fisher's Hill, separating it from ground the Federals occupied before the battle, ran Tumbling Run. That stream lives up to its name by bubbling cheerfully through the fields on a twisting course. The run served as a moat of sorts below the southern line, too small to pose a major military obstacle but indicative of a deeply cut ravine that separated the armies. Northerners attacking across the run would have to descend to it under fire, then clamber up slopes so formidable as to be virtually impregnable if defended with even moderate strength.

The only weak point in Early's line lay on his left, and even that zone included some points useful for defense. The western wall of the Valley loomed there, as though designed for a line to anchor on, and while Fisher's Hill lost much of its elevation and regularity on the left, good ground nearby gave Early terrain advantages. The immense strength of the Confederate right must have been apparent to the most unlettered private soldier on either side (though Sheridan's first plan was to attack there, before wiser heads prevailed). By the same token, the need for Confederate caution on Early's left was strikingly apparent.

In what must be adjudged an egregious tactical blunder, perhaps his largest of the long campaign, Early packed his seasoned infantry into the powerful

40. Colonel George H. Smith, "Imboden's Brigade," *Richmond Whig*, October 12, 1864. Smith's narrative was in the form of a letter to the *Whig* dated October 4.

position on his right and scattered his unreliable cavalry out on the more sensitive left. The only faint mitigation that might be offered for Early's dreadful misjudgment is the fact that the Valley Pike ran through his right. To have his line broken atop that crucial artery would have constituted a marginally greater disaster than a rupture on the left. It seems certain, however, that neither end needed to face destruction had Early distributed his forces rationally.

On the afternoon of September 22, Early reaped the bitter fruits of his faulty alignment. Federals under George Crook moved up the mountainside, then south beyond the southern flank, then roared down the slope and shattered the Confederate cavalry along Early's left. It is, of course, impossible to say precisely what would have happened had veteran Confederate infantry stood in the way. What is of record is that the horsemen ordered to hold that ground dissolved in record time. The Confederate cavalry had too few numbers and, more important, neither the spirit nor the efficiency to repulse or even impede Crook's assault.

The scampering cavalrymen disgusted, though did not surprise, their infantry mates on up the line. After the war, one of the foot soldiers recorded with undisguised disdain the demeanor of the first straggler who dashed past: "After a slight fire on the left a cavalryman came down our line telling the men they were flanked. This did much for Sheridan and that fellow should have a [Yankee] pension. I have often regretted I did not shoot him and shall always regret not having arrested him. It might have saved us from a disgraceful defeat. It certainly would have been stopped further to our left. He passed over three-fourths of our line telling every man 'we are flanked' and 'the enemy is behind us.'"[41]

The vacuum on the left quickly unraveled Early's line, and his men fled in complete rout up the Valley, replicating in excruciating detail their unhappy experience three days earlier. Virginian artillerist Micajah Woods watched as the dismounted cavalrymen "rushed from the works in confusion—neither officers nor men seeming to know what to do." A North Carolina infantry officer described the weary loathing with which his colleagues viewed their cavalry detachment. To the infantry, he wrote, the mounted men in the Valley seemed to dash "hither and thither with no object apparent to prejudiced eyes, except that of keeping as much space as possible between themselves and the foe."[42]

---

41. Samuel D. Buck, *With the Old Confeds: Actual Experiences of a Captain in the Line* (Baltimore: H. E. Houck, 1925), 114.

42. Micajah Woods to father, September 23, 1864, Woods Papers, Alderman Library, Univer-

The Fisher's Hill rout gave a disgusted Jubal Early the chance to use the battle's name as an epithet. Some soldiers jeered at their army commander a bit later as they passed him near a roadside house, waiting for a drink of water. "Give that dog a bone and let him go," yelled an irreverent Confederate. Early snarled back: "Fisher's Hill, God Damn You." The general obviously had concluded, not without cause, that merely citing the name should embarrass the soldiery that had fled from the place so precipitately.[43]

During the frightful ordeal of racing away from Fisher's Hill, a North Carolinian officer passed a Confederate who had composed a ditty in tribute to the shortcomings of the Valley cavalry. "For some cause known only to their whimsical philosophy," the foot soldiers held Imboden's cavalry as "an especial object of their disesteem. By way of derision they called it 'Jimboden's' cavalry." The embittered lyricist near Fisher's Hill aimed his song at "Jimboden," though in fact the cavalry at fault on that day had been under L. L. Lomax. As the North Carolinian rode southward amid the discouraged mass, he noticed,

> close beside the road along which the troops poured in confusion, a ragged, dejected, unkempt "Confed" crouched over a little fire, regarding naught, absorbed alone in warming numbed fingers and toes, for the day was chilly. As he crouched and shivered he droned a song in whose tone disgust, despair and disdain all strove for the mastery. The song, which must have been rich, was lost except the following stanza caught as a group of officers rode by:

> > "Old Jimboden's gone up the spout,
> > And Old Jube Early's about played out."[44]

A few weeks later "Old Jube" Early proved to the astonishment of many on both sides that he was not played out. Precisely one month after the disaster at the Third Battle of Winchester, Early was back at Sheridan's throat and close to destroying him north of Strasburg. Before he completed his metamorphosis, though, Early faced the misfortune of picking up the pieces after yet another cavalry debacle.

The cavalry embarrassment at Tom's Brook on October 9 had its roots in the savage destruction of much of the Valley's substance under Sheridan's or-

sity of Virginia, Charlottesville; Clark, ed., *Histories of the Several Regiments and Battalions from North Carolina*, 2:257.

43. James Alexander Milling (3rd South Carolina Battalion), "Jim Milling and the War," typescript copy in the author's possession.

44. Clark, ed., *Histories of the Several Regiments and Battalions from North Carolina*, 2:257–58.

ders. As northern troopers moved down the Valley in early October, they methodically destroyed everything in their path. Tom Rosser did not need to prod his southern horsemen after the burners; many of the pursuing riders saw their own homes and families brutalized during those terrible days. Some Federal detachments with arson on their minds ran into Confederate parties who butchered them as part of a new sort of war even uglier than the old variety. On a larger scale, though, the Confederate mounted units suffered a marked disaster when their outraged ardor led them too far from infantry support in desperate pursuit of vengeance.

When Rosser and Lomax came under heavy attack just south and southwest of Tom's Brook on October 9, their troopers stood and fought against enormous odds for some time. In the end, they succumbed and raced south up the Valley in abject rout, not stopping until back behind the far-distant infantry front. Many threw away their arms. An artillery colonel wrote two days later that the cavalry force "has been almost ruined." The "poor creatures, officers and all," had become deathly afraid of Federal sabers, an "almost harmless weapon." The colonel predicted, accurately if obviously, that the cavalry never again would stand up to the Federals, and the infantry's awareness of that fact made the whole army subject to almost inevitable disaster. An infantryman in the 4th Georgia played to the same weary refrain in a letter home: "All of our misfortunes were caused by depending on our cavalry. . . . It is worth very little." In similar spirit an ordnance officer called Lomax's division "not worth the powder necessary to shoot them down. . . . May the devil get all those fellows."[45]

Rosser's own Laurel Brigade scattered no more widely or rapidly than any of the others at Tom's Brook, but its proud reputation and distinctive name prompted Early to pick on it in the aftermath. In a bitter (and botanically inaccurate) aside, Early cracked that "laurel is a running vine." Had the army commander been present, he would have greatly enjoyed another episode in the aftermath of Tom's Brook. As the rout slowed in exhaustion, Tom Rosser spied a regimental fragment carrying one of the unique Laurel Brigade flags. The general turned to Lomax and exclaimed with vestigial pride, "You see the Laurel Brigade brings out its flags." As the weary riders drew closer, Lomax said, "If I am not mistaken, that is one of my regiments coming out." Lomax

45. J. Floyd King to "Dear Friend," October 11, 1864, in King's CSR, M331, NA; J. L. Johnson to Lizzie Hitchcock, October 14, 1864, J. C. Bonner Collection, Georgia College, Milledgeville; Oscar Hinrichs journal, October 9, 1864, copy in the author's possession.

was right. His men had either recaptured the laurel flag from the enemy or, more likely, had salvaged it from abandonment. Infantry brigadier general Bryan Grimes told his wife in disappointment that Rosser had failed to reverse the cavalry trend: "There must be something contagious in this atmosphere, or in this valley cavalry for they cause everything to stampede that comes in association with them." Grimes indignantly suggested that "at least one hundred of them" ought to have been hanged the next morning.[46]

Jubal Early's greatest success in the campaign came on October 19 at Cedar Creek. As had happened twice before within a month, Early's army won the first three-fourths of a battle despite the odds against it. The opening success at Cedar Creek ran farther and deeper than at Winchester or Fisher's Hill and in fact was equal to anything done by the Army of Northern Virginia in its storied campaigns of the war's middle phase. Almost all of the Confederate success on October 19 sprang, once again, from strong infantry performances. While John B. Gordon, Stephen Dodson Ramseur, and Joseph B. Kershaw drove three Federal corps from their positions, Early's cavalry accomplished almost nothing. Old Jube himself deserved half of the blame because he sent about one-half of his available mounted force off to his right under Lomax on an ill-defined and hopeless mission. Having dissipated a large part of his already inadequate cavalry strength by executive fiat, Early could hope for results only from Rosser's men and a few other tiny detachments.

Rosser and his force spent October 19 where Early habitually posted his cavalry—on the army's far left. In that zone Rosser virtually disappeared during the course of the day. Federal cavalry responsible for keeping him in check gradually recognized the absence of threat, and eventually most of them went off to take part in fighting to the east. When Sheridan retrieved his fortunes late in the afternoon, Federal cavalry roared across the Confederate left, as at Winchester and Fisher's Hill. Giddy victory on the morning of October 19 transmogrified into defeat of the most total scope by nightfall. Attempts to hold back the triumphant Federals and to salvage something from the chaos fell yet again to a rear guard composed of infantry, not cavalry. The formula for disaster, vintage 1864 Valley, applied yet again at Cedar Creek.

Early's disorganized retreat from Cedar Creek marked the end of serious infantry fighting in the Valley. There remained still another cavalry failure that fall, as the Confederate horsemen drained the last bitter dregs from a cupful

46. Peyton, *Civil War Record*, 91; Bryan Grimes to wife, October 10, 1864, Grimes Papers, SHC.

of defeats. On November 12, while infantry skirmished in desultory fashion, Rosser and Payne fought northern cavalry with some success near Strasburg. At the same time around Nineveh, north of Front Royal on ground that had been the scene of Stonewall Jackson's triumphal affairs on May 23–24, 1862, McCausland repulsed two attacks and concluded that he had finished a good day's work. As his men nonchalantly ate dinner and fed their horses, ignoring as usual the basic disciplinary and security measures necessary in disputed country, a renewed Federal surge caught and destroyed them.[47]

Early responded to this latest debacle by publishing names of cowards in a written special order. The poltroons were to be "transferred from Cavalry to Infantry, for misbehavior before the enemy on Nov. 12th 1864." They also were to forfeit their mounts—a serious punishment because the horses were private property and at that stage of the war carried a value almost as great as their weight in depreciated Confederate currency.[48] The fuming general doubtless found some catharsis in being able to pinpoint even in a small way his frustrations with the cavalry that had caused him so much grief. As the fall of 1864 ended, though, anything that Jubal Early might attempt to do with his frail cavalry arm was far too little and far too late. The Valley horsemen had long been ill-disciplined. Now they constituted a gaggle scornfully, but aptly, described during the war's last winter as the "straggling cavalry that infested the Valley . . . a greater terror to their friends than their foes."[49]

The question remains whether there ever was a time at which Early could have straightened out the Valley cavalry or a means that could have achieved that end. During 1864, the more regular cavalry supporting the Army of Northern Virginia east of the mountains faced odds and disadvantages not unlike those that overwhelmed Early's troopers. Lee's horsemen performed their assigned tasks and maintained a precarious equilibrium. They contained hostile raids, scouted advances, and screened retreats. Despite the loss of Stuart, they deflected Sheridan's Richmond raid in May, and in early June they thoroughly bludgeoned that officer's force during its threat to the railroads in the Battle of Trevilian Station. The era of rides around the Army of the Potomac was long gone by the summer and fall of 1864, but dedicated and disci-

47. Hotchkiss, *Make Me a Map*, 243.

48. Special Orders No. 125, December 1864, signed by Early, reproduced in manuscript in the CSR of Benjamin R. Pennybacker, 17th Virginia Cavalry, M324, NA.

49. "The Shenandoah Campaign," *New Orleans Daily Picayune*, January 14, 1865. The author of this article probably was Major John P. H. New, aide to Generals Ramseur and Pegram.

plined cavalry continued to play its assigned role for Lee at the time that Early languished without effective mounted support.

Early's own infantry and its leaders also offered an abrupt contrast to the demeanor of the Valley cavalry. Rodes, Gordon, Ramseur, John Pegram, and Kershaw each displayed steady competence and often brilliance. Their men performed in like manner, in the healthy positive spiral that results from good leadership nurturing good support, and vice versa.

By contrast, not one officer among Rosser, McCausland, Vaughn, Imboden, W. L. Jackson, B. T. Johnson, and Payne offered assets nearly as good as the worst of those infantry leaders. We owe it to those men to consider the salient question: Could *anyone* have done the job? The answer must be, probably not. Those cavalry leaders most susceptible to criticism for problems during Early's campaign, however, were the ones who had been in their roles for a long time and therefore had contributed to the lack of discipline and the ineptitude of troops and units that fell apart under the demands of that difficult period.

The irregular Valley cavalry, by its nature, required especially strong leadership, but more often than not it had done without that important guidance throughout the war. The circumstances of Early's 1864 Valley campaign redoubled the demand for strong leaders. Time and again the events of the campaign resulted in a requirement that the cavalry do near impossibilities at moments of decision. In consequence, the poor caliber of the men and units was exposed under an unblinking spotlight, and the shortcomings of their leadership were magnified manifold. To compound and redouble this unhappy mix, General Early for his part was maladroit in his desperate attempts to make the best of a bad deal.

9

Confederate Books: Five Great Ones and Two Bad Ones

No historical event has been the subject of nearly so many books in the English language as the American Civil War. The flood of ink spilled on the subject has yielded some very good things, both as history and as literature. It also has resulted in tens of thousands of ordinary books and a good many truly dreadful volumes. The reflective essays that make up this chapter discuss five of the best Confederate titles. All five books are from the first-person genre—the most important and interesting sort of books about the war, or about any other historical period. The book essays reveal, it must be admitted, the author's intense love of books as books, in addition to interest in their contents. Two brief reviews of wretchedly tendentious modern books offer a counterpoint at the end of the chapter. That the five books lauded here are primary sources and the two panned are secondary is entirely coincidental. Innumerable bad primary books reached print, of course, and splendid secondary studies abound.

A FIRE BOOK

Almost every battlefield has a Bloody Pond, a railroad cut, a ghost or two, and some sort of sunken lane.[1] Rare books often have their own distinctions: limited editions, numbered editions, private printings, special papers and bindings, and books rendered exquisitely rare because most copies have been

1. This article first appeared in *Blue & Gray Magazine* 6 (December 1988): 40. It is reprinted here, with a few modifications, by permission.

destroyed by fire.[2] This essay is about one of those rare books singed with fire, *Rebel Private, Front and Rear.*

Crackling flames became frightfully commonplace during the 1860s in the brutalized regions of the Shenandoah Valley, Georgia, and South Carolina. The book-consuming flames under discussion here, though, actually crackled in 1924, half a century after legally sanctioned arson had grudgingly gone out of vogue. They burned up "the greater part" of the supply of W. A. Fletcher's memoir, *Rebel Private, Front and Rear,* which had been published sixteen years earlier in Beaumont, Texas.

William Andrew Fletcher was born in St. Landry Parish, Louisiana, on April 23, 1839. His father was an overseer who did not like slavery and escaped that elemental incongruity by moving away from dense slave country to Texas in 1856. The elder Fletcher earned his living as a millwright in Beaumont when war came and young William left to become a soldier.

Fletcher enlisted two days before the firing on Fort Sumter in a unit that eventually came to be designated Company F, 5th Texas Infantry. The 5th Texas became an integral part of one of the most renowned units in the Army of Northern Virginia—Hood's Texas Brigade it was called, long after Hood had gone. William A. Fletcher fought among those redoubtable shock troops and fought hard, at the cost of severe wounds suffered at Second Manassas and Chickamauga.

Early in 1864, Fletcher followed the popular road from infantry to cavalry service, becoming a member of Company E, 8th Texas Cavalry. Unfortunately for students of the campaigns in the Virginia theater, fully one-half of Fletcher's published memoir deals with his late-war experiences amid the less interesting bushwhackery in Tennessee and the Carolinas.

Back home in Beaumont after the war, veteran Fletcher married in 1866 a local girl with the peculiarly masculine name of Julian Long. He proceeded to get comfortably wealthy in the lumber business before retiring to a large ranch after the turn of the century. Fletcher died on January 5, 1915.

Seven years before his death, Fletcher published his war story in a prettily

---

2. Other "fire books," according to bibliophilic lore, include the Confederate poem by Stonewall Jackson's sister-in-law published in 1865 and a superb standard reference on Georgia in the war. Those are Margaret Junkin Preston, *Beechenbrook: A Rhyme of the War* (Richmond: J. W. Randolph, 1865); and James M. Folsom, *Heroes and Martyrs of Georgia: Georgia's Record in the Revolution of 1861* (Macon: Burke, Boykin, 1864). The Preston Confederate imprint appears for sale intermittently at huge prices ($3,500 in 1999), but no copy of Folsom has been seen for many decades.

bound beige volume, bedizened with colorful Confederates flags on the front cover. When fire destroyed the family home in 1924, the surviving undistributed books were either completely burned or at least stained badly by smoke. Most known copies show traces of the smoke. Good specimens are lightly stained or at least evenly stained. Ordinary copies suffer from varying degrees of ugliness. Only a few fortunate collectors own precious copies that were distributed before the fire and have somehow come onto the market.[3]

Bibliophilic lust for the first edition of Fletcher is fed by all of the usual fires, as well as by the scarcity resultant from the literal fire in 1924. There are ample reasons to love even the 1954 reprint (University of Texas) for its colorful but down-to-earth contents. Fletcher wrote with rambunctious good humor and deadly realism. He reported his own drunken sprees. He evinced unmistakable relish over the number of dead Federals in evidence at Fredericksburg: "the more dead the less risk." He also saw no harm in stripping clothes from dead enemies for reuse. In a remarkably un-Victorian passage, Fletcher apparently intimated that evidences of venereal disease were prevalent among those stripped Federal dead. On balance, William A. Fletcher rates as a Deep South equivalent of hard-eyed Stonewall Brigade memoirist John O. Casler (who wound up living for a time not far from Fletcher after the war, by coincidence).

A small pamphlet about Fletcher by his maiden daughter is a nice associative piece for book collectors who appreciate the veterans' memoir. *A Biographical Sketch of William Andrew Fletcher, Author of Rebel Private—Front and Rear, by his Daughter Vallie Fletcher* was published in 1950 in Beaumont, although not by the same small-town press that issued the earlier book.[4] The pamphlet measures 21½ centimeters tall, includes twenty-seven pages, and is ephemeral to the point of being virtually unknown. The only copy I have ever seen was one given to the late Bell I. Wiley by Vallie Fletcher and eventually sold when Wiley disposed of his library.

VIRGINIA'S CONFEDERATE MAURYS—ESPECIALLY BETTY

In 1938, Alice Maury Parmelee of Washington, D.C., "caused to be privately printed twenty-five copies" of her mother's Confederate diary kept in war-

3. Another anomaly affects *Rebel Private*: a number of copies were bound upside down, which of course cannot be blamed on the fire.

4. "Press of the Green Print" printed *Rebel Private*. Vallie's pamphlet came from Lamb Printing Company. William Fletcher's great-granddaughter Vallie Fletcher Taylor addressed the Houston Civil War Round Table about her ancestor in November 1999.

A BIOGRAPHICAL SKETCH

of

William Andrew Fletcher

Author of

REBEL PRIVATE—FRONT AND REAR

For Dr. Bell Irwin Wiley
With sincerest thanks
to you for work on my
father's book.
Vallie Fletcher

by his daughter

VALLIE FLETCHER

Printed by Lamb Printing Company

Beaumont, Texas

May, 1950

torn Fredericksburg, Virginia.[5] Alice called the book *The Confederate Diary of Betty Herndon Maury*. Most of this chapter, and of the remainder of the book as well, focuses on Confederate military matters. This superb female diary constitutes such a striking original source, though, that it well warrants attention from both military and social historians. Few things are more inclined to fire a book collector's passions than a solidly produced hardbound book, with substantive subject matter, documented as existing in so minuscule a printing. That the subject is Fredericksburg, about the most congenial latitude in the Old Dominion, adds to the fascination.

Elizabeth Herndon Maury was born in 1835 to one of Virginia's most renowned historical figures, Matthew Fontaine Maury, and his wife, Anne Hull Herndon. In 1857, Betty married William A. Maury (1832–1918).[6] William was a cousin, which made him a particularly fitting mate by the traditions of mid-nineteenth-century Virginian society. William served the Confederacy in the office of the judge advocate general and then was an assistant attorney general of the United States after the war. Late in his life Maury was a law professor in Washington and represented the United States on the Spanish Treaty Claims Commission. Betty and William had two children: Nannie Belle Maury (1858–1939), who is mentioned frequently in her mother's war diary and who died unmarried; and Alice Maury Parmelee (1863–1940), who left no issue.

Betty Maury was brimful of southern enthusiasm and "a *hundred* times prouder" of her famous dad for seceding with the Confederacy than she had been for all of the scientific accolades he had won. As Betty and little Nannie Belle ran the picket blockade from Washington to Fredericksburg at the beginning of the war, the youngster's inherited Confederate spirit posed difficulties: her endless, noisy choruses of "Dixie" were giving the northern pickets reason to wonder about letting the Maurys pass. In hopes of corking the audible portion of her daughter's pronounced southern chauvinism, Betty began feeding the

5. This description of the Maurys and their books first appeared in *Blue & Gray Magazine* 4 (May 1987): 25–26. It is reprinted here, with a few changes of limited scope, by permission of the publisher of that serial, the gallant and distinguished Brevet Corporal David Roth. The same generous fellow granted reuse rights for the four other articles in this chapter that first appeared in *Blue & Gray*.

6. The best source on this storied Virginian clan is Anne Fontaine Maury, ed., *Intimate Virginiana: A Century of Maury Travels by Land and Sea* (Richmond: Dietz Press, 1941). The Maurys also are writ large upon the pages of Robert Alonzo Brock, comp., *Documents, Chiefly Unpublished, Relating to the Huguenot Emigration to Virginia* (Richmond: Wm. Ellis Jones, 1886). The Brock compilation constitutes volume 5 of *Collections of the Virginia Historical Society, New Series*.

Betty Herndon Maury

child a sugar cracker each time a sentinel loomed ahead. While little Miss Maury had never heard of Pavlov's dogs, she knew her pastries and began looking alertly for pickets: "Mama, here is another soldier, give me a sugar-tacker."

Although Betty Maury's published diary is replete with entries that show strong, tender family ties at all levels, her entries often deviate from the sugar-and-lace Victorian norm seen in female writings of that period. Her brother Dick's fiancée (he was lieutenant colonel of the 24th Virginia Infantry), Betty pronounced "not so pretty with her bonnet off." When her husband made especially careful preparations for a short trip to Richmond, Betty fumed: "From the preparations he is making, he must intend to spend eight or ten months at least. Never saw such a 'Miss Nancy.' Oh me! I wish I was more amiable and more charitable." Her cousin (and Will's cousin too) Betty called "the prosiest and most tiresome old man in Fredericksburg!" Finally, in a fit of dismay over what seemed to be inadequate attention from her spouse, Betty dipped her pen in sarcasm and screeched: "I have my baby, a novel, and a paper of candy. What more can any *reasonable* woman want?"

There is really very little military insight to be gleaned from Betty's diary. Her reports of her father's struggles with bureaucracy and her own outrage over such difficulties offer some interesting footnotes to military matters.[7] When war came in earnest to Fredericksburg in November 1862, Betty and her baby were well away from the town, staying with a relative near the county seat of Caroline (which she styled "*the* Bowling Green"). Male friends and kin going into town reported back with tales of looting, gore, and destruction. Betty faithfully recorded their tales in her diary, but they obviously do not have the immediacy of eyewitness material.

The great value of *The Confederate Diary of Betty Herndon Maury* comes, predictably, from the unaffected, close-up view it affords of a Virginia town in wartime conditions: depreciation of currency, increasing shortages, gradual desertion by the slaves, facing and coping with an invading army, and endless worry about loved ones under fire. The large and small crises of domestic life, inflamed far beyond their normal scope by war's pressures, are the warp and woof of Betty's story.

The largest of those crises brought about the end of the diary. In early 1863, as Betty Maury was approaching the term of her second pregnancy, the cousins with whom she and her family had been boarding (for $200 per month) quietly evicted them and ceased speaking to them. The diary's last line mentions an importunate letter to an aunt in central Virginia, asking for shelter. The aunt did not come through either, and Betty took Nannie Belle off to seek help from relatives near Charlottesville; her husband's duties obliged him to stay in Richmond. Betty traveled west, terrified the whole trip "of being delivered on the public highway." Soon after she reached Charlottesville, Alice was born, June 7, 1863. Precisely three-quarters of a century later, Alice was responsible for the twenty-five-copy printing of her mother's diary, in Washington, D.C. By then Elizabeth Herndon Maury had been dead for thirty-five years.

There is, of course, a vast body of nineteenth-century Maury literature extant because of Betty's brilliant father. His own fecund pen spawned books

---

7. A fine early biography of Betty's distinguished father is John W. Wayland, *The Pathfinder of the Seas* (Richmond: Garrett & Massie, 1930). The more modern, and clearly definitive, work on the subject is Frances Leigh Williams, *Matthew Fontaine Maury, Scientist of the Sea* (New Brunswick: Rutgers University Press, 1963). Wayland's book is graced by a lovely Charles W. Smith dust jacket.

and papers without end, many of them breaking exciting new ground in matters of national or international importance. After the commodore died in 1873, writings about him proliferated, including several by members of his own family. All of that literature lies far beyond the capacity of this essay to discuss in any detail. Two Civil War pieces written by Maurys but not concerned with the renowned commodore might be cited, though, to round out the picture of this Confederate family.

Betty's brother, Colonel Richard L. Maury (1840–1907), recorded the bravest moment of his regiment in a nice little twenty-page pamphlet, *The Battle of Williamsburg and the Charge of the 24th Virginia* (Richmond, 1880). Richard's account also appeared in *The Southern Historical Society Papers* twice, in somewhat variant form, in 1880 and 1894. The later account affords something more of the shared glory of the charge to the 5th North Carolina Infantry, which clearly deserved its generous portion. A modern reprint, without new imprimatur, has been around for about twenty years.

The largest Maury book about the Civil War should by all odds be the best, and one of the best about the war. Dabney Herndon Maury (1822–1900) was a Fredericksburg man who became a Confederate major general. Matthew Fontaine Maury was his uncle and guardian. Dabney Maury's *Recollections of a Virginian in the Mexican, Indian, and Civil Wars* (New York, 1894) is warm, sometimes charming, and sometimes interesting.[8] But it never rings the big brass gong that the reader of so promising a title has in mind. When some of the anecdotes are susceptible to cross-checking, they do not always survive intact. Some of that disappointment may reflect the predilections of this reviewer, who has very little adrenalin available for response to tales about western-theater bushwhackery, and that's where Maury had the misfortune to spend his war.

Perhaps a major reason that Betty's book is so much more entrancing than cousin Dabney's is simple rarity. There were only twenty-five of Betty's ever produced; surely some have been destroyed, most of the rest imprisoned in institutions.[9] The odds are, though, that somewhere out there are two or three

8. The publisher issued a very few copies of Dabney Maury's *Recollections* in elegant three-quarters leather. The familiar trade edition in gray cloth is quite common; the leather edition is extraordinarily uncommon.

9. Robert A. Hodge, then of Fredericksburg, made a typescript from the manuscript of Betty's diary at the Library of Congress in 1985. He produced a dozen or so photocopies, had them very simply bound (some in pressboard covers with interior metal clips, some in homemade leatherette buckram), and sold them in town.

copies passively awaiting the chance to brighten a collector's eye. So you'll know when you've seen one, here are the specifications: quite tall (24½ centimeters); quite slender (102 pages); printed on very fine paper; bound into either half-leather with boards or rather unprepossessing cloth of ecru gray (something like Freeman's *Last Parade*); paper labels. When Richard Barksdale Harwell included Betty's diary in his list of the two hundred "most important Confederate books," a distinction it richly deserves, he ensured an immense price for any copy that may eventually reach the marketplace.[10]

J. F. J. CALDWELL'S WONDERFUL BOOK WITH THE ENORMOUS NAME

Some Confederates echo down through the years and reach us in images larger than life because of their particularly dazzling battlefield performances.[11] Others are especially memorable because we can discern attractive qualities in their personal lives or their public behavior. Yet another niche in the pantheon of important Confederates is reserved for participants in the historic events who produced the best written records of their experiences. Among the literary stars in the last category must be included such familiar names as Jedediah Hotchkiss, William A. Fletcher, Mary Boykin Chesnut, William Allan, John Casler, and J. F. J. Caldwell.

James Fitz James Caldwell (1837–1925) was a South Carolinian, first and last. His Confederate service was distinguished by honorable wounds and by promotion from the ranks to a commission as lieutenant in the 1st South Car-

---

10. Harwell's book is *In Tall Cotton: The 200 Most Important Confederate Books for the Reader, Researcher and Collector* (Austin, Tex.: Jenkins Publishing Company and Frontier America Corporation, 1978). Betty appears on page 44. (The Caldwell book reviewed in this chapter also made *In Tall Cotton*, on page 5.) Harwell was the preeminent Confederate bibliographer of his era, and *In Tall Cotton* is a splendid book; but the frantic enthusiasm for collecting books it lists exceeds reasonable bounds and surely would have amused its author. Bookmen insist that a listing in Harwell at least triples the price of books, even of the most common sort. *In Tall Cotton* itself now fetches $600, twenty-three years after publication. When two wonderful Maury women of mature years visited me a few years ago, I asked about Betty's diary. They knew of several distributed about the family but implored me to let them know if I ever saw one for sale, since descendants probably would be glad to pay $100 to get a copy. The ladies were nonplused when I told them the price would surely be in the vicinity of two hundred times that much, in the unlikely event that a copy surfaced. In 1995, an avid collector and devotee of *In Tall Cotton* offered $10,000 plus another great rarity for one copy of the Betty Maury book that is in private hands.

11. This essay first appeared in the September 1983 number of the *Maryland Line*, organ of the Montgomery County, Maryland, Civil War Round Table. This printing includes a few modest revisions.

olina. That regiment and four others (12th, 13th, and 14th South Carolina
and Orr's Rifles) made up the famed brigade commanded by Maxcy Gregg
and then by Samuel McGowan. Caldwell's creditable service was equaled by
any number of infantry lieutenants from his home state; but he stands out
today in bold relief because of the proverbial relative might of pens and
swords. Caldwell wrote a great book.

It cannot have been many weeks after Lee's surrender at Appomattox that
Caldwell began to sift his records and his memories in preparation for writing
a history of the brigade he had served so well. The product of his labors was
published in Philadelphia in 1866 under the tortuous title *The History of a
Brigade of South Carolinians Known First as "Gregg's," and Subsequently as "Mc-
Gowan's Brigade."* In the introduction to his work, Caldwell devoted a full
page to a careful explanation of the purpose of the book in a dozen or so different categories. He concluded with the hope that "it will be found a fair
account of the Confederate soldier's life, and I know that it will be strictly
true." With the perspective of a century and a third, it is hard to see where
Caldwell missed any of his targets.

The published product sported stiff paper wraps of a soft beige hue and
text printed on rather poor paper. To the eye of a modern bibliophile, the
book is a comely physical package, but that is probably the result of the pious
antiquarian reverence we bring to such things.[12] In truth, the printing was less
than exquisite; typographical errors abound. The substance of the book, however, is a bonanza of gilt-edged words and historical pearls. Writing from the
literal ashes of the war, with fresh memory undistorted by the incipient quarrels among participants, Caldwell produced one of the very best books ever
written about the Army of Northern Virginia.

The History of a Brigade is remarkable for its historical content, but there is
reason to savor its prose for its own merits as well. The subject provides drama
and pathos aplenty; Caldwell adds verve, droll humor, and wry deprecation by
turns as spice. The flavor of Reconstruction in the South Carolina of 1866,
for instance, is nicely conveyed in the last phrase of the main narrative, in
which Caldwell imagines the typical brigade veteran "enjoying as best he
might, that state which certain imaginative persons have denominated peace."

Many years after the war, Caldwell applied his pen to a very different venture when he wrote a novel called *The Stranger*, which was published by the

---

12. The price of a first edition of this classic work in the rare book market, with crisp wraps
and in generally nice used condition, is now in the vicinity of $2,000.

Neale Company of New York and Washington in 1907.[13] The publisher, not surprisingly, slathered mention of Caldwell's war history across the title page of the novel and throughout its various advertisements. The successful war book doubtless prompted Neale to handle Caldwell's fictional effort. *The Stranger* is a large book (520 pages), full of intersectional strife set in South Carolina during Reconstruction. It really is quite well done, although not much turn-of-the-century fiction will hold up to modern tastes.[14] There is in the surviving record just a hint that the novel was not popular with some of Caldwell's fellow South Carolinians, for one reason or another.

Although *The Stranger* is interesting in its own right and as an association piece, *The History of a Brigade* is what made Caldwell famous and won for him an undying name. Ten centuries from now (assuming that North Carolina does not spread across its borders and destroy civilization as we know it), mankind will be writing about the epic military history of the nineteenth century and quoting J. F. J. Caldwell in the process. The redoubtable Confederate authority Douglas Southall Freeman pronounced Caldwell's book "altogether the best history of a Brigade in Lee's Army. A wise, well-written book." The standard annotated bibliography of Civil War literature came close to the same judgment when it called Caldwell's book "the best unit history from the Palmetto State."[15]

Three reprinted versions of Caldwell reflect a continuing demand for the book. A 1951 edition published in Marietta, Georgia, and a 1974 edition (both hardcover and paperback) published in Dayton, Ohio, reproduced the original 248 pages by photographic process. The definitive reprint version appeared from Morningside Press in Dayton in 1992, completely reset. It includes all the trappings of thorough scholarship: an introduction, a useful appendix, many notes, and a fine index, all prepared by an admirable—indeed incomparable—Confederate scholar, the late Lee A. Wallace, Jr. Lee also found several unpublished photographs for inclusion in the 1992 edition, in-

---

13. For full bibliographical details and a plot outline, see Robert K. Krick, *Neale Books: An Annotated Bibliography* (Dayton, Ohio: Press of Morningside Bookshop, 1977), 5–26.

14. The author of this essay, who suffers from bibliomania as acute as any on record, has seen *The Stranger* for sale only three times in more than three decades of close attention to such things—never with a dust jacket and always in rather poor condition. That scarcity likely results more from the obscurity of quotidian elderly fiction than outright rarity.

15. Douglas Southall Freeman, *Lee's Lieutenants*, 3 vols. (New York: Charles Scribner's Sons, 1942–44) 3:821; Allan Nevins et al., eds., *Civil War Books: A Critical Bibliography*, 2 vols. (Baton Rouge: Louisiana State University Press, 1967, 1969), 1:66.

cluding two of Caldwell. The reprint adorned with Wallace's rich new material certainly will remain the standard version indefinitely.[16]

GENERAL NAT HARRIS'S DIARY: THE RAREST ARMY OF
NORTHERN VIRGINIA BOOK

General Nathaniel Harrison Harris rose through the ranks of the 19th Mississippi to command a sturdy brigade of veterans in Lee's army and led it on two memorably desperate days—but he is best known for the imprint of his pen rather than that of his sword.[17] Harris's diary, published in Duncansby, Mississippi, the year after his death, may be the rarest book by a member of the Army of Northern Virginia. It unquestionably is the rarest written by a Confederate general.

Nat Harris was born in Natchez on August 22, 1834, and graduated with a law degree from the University of Louisiana (now Tulane).[18] He set up practice in Vicksburg, living in the household of his elder brother James, also an attorney. By 1860 the novice lawyer had accumulated very little wealth: the census showed Nat's net worth as $1,600 in personal estate (most of that in the form of one twenty-four-year-old female slave) and no real estate at all.[19] Counselor Harris raised a volunteer company called the Warren Rifles, which he led into state service on May 8, 1861, as its captain. Three weeks later the company mustered into Confederate service, where it soon became Company C of the 19th Mississippi Infantry.

Captain Harris and his Vicksburg volunteers marched toward the First Manassas battlefield as part of Kirby Smith's Brigade, but a railroad accident

16. I have Lee Wallace's retained copy of a 1953 letter to a friend, touting the then-new Marietta reprint as one of the finest Confederate books. The notable Caldwell event since 1992 has been the publication of three short articles that he wrote. South Carolina Division, United Daughters of the Confederacy, *Recollections and Reminiscences, 1861–1865*, 10 vols. (Columbia: United Daughters of the Confederacy, 1990–2000), 5:81–84, 354–56, 10:523–25. The 1992 Morningside reprint is one of a tiny handful of books published by that specialty house that sport a dust jacket (a bright red one in the case of Wallace/Caldwell).

17. This sketch first appeared in *Blue & Gray Magazine* 8 (August 1991): 30–31. It is reprinted here, with a very few modifications, by permission.

18. His parents were William Harris, born in New York, and Caroline Harrison (whence his middle name), born in Mississippi. Biographical sheet executed and signed by N. H. Harris, Dreer Collection, Series 67, Box 2, Historical Society of Pennsylvania, Philadelphia.

19. 1860 Mississippi Census, City of Vicksburg, p. 985, and Mississippi Slave Schedule, Warren County, p. 31, NA.

delayed their arrival until after the fighting ended. Harris led the company at the Battle of Williamsburg the following spring in its first significant action, where he exhibited enough skill and élan to elicit public praise in the official report of Colonel L. Q. C. Lamar. The captain's performance earned him promotion to major with rank to date, fittingly, from May 5, 1862. The 19th Mississippi fought through the summer of 1862 as part of W. S. Featherston's Brigade in a small division commanded by Cadmus M. Wilcox. Harris emerged from that spell of strenuous fighting as a lieutenant colonel, to rank from November 24, 1862. On April 2, 1863, he received a commission as colonel of the 19th. Colonel Harris led his command to Chancellorsville and Gettysburg as one of four Mississippi regiments in General Carnot Posey's Brigade. When Posey went down with a mortal wound in the midst of A. P. Hill's fiasco at Bristoe Station, Nat Harris stood in line to take his place. Harris received his appointment as brigadier general on February 17, 1864, to take rank from January 20.[20]

When he accepted the mantle of brigade commander, General Harris was twenty-nine years old. Although he had had neither antebellum training nor experience in martial matters, the new general had survived three years of intense military service, including some of the severest fighting in American history. If he had any trepidation about his responsibilities, no record of it survives, nor did his performance display any signs of hesitation.[21] Just one week into his first campaign as brigadier, Nat Harris occupied center stage during savage hand-to-hand fighting at Spotsylvania's Bloody Angle on May 12, 1864, which must be reckoned among the bloodiest and most desperate days of the entire war. His Mississippians and a single brigade of South Carolinians stood for some twenty hours within a few yards of thousands of Federals as the two sides contended for a critical earthwork line in a pelting rain. The Carolinians have received more attention for their role than have Harris's men because of several fine accounts written by Carolinian survivors. General Harris was the ranking officer present, however, and his brigade deserves at least half of the credit for the epic southern stand on that dreadful day. One of the Mississippians "saw a man fall dead in the arms of Gen. Harris. This

20. Harris's dates of rank are from his official CSR in M331, NA. An obscure and important source on the brigade of which he assumed command is John J. Hood, "Reference to the Featherstone-Posey-Harris Brigade," *New Orleans Picayune*, June 8, 1902.

21. A thorough, thoughtful explanation of regimental and brigade tactics by Harris, which reveals a firm grasp, is in G. F. R. Henderson, *Stonewall Jackson and the American Civil War*, 2 vols. (London: Longmans, Green, 1898), 2:584–85.

brave and good man, in this hail of death, laid him gently on the ground, with the exclamation, 'Oh, my poor fellow!'" The toll of dead among both officers and men mounted painfully high. In 1866 Harris wrote mournfully of "the noble sons of Mississippi, who upon that deadly field, made the final and greatest offering upon the altar of duty—life itself."[22]

General Harris led his brigade with steady competence through the Confederacy's last year of life. A Pennsylvania-born private in the 16th Mississippi grumbled that Harris "got lost" frequently on marches, but a member of the 3rd Georgia observed from the neutral vantage of a bystander in early 1865 that Harris's Brigade was the "grandest body of men that I ever saw (taking the whole war through)."[23] As the southern lines around Richmond and Petersburg collapsed in April 1865, General Harris and his men contributed another famous stand to the army's lore when a few score Mississippians bravely clung to Fort Gregg in a forlorn rear-guard action that bought time for Lee. A field return dated April 8 reveals the extent of their sacrifice: the brigade had a pitiful total of 127 men for duty on that date. The table of organization called for more than 4,000.

After Appomattox the former general returned to Vicksburg for a time. He became president of a Mississippi railroad, then held a government office in South Dakota. Harris visited San Francisco in 1890 and promptly fell in love with the place.[24] He made the city his home for the rest of his life. General Harris died at the Imperial Hotel in Worcester County, England, on August 23,1900, of heart disease while on a business trip.[25]

In 1901, Nat's younger brother William, who had served on the general's staff as a lieutenant and aide-de-camp, published in Duncansby (apparently a suburb now absorbed by Jackson) a small book that survives in only a tiny handful of copies. *Movements of the Confederate Army in Virginia and the Part Taken Therein by the Nineteenth Mississippi Regiment from the Diary of Gen.*

22. Mamie Yeary, comp., *Reminiscences of the Boys in Gray* (Dallas: Smith & Lamar, [1912]), 148. The most detailed tactical examination of Harris and his brigade on May 12 at the Bloody Angle is Robert K. Krick, "An Insurmountable Barrier Between the Army and Ruin: The Confederate Experience at the Bloody Angle," in Gary W. Gallagher, ed., *The Spotsylvania Campaign* (Chapel Hill: University of North Carolina Press, 1998), 80–126.

23. Eugene Matthew Ott, Jr., "The Civil War Diary of James J. Kirkpatrick, Sixteenth Mississippi Infantry," entries for November 8, 27, 1863, M.A. thesis, Texas A&M University, 1984; C. W. Reynolds (3rd Georgia Infantry), "Comrade's Tribute to Gen. G. M. Sorrell," *Atlanta Journal*, August 17, 1901.

24. As have many others over the years, including the author of this book.

25. Copy of death certificate DA790897, in the author's possession.

Nat H. Harris is a forty-five-page volume printed in very fine type, with paper wraps, measuring 22 centimeters. It opens with a detailed roster of the commissioned officers of the 19th Mississippi, including those holding elusive staff ranks. Most of the book consists of diary entries made by the general between January 15, 1863, and April 13, 1865. The accuracy of the printed narrative is conveniently validated by a long letter that Harris wrote on August 2, 1866, to General William Mahone, who as division commander had been Harris's superior late in the war.[26] Harris obviously drew on the diary for that letter because some of its passages are nearly identical to the printed version: most deviations represent changes in the person of pronouns. The diary affords particularly lengthy coverage of Harris's famous actions at the Bloody Angle and at Fort Gregg—a predictable and gratifying circumstance.

Nat Harris's little book shows up in the holdings of just three of the thousands of libraries that participated in the modern *National Union Catalog* project. In fact, none of those three has a complete copy today; one has a fragment that ends with the introductory roster segment and the other two now report no copy in hand. A Mississippi library recently acquired the single known complete public copy, and one private collector owns another.[27] While a few additional copies must exist somewhere, they cannot be many in number. The dreadful quality of the book's stock—the first half of one surviving copy is on brittle paper as brown as a grocery bag—probably contributed to the low survival rate. Is there a rarer book from the pen of a Confederate general? None comes close.

A GREAT RARITY WITH A MODEST PRICE TAG: ALEXANDER CHEVES HASKELL

By the time he led a frenzied saber-swinging charge down the Darbytown Road on October 7, 1864, Colonel A. C. Haskell had seen Death's leer at close range on more than one occasion.[28] He had been shot and seriously hurt at Fredericksburg and again, even more gravely, at Chancellorsville. In those earlier instances he had been serving as a staff officer with the rank of captain.

26. The Harris letter to Mahone is in the William Mahone Papers, Virginia State Archives, Richmond.

27. The public copy is at Mississippi State University, Starkville.

28. *Blue & Gray Magazine* published this look at Colonel Haskell and his book in 2 (July 1985): 23–24. It is reproduced here, with a few editorial changes, by permission.

Both of those dangerous experiences paled into insignificance by comparison with the affair on October 7.

Haskell had taken the 7th South Carolina Cavalry, of which he was colonel, through a hole in the enemy position that fall day in 1864 and had gotten into a very tight spot. Two enlisted men rode at his side as Haskell hurried along a narrow, confusing, shrub-crowded lane. Immediately after turning a tight corner, the three southerners found themselves right upon a full squadron of Federal cavalry, with a general and two staff officers abreast in front. No decent options existed, so Colonel Haskell hoarsely screamed "Charge" and threw himself into the mass. He shot down two of the three officers in a frozen moment and was about to kill the third when he saw a carbine thrust over the officer's shoulder. Before Aleck Haskell's finger could finish pulling the trigger, the man with the carbine shot him squarely in the head.

One of the classics of Confederate literature exists because the Federal carbine ball was not quite as deadly as it appeared, though it did an ample dose of harm. The ball struck Haskell's left eye and came out behind his left ear. The victim later narrated his stunned reactions: "I felt the sensation of death. . . . Time, space, all lost its limit or measure. . . . Just as the smoke was beginning to clear from the carbine . . . I saw, with my right eye, my right hand up in the air with the pistol in it pointed at this General. Then the silence was broken, and as the hand sank towards the horse's neck, the cry burst out, 'We have killed the General!' As I fell heavily to the ground, I said to myself, with a sort of a grim mental smile, 'Only a Colonel, Gentlemen, only a Colonel!'"

Alexander Cheves Haskell was born in Abbeville District, South Carolina, on September 22, 1839. Aleck was one of a round dozen children, six of whom were boys who served the Confederacy well and at high cost to themselves. The young man's life was consumed by war as though it had been scheduled that way, since South Carolina seceded within weeks after he had graduated from South Carolina College. Aleck joined almost at once with a company that became Company D, 1st South Carolina Infantry. The regiment was commanded by Maxcy Gregg, a stalwart Confederate with whom Haskell's destiny would be inextricably intertwined.

Not many days after his enlistment, Haskell became adjutant of the regiment. When Gregg won promotion to the rank of brigadier general, Aleck went with him under a commission as lieutenant and aide-de-camp. The commission bore precisely the same date as Gregg's promotion—December 14, 1861. Gregg had exactly one year, to the day, to live. During that time Haskell served him well and won promotion to the rank of captain. After his general's death Haskell stayed on staff duty with Gregg's successor in command of the brigade, Samuel McGowan, and with fellow South Carolinian Abner Perrin.

On October 31, 1863, Perrin wrote a glowing recommendation of Haskell for promotion into a line command. The manuscript survives as a summation of Haskell's qualities. The young officer was distinguished for "gallantry and skill" in every battle, wrote Perrin, with particular emphasis on Fredericksburg and Chancellorsville. At the first-mentioned battle he was "mainly instrumental" in stabilizing the brigade after Gregg's mortal wounding. Perrin cited Gregg's dying request that Haskell should be promoted. In conclusion, the general declared that Aleck should have a cavalry command if possible: "As the commander of a Regiment of Cavalry he would have no superior." Four days later R. E. Lee added a handwritten endorsement in which he echoed Perrin's assessment but grumbled that he would not countenance losing Haskell from the Army of Northern Virginia and wanted any arrangement to include that condition. Before the Perrin note had reached Richmond (it was addressed to General Samuel Cooper), J. E. B. Stuart and Wade Hampton also had added fulsome tributes. A few months later General Cadmus M. Wilcox, a veteran division commander, recommended Haskell for promotion to brigadier general.[29]

A few months later, Haskell was indeed a line commander of cavalry, as lieutenant colonel of the 7th South Carolina Cavalry, to rank from April 1864; he eventually replaced William P. Shingler as colonel of the regiment, in June. Then came the painful October day on Darbytown Road. Incredibly, by January 1865, Aleck had recovered enough from his ghastly wound to resume command of his cavalry. He reported home: "My wound is doing well and my health is good. My appetite is outrageous and my rations small." When Haskell surrendered a few weeks later as part of the faithful remnant at Appomattox, he was a very old and somewhat battered twenty-four years of age.

Haskell had written to his family regularly and extensively all through the conflict. After the war he put down on paper his recollections of his life, with particular emphasis on his war experiences, as might be expected. Extracts from both sources were blended into a fine book by the third of Haskell's eleven children, Louise Porter Haskell Daly (1872–1947). *Alexander Cheves*

29. Haskell's official CSR in M267 and M331, NA. The Wilcox letter, dated May 29, 1864, is in the CSR of Thomas M. Logan, M331, NA.

Haskell: The Portrait of a Man was privately printed at the Plimpton Press in Norwood, Massachusetts, in 1934. It was bound into a comely cloth of light blue-gray, which has had a tendency to fade and weather a bit on the spine, but not flagrantly. All copies of the book seem to have been inscribed by Louise Daly, in some instances with a message mentioning the Christmas of 1934. The private printing ran to either 100 or 125 copies, the exact number not being known with certainty.[30]

The book promptly got favorable attention in the best Confederate circles. In his landmark bibliographical essay, *The South to Posterity* (New York, 1939), published just five years after *Haskell*, Douglas Southall Freeman was nothing short of effusive in his comments. He called *Haskell* "among the dozen most charming books of Confederate history" and rued the fact that its small printing and private circulation would keep it from wide availability. Freeman's ardent interest was made apparent by the fact that he devoted more space to the book than any other and reproduced a passage many times longer than any other quote in *The South to Posterity*.[31]

The merits of the Haskell book rise from circumstances typical of many others that we consider Confederate classics: he had wide and interesting battle experience; he was in a position to see things many others could not see; he was an intelligent and articulate individual; and the basis for much of the book is contemporary material, unclouded by the fog of time. Battle descriptions are of extraordinary vividness and even savagery, including not a little of the mounted swordplay which revisionists would have us believe is pure fantasy.

In marked contrast are the sensitive and pathetic letters Aleck wrote when his life was devastated by the death of his wife in 1862. He had courted Rebecca Singleton (1839–62, known as "Decca") very briefly before marrying her on September 10, 1861. She bore a daughter on June 20, 1862, and died six days later. Aleck's long, soul-wrenching letter home with that news was what Freeman quoted extensively in *The South to Posterity*. For the rest of the war, Haskell maintained a resigned tone in his correspondence, typified by his unpublished letter of April 2, 1863: "The sword may fall heavily again but its keenest edge has gone." Mrs. Daly's book is laced not only with the death of

30. Both of those numbers have been asserted as the size of the print run in catalogs and have seeped into bibliographic lore. Correspondence with Mrs. Daly's descendants yielded no proof on the matter; they had no idea.

31. Freeman mentions Haskell on pages 6–11, 17, and 204.

her father's first wife but with the effect of the whole business on his second wife, in a fashion that to modern tastes verges on the mordant. The second Mrs. Haskell told her children (there were ten) "that Father never recovered from the wound of Decca's death." One is reminded of T. J. Jackson's anxiety to meet Elinor Junkin Jackson (1825–54) in heaven, expressed in one of the last letters he wrote before going into the battle that made Mary Anna Morrison Jackson (1831–1915) the nation's most visible widow for more than fifty years.

Military matters, of course, are what make Haskell of special interest. It is the primary source—virtually the only source—for substantial information about Maxcy Gregg. One of the most memorable passages covers an 1861 episode that involved Gregg with Robert Toombs in one of the Georgian's unbalanced forays. Its denouement found Haskell in the presence of Jefferson Davis while the president threw a tantrum as he sided with Toombs against Gregg. At the other end of the war, the book shows Haskell in strong support of arming slaves to fight Yankees, remarking that "in this [I] think that I recognise the principal element of our success." The four years between those bookends were full of close-up war as infantryman, staff officer, and cavalry leader.

Although there are precious few copies of *Haskell* in existence, those that come on the market command a modest—even relatively paltry—price. One of the leading dealers in the field had asked $60, then $120, then $250 for copies between 1975 and 1985. Today he suggests $500 as the reasonable retail. Even after doubling the price at each renewed offering, the level remains a bare fraction (about one-tenth) of that asked for parallel books. Consider the case of the renowned Eppa Hunton book. Hunton's *Autobiography* appeared in 1933, one year before *Haskell*; it was privately printed, just as was *Haskell*; it was limited to one hundred copies, as was *Haskell*. Although the two books are virtually twins in antiquity, scarcity, and private circulation, Hunton commands vast prices, limited only by the venality of dealers and the lust of collectors, and both of those commodities are virtually inexhaustible. Eppa Hunton fetches $5,000; *Haskell* seems to be worth $500. There's no good reason for the anomaly, and no bad reason comes readily to mind either.[32]

32. Broadfoot Publishing Company of Wilmington, North Carolina, issued an excellent new edition of *Haskell* in 1989, with binding closely matching the original. It features a fine introduction by Lee A. Wallace, Jr., and—even more important—a thorough new index.

Aleck Haskell married in 1870 the sister of General E. P. Alexander, Alice Van Yeveren Alexander, thus uniting two of the most literate of Confederate families.[33] At the time, the young-old soldier was in the midst of the movement that redeemed South Carolina from the vile clutches of Yankee Reconstruction. He died in Columbia forty-five years and four days after he had surrendered at Appomattox. The book his daughter assembled in tribute to Haskell, by which we know and judge him, is a real treasure.

BOOK ON LEE LACKS PERSPECTIVE, RESEARCH

The tendentiously anti-Lee book *Lee Considered* appeared in 1991 from the University of North Carolina Press.[34] It was written by an Indiana lawyer, Alan T. Nolan.

This book establishes after ponderous effort what might have been readily stipulated: that R. E. Lee, unreconstructed and unrevised, could not function comfortably as the soulmate of a midwestern lawyer of 1991 vintage. Neither could Abraham Lincoln or even the notorious Federal hero Benjamin F. "Beast" Butler. The most convenient equipment for a bootless revisionist is a total lack of perspective of historical time and sense. Much of Nolan's premise is supportable only on those terms.

The author posits in one chapter that Lee's frequent comments about the impropriety of slavery and his pious hopes that God's plan for human progress would result in its abolition were not nearly aggressive enough to earn him modern respect. That premise is inarguable but well-nigh irrelevant to historical inquiry.

In another chapter, Nolan describes Lee's commitment to behaving with personal honor as "self-serving," "simply rhetorical," and "an incantation." Lee's reaction to the upheavals of the secession crisis revealed an "unusual gift for self-justification" and "an unusually high tolerance for ambiguous loyalty."

---

33. Alexander's writings are among the very top rank of Confederate literature. Some of them are cited elsewhere in this book. A. C. Haskell's brother John wrote a charming memoir of artillery service in the Army of Northern Virginia, but it is late and rambling and not remotely as important as Aleck's book. Gilbert E. Govan and James W. Livingood, eds., *The Haskell Memoirs: John Cheves Haskell* (New York: G. P. Putnam's Sons, 1960).

34. This review first appeared in the Fredericksburg *Free Lance-Star*, July 20, 1991, and is reprinted here—with an introductory paragraph, a few minor emendations, and a new concluding paragraph to update the book's history—by permission of the congenial Josiah P. Rowe III, owner and publisher of the newspaper.

Nolan is particularly chagrined that historians have naively accepted Lee's own statements as honest declarations of his sentiments and intentions.

In a chapter by far the longest in the book, and probably the best and most important (even though stridently inaccurate in this reviewer's opinion), Nolan analyzes Lee's generalship in a warwide context and—predictably—concludes that his aggressive style lost the war.

Although "Lee's campaign and battle strategy and . . . tactical performance were largely . . . brilliant," Nolan's *own* incantation, by now oft-repeated, insists that Lee should have hunkered down to await foolish Federal attacks. That desirable result, of course, required a fabulously pliant enemy—who, in fact, almost certainly would refuse to cooperate: Ambrose E. Burnside had only one opportunity to show his ineptitude at the head of the northern army in Virginia. The need for Lee to use initiative in attempts to control strategic arrangements within the theater seems patently apparent, albeit not to Nolan.

During a seventeen-month period that included Gettysburg, for instance, Lee fought precisely two substantial battles. Fewer than that in like time would be difficult to imagine; to fight them with an attempt at choice of site and ground seems wholly reasonable strategically, results and particulars aside.

Chapter 5 insists that Lee actually did *not* like Yankees and was churlish enough to complain about their "pillaging," "robbing," and "disregard of civilized warfare and the dictates of humanity." Since Nolan is able to document Lee's grief "over the desolation of the country and the distress of innocent women and children," the general's supporters will have little choice but to acknowledge that egregious character defect.

Lee should have surrendered sometime in mid-1864, Nolan insists, had not his pride and personal considerations prodded him foolishly to squander lives. Nolan's favorite source, E. P. Alexander (which befits the oracular status of that fine memoir, especially given Nolan's avowed avoidance of original research), appears at length as a witness to the fact that the cause became irretrievable sometime during the siege of Richmond and Petersburg. Alexander's further vivid testimony about the army's attitude toward fighting out the war through 1864 and into 1865 ("the only proper & dignified & worthy end"), Nolan of course fails to adduce. Alexander actually was eager to extend the war by guerrilla fighting after Appomattox, but by then he had long since veered from Nolan's preferred course and therefore had been exorcised from the witness stand.

One of the most basic premises of historical discourse is the requirement to imagine events for those who lived them, without unfair employment of hindsight. While history of course is written in retrospect, its principals lived the events without knowing the end from the beginning. We cannot ever entirely understand the sensation of knowing only the beginning acts of dramas now long over—but we must try. Nolan is not remotely interested in that effort.

Lee's heartfelt tribute to the "most gallant" defenders of Fort Gregg early in 1865 actually reveals his brutal bloodlust, we are told, since Lee had long before ignored Nolan's optimal surrender point. Nolan then offers one line from a Michigan soldier asserting that joy swept the rebel army when Lee surrendered, setting at naught the tens of thousands of words from primary, contemporary accounts that had deluded us into believing the myth of Confederate desolation at Appomattox.

The silver lining is that the exuberant new prisoners at long last win Nolan's approbation, after his long and steady rejection of their wartime testimony and bona fides: they had been viewed as lying incessantly, massively, and uniformly, until at last one source suggested that they agreed with Nolan's premises. A more vivid example of selective use of evidence than Nolan's performance with the Appomattox story would be hard to find anywhere in historical literature, although there are other lively competitors for that dubious prize elsewhere in *Lee Considered*.

After the war Lee assumed a pose far more conciliatory than that of most former Confederate heroes, and he contributed thereby to early progress on the essential healing process. By not embracing Radical Reconstruction, however, and by defending his cause and his section, Lee earned another dose of Nolan's disdain. The "tradition of the conciliatory postwar Lee does not hang together," Nolan declares. The recidivist Lee even called the Joint Congressional Committee on Reconstruction, a starkly Jacobin group, "the most bitter and implacable foes of the South." What are we to do with so outrageous and confused a fellow as this, actually believing that the committee was hostile to the South? Melt all of his bronzes, at the very least.

Federal general John M. Schofield wrote to U. S. Grant in horror in 1868 about the desolation of Virginia by radicals: "They could only hope to obtain office by disqualifying everybody in the state capable of discharging official duties, and all else to them was of comparatively slight importance." In the same vein, Nolan (who would, of course, find the conciliatory Schofield fatally flawed) makes his way through his analysis of R. E. Lee by the convenient device of rejecting most southerners of temperate mien as dishonest, calculating purveyors of the Lost Cause and therefore unworthy of belief. Having disqualified everyone sympathetic to the South, all else falls cozily into place.

Under this self-fulfilling evidentiary system, when Lee is reported as dealing with a black man in his customary dignified fashion, the tale must be a fabrication for the irrefragable reason that Nolan *knows* that Lee was "personally hostile to blacks."

Nolan did no original research and openly acknowledges that circumstance. This reviewer's initial horror that anyone should attempt so arrant a revisionist commentary without deigning to do research soon dissolved into indifference. New sources would only have supplied further opportunities for disdainful rejection of the new evidence as readily as the old.

Nolan's book sold well, has gone through several printings by this writing early in 2000, and unquestionably will remain popular in the current climate. It wonderfully suits the Zeitgeist by appealing to the sempiternal yearning to smash idols, which inevitably afflicts a noisy segment of the race. The itch to fling dead cats into sanctuaries usually does more good than harm. In this instance, it also affords a limitless appeal in a smug way to the political-correctness wowsers. Fortunately for the historical record, Lee himself is readily accessible to anyone who genuinely cares to see him. Hundreds of thousands of words from his pen—official, semiofficial, and unofficial—can be found without much effort. They reveal the original Lee for each individual to review for himself, without recourse to historians of the Nolan stripe—or of the Krick antinomian heresy either.

A Dreadful Longstreet Book

James Longstreet looms large in the annals of the Army of Northern Virginia, but his development and accomplishments remain unclear because the general never has been subjected to the scrutiny of a carefully thorough biography based on the rich available manuscript sources.[35] W. G. Piston's book *Lee's Tarnished Lieutenant* is not a biography but rather an explication of the general's postwar scourging by his former comrades in arms and of the resultant diminution of Longstreet's rightful place in the Confederate pantheon. Piston achieves that stated aim to some degree by avoiding an overstatement of his subject's virtues.

In the process, however, the author indulges in an orgy of conspiracy-bash-

35. This review of W. G. Piston, *Lee's Tarnished Lieutenant: James Longstreet and His Place in Southern History* (Athens: University of Georgia Press, 1987), appeared in *Blue & Gray Magazine* 5 (May 1988): 26. It is reprinted here, with a few slight revisions, by permission.

ing frenzied enough to suggest that the work might aptly have been titled
Marble Man Redux, or be used as screenplay for a feverish Oliver Stone mo-
tion picture. The fairness displayed toward Longstreet, and overextended
amusingly to those pathetic military caricatures Robert Toombs and Louis
Wigfall (pp. 21, 29, 65), exhausts the author's supply. The fabulous conspiracy
he perceives in favor of Lee—fueled by self-serving motives—prompts Piston
to the extravagant conclusion that Douglas Southall Freeman willfully depre-
cated even Stonewall Jackson in order to complete the artificial apotheosis of
Lee! In *R. E. Lee*, Freeman "took pains . . . to reduce the status of Stonewall
Jackson" (p. 175), and in *Lee's Lieutenants* he expended far too much space on
Jackson, "little . . . complimentary" (p. 177). Few veterans of those seven volumes will be anything less than astonished to learn that they somehow missed
the anti-Jackson message and will conclude that someone who will believe
that will believe anything.

The biographical summary of Longstreet's career does not share the selective virtues of Piston's postwar analysis. The author's unfamiliarity with military details yields an astonishing flood of objective errors, these few among a
great many: Sandie Pendleton identified as his own first cousin (p. 87); allu-
sion to a nonexistent "clerical element" on Lee's staff (p. 35); the wrong given
name for McDowell (p. 12); at least three mistakes in identifying institutions
(pp. xiii–xiv); and Winchester captured on the wrong day (p. 46). Discussion
of the numerous more substantive errors of fact (interpretations aside) would
require more space than this forum offers. The biographical sketch concen-
trates much of its limited scope on Gettysburg. That leaves no room for examination of Longstreet's independent operations on which, finally released from
the shadow of what he perceived as Lee's military deficiencies, he had opportunity to blossom. The siege of Knoxville, during which a free-at-last Longstreet stumbled into the path of that military juggernaut, Ambrose Burnside,
occupies just six lines.[36]

Piston evaluates the morale of the army in early 1864 in the context of
"Lee's bloodbaths which had resulted in mass desertions." He proffers no support for that fanfaronade for the good reason that there is none. Readers who
have somehow divined that kind of consensus in their exposure to war-dated
Confederate attitudes toward Lee, despite the massive evidence to the contrary, will like this book. Others won't. Meanwhile, someone needs to write a
Longstreet biography.

---

36. A detailed review of Longstreet's operations around Knoxville and of his incredible behavior in their aftermath is found in Chapter 4 of this book.

10

Confederate Soldier Records:
Finding Them and Using Them

The southern men and boys who answered war's klaxon in 1861 and their neighbors and kinfolk who entered service later in the war under various promptings marshaled into units and armies that are among the most famous in all of recorded military history. Until recently, however, no comprehensive listing of the Confederacy's fighting men had ever been published. During the war, some states made laudable but ill-focused attempts to prepare rosters of their sons in Confederate service. Starting as early as 1862 and running down to the present day, regimental histories have included lists of soldiers. Some such rosters are thorough; most are defective. Virginia appointed in the 1890s a commissioner of Confederate records and directed that he prepare a thorough roster of all Virginia organizations. The Virginia effort yielded much of value but came nowhere remotely near a definitive result. In fact, the project failed completely with some units—leaving nothing but absolutely blank pages for entire companies.[1]

Most of this chapter appeared as an introduction and finding aid in Janet B. Hewett, ed., *The Roster of Confederate Soldiers, 1861–1865*, 16 vols. (Wilmington, N.C.: Broadfoot, 1995–96). The version printed here is substantially revised, with notes added. It is used by permission of Thomas W. Broadfoot, the leading Civil War book dealer in the land. Tom's surname has achieved the dignity of an adjective in the bibliophilic world: the "Broadfoot price" is what a rare book ought to cost, without either cheating the dealer or bludgeoning the customer.

1. The Virginia commissioner was Virginius Bidgood, and the papers at the Library of Virginia, Richmond, that resulted from the efforts of the commissioner's office still are referred to familiarly by researchers as the "Bidgood Papers." An interesting attempt at regional cooperation to stimulate roster projects is reported in *Proceedings and Memorial of a Conference of Confederate Roster Commissioners* (Montgomery: Alabama Printing Co., 1903). For an intelligent discussion of

As soon as the Civil War ended, the dead Confederacy's official records (often stamped with the "Rebel Archives" rubric familiar to historians and collectors) belonged to the victorious Federal government. Only those official records contain the information necessary to reconstruct an accurate list of a unit's soldiery—or of the entire Confederate nation at arms.[2]

Compilation of individual service records from the vast array of "Rebel Archives" manuscripts did not begin until a half-century after the war's end. An act of Congress passed in 1903 directed that the War Department amass a complete roster of Civil War soldiers of both sides and then have it printed. The act appropriated the lordly sum of $50,000 to achieve that laudable goal. Nine years later the department promulgated an order establishing a mechanism under which rudimentary public inquiries could gain access to the developing project. (It stopped short, however, of fulfilling the casual demand in that year by a Floridian congressman for the complete record of every soldier from his state.)[3]

As late as 1917 the War Department remained sanguine about printing the lists "in the not distant future," as a sort of appendix to the published *Official Records* set. That never happened, of course. It remained for Tom Broadfoot to get the job done as a private venture more than three-quarters of a century later. The result is a set of books that has literally changed the life of every serious student of the American Civil War. "The book that changed my life" has the ring of a proselytizing tract that perfectly suits a pietistic reader: in this case, the epiphany comes from a listing, tedious to the noncognoscenti, of more than 1,200,000 names with units appended.[4]

Brigadier General Fred C. Ainsworth superintended the start of the service records project as head of the War Department's Record and Pension Office.

Virginia records, which also will be useful as background for anyone deeply interested in Confederate records, see Meriwether Stuart, "The Record of Virginia Forces: A Study in the Compilation of Civil War Records," *Virginia Magazine of History and Biography* 68 (January 1960): 3–59.

2. Much of the information in the opening section of this chapter, that portion dealing with the history of National Archives manuscripts, comes from the matchless oracle on Civil War records there, Michael P. Musick. No person has been more important to Civil War research in primary official documents during the past thirty years than the nonpareil Professor Musick.

3. Congressman Frank Clark to the Adjutant General, January 4, 1917, and reply dated two days later, Document File—Correspondence, 1890–1917, AG 915872, Record Group 94, NA. At that same point there is filed a detailed and highly useful four-page typescript, dated February 1916: "Report relative to the printing of the 'Roster of the Officers and Enlisted Men of the Union and Confederate Armies.'"

4. That work is the sixteen-volume set cited in the first, unnumbered note above.

The essential substance of most soldiers' records, it quickly became apparent, could not be original documents. Most surviving manuscripts covered more than one man—often an entire company of men. Ainsworth's swarm of helpers therefore expended massive effort in extracting individuals' data onto preprinted slips.[5]

During the 1890s, Fred Ainsworth had resisted the notion that individual service records (as opposed to the broadly historical material then appearing in the *Official Records*) should be generally accessible. He cited six reasons good enough to sink the project for a decade: potential for damage to fragile manuscripts at the hands of researchers; danger of loss of records the same way; the government would forfeit an edge in detecting bogus pensions and other claims—in fact would give away material useful to frauds; confidential material might embarrass living individuals; clerical staff could not deal with the traffic; and there simply was no room to accommodate people wanting to look at records. By 1903, however, Ainsworth was ready and willing to assume the daunting task despite the obstacles in its path.

The impetus for arranging service records into the now familiar official Compiled Service Records sprang far more from pragmatism than from scholarly or preservationist impulses. Pensions by this time had become a veritable cottage industry—often on bogus claims of service, as Bill Marvel's research has demonstrated.[6] The Federal government understandably wanted a reliable set of records against which to check pension applications. The various southern states (Confederates of course got no Yankee pensions) obviously shared that need for the support of their own local pension programs.

General Ainsworth's herculean challenge was compounded by frightfully inadequate space and facilities. His allotted fifty-five thousand square feet could not hold the bulk, and he had to store the overflow across town at rundown (if famous) Ford's Theater. Ainsworth worried about floors collapsing under the weight of paper. Stacked documents climbed toward ceilings, stretching out of ready reach and blocking out light. "Many of the clerks," the general wrote in alarm, "are compelled to do their work standing in narrow aisles . . . because, in order to make room . . . it has been necessary to do away with the desks at which the clerks formerly sat."[7]

5. An invaluable work on Ainsworth, with much of interest concerning the service records and other Civil War manuscripts, is Mabel E. Deutrich, *Struggle for Supremacy: The Career of General Fred C. Ainsworth* (Washington, D.C.: Public Affairs Press, [1962]).

6. William Marvel, "The Great Impostors," *Blue & Gray Magazine* 8 (February 1991): 32–33, shows beyond doubt that all of the last ten surviving "veterans" were the impostors of his title.

7. Deutrich, *Struggle for Supremacy*, 70.

The cramped and hampered transcribers did a really splendid job. Comparison and cross-checking refined the finished product to an admirable level of excellence. It is impossible to imagine achieving a labor-intensive project of this bulk in today's world at all, to say nothing of accomplishing it with such fine-honed quality. Fred Ainsworth and his merry band deserve our gratitude.

The published Broadfoot index to Confederate soldiers is based on one of the results of Ainsworth's labors. It reproduces intact, with additions to correct errors, the National Archives's consolidated index of Confederate soldiers. That index consists of a vast body of slips arranged in alphabetical order. Each soldier who has a surviving record of any sort—with state troops, central government units, or in staff functions—has at least one slip. It contains his name and unit and rank. Many slips also include printed matter about the units, some of which passed through various incarnations.

Alphabetization conforms to a system at variance with what most of us are accustomed to using. Initials are disregarded as such and are alphabetized as though they spelled a name. J. J. Aaron is situated before John Aaron but after Jefferson M. Aaron. So too is Joseph Aaron after J. J. yet before J. P. Aaron. Most of us would consider a simple first initial as falling before any full first name that begins with that letter, for instance: J.; J. J.; J. P.; J. W., James H., Jefferson M., John P., Joseph A. The National Archives system instead arranges the same set of names by disregarding periods for initials and arranging the letters given strictly in alphabetical order, as follows: J., James Y., Jefferson M., J. J., John P., Joseph A., J. P., J. W. Anyone who sallies forth into Confederate records at the National Archives must bear that anomaly firmly in mind.

Modern indexers, researchers, and publishers are pretty much obliged to stick with that peculiar alphabetization configuration for reasons simple and probably obvious: it is essential that any index steer users smoothly to the main body of information being indexed. Since the service records themselves use that unusual system (and it is inconceivable that they ever will be redone), the index must do likewise. In the same vein, indexers must resist the urge to expand or correct any entries. Supplying more complete names sometimes would be easy. Such helpful editorial work has dramatically improved many documents upon publication. In indexing service records, however, such additional information is inappropriate. Correcting misspelled names would leave corresponding service records unknown and inaccessible, especially given the Archives's unusual notions of alphabetization.

A few men in the National Archives indexes show no company next to their names. In some instances that is because the individual belonged to no company, being part of the headquarters establishment of a larger unit (usually a regiment). The original cards for such men put in the company blank the notation "F & S"—for "Field and Staff." The ranks of colonels and adjutants and quartermasters convey the fact that they belonged to a regiment at large, not to a company.

Ranks of Confederates as revealed in the index to service records—both the printed Broadfoot edition and the microfilmed version at the National Archives—hold the potential for confusion. Each original slip reports two ranks: rank at entry into service and rank at the end of service. Typically, though by no means inevitably, the first rank is lower than, or the same as, the last rank. The index slips offer no space, of course, for a full survey of ranks at various stages of the war; the service record itself is the place to look for those details. Some men entered as privates, rose to commissioned ranks of various levels, and wound up as privates again at the end. The index slip carries only the two outer benchmarks. Neither, of course, is necessarily the highest rank ever attained by the soldier, but in most cases it will report that pinnacle accurately.[8]

Original compilers who recognized variant names on slips as belonging to the same individual, for service in the same unit, made an intelligent estimate (almost invariably accurately, upon further review today) of the right name and consolidated the slips into a single record. To be helpful, they generally prepared separate slips for the variants with the legend "Original Filed Under ———." Many "Original Filed Under" cross-reference slips in Confederate Compiled Service Records reflect nothing more than simple mistranscriptions by clerks, whether in the 1860s or in the Ainsworth era.

Both the microfilmed and published indexes to Confederate service records necessarily include many abbreviations. Most were chosen with care, make sense, and have stood the test of time. They do, however, require some familiarization before efficient and accurate use of the records can be assured.

The correct name for some Confederate soldiers may not turn up in the indexes, at least not at the first attempt. The astonishing indifference to spelling in the mid-nineteenth century, even of surnames, sometimes leaves modern searchers bewildered. Anyone who has tangled with Virginia's Robersons, Robinsons, and Robertsons will recognize the ambivalence with which Con-

---

8. The published Broadfoot index goes another step toward simplicity, printing only the highest of the two ranks, initial and final, shown on the National Archives filmed index. The printed index further simplifies listings by omitting rank for private soldiers—by a huge margin the most common subspecies, of course—leaving that rank implicit unless otherwise specified.

federates rendered their own family names. (A river bearing that name on the Madison-Culpeper County line appears variously, almost randomly, spelled.) The lieutenant colonel of the 12th Virginia Infantry repeatedly signed himself J. Richard Lewellen (three "l's" and three "e's") on Confederate documents but is buried under a tombstone spelled Llewellyn (four "l's", two "e's") and surrounded by Llewellyn family members.

The nonchalant Confederate approach to military record keeping compounds the problem of finding service documents. Even carefully compiled southern records suffered devastating losses, especially by destruction late in the war. A few men coming of military age after the summer of 1864, for instance, served without leaving any paper residue for our enlightenment.

Despite those caveats, the Confederate Compiled Service Records index is an invaluable research tool, wonderfully accurate and essentially complete. The microfilmed index at the National Archives and the more readily available published version in sixteen volumes are a *vade mecum* for anyone serious about Confederate history—or interested in nineteenth-century southern history and genealogy. The published version has indeed become for many students of the war that evangelical-sounding epiphany: the books that changed their lives.

One fascinating result of the published index is the chance to be able to count the precise number of service records for each Confederate state. Years of gasconade about the number of soldiers contributed to Confederate service by the various states (much of it generated by North Carolinians sensitive to their state's record) now can be put to rest. The computerized count of official service records shows conclusively that Virginia put more soldiers into the Confederate army than any other state, and by a wide margin; North Carolina stands only fourth.

Virginia	214,476
Georgia	181,033
Tennessee	141,728
North Carolina	137,527
Mississippi	127,069
Texas	115,603
South Carolina	102,245
Louisiana	93,120
Missouri	53,007
Kentucky	37,385
Florida	23,380
Maryland	4,433

That total of 1,231,006 Confederate soldiers includes a great many men who served in more than one unit and therefore have more than one service record. It also excludes the men in the general and staff files and the Confederates in units with central government (and thus no state) identities.[9] There is, of course, no reason whatsoever to believe that either of those factors would markedly (or even marginally) change the proportions between states.

Identifying Confederate Soldiers and Finding Their Traces

Identifying Confederate soldiers and following them to their personal records, formal and informal, is a task that a thoughtful researcher can accomplish successfully in almost every instance. The rest of this chapter offers suggestions on sources that identify Confederates and on other sources that provide material about their military service and personal lives. The chapter is arranged in a manner designed to help anyone looking for a Confederate soldier, whether he appears in the central indexes or not.

Indexes to the Compiled Service Records

The initial step for any work on a Confederate is to identify his unit or units. No other step is nearly so important. A soldier's official records will be filed with those of his unit, and his war experiences will be tied up with that unit. The cumulative index to the official compiled military service records issued by Broadfoot Publishing in 1995–96 (cited in the first, unnumbered note for this chapter) will solve most researchers' questions about soldiers' units. A sizable minority, however, still will find useful the state-by-state indexes on microfilm from the National Archives and other sources.[10] The most frequent instance suggesting use of an index for a single state will be when stymied by the bulk of the printed cumulative index for a common name. The main index, for instance, includes some twenty-two thousand men named Smith.

9. Computerized tabulations by the Broadfoot Company based on the completed index, in Joyce [Lawrence] to Tom [Broadfoot], April 24, 1997, copy in the author's possession.

10. The Broadfoot Publishing Company also is issuing printed Confederate indexes by state. As of March 2000, Alabama, Georgia, North Carolina, South Carolina, Texas, and Virginia were in print. The Mississippi index is pending. Broadfoot at that time had no plans to publish individual volumes on the other Confederate states. The state sets include a statewide alphabetical listing and then a listing of names arranged by unit.

A search for a Smith known to be from a specific state would therefore go much more smoothly in the far narrower universe of that state's index.

The microfilmed National Archives indexes for each Confederate state include those who served in a unit from that state. Many Marylanders, for instance, served in Virginia regiments. Those fellows will be indexed under Virginia, not Maryland. Publication numbers follow for the various microfilm indexes issued by the National Archives. The number of rolls of film for each index gives some indication of the size of the task involved. That number is shown in parentheses after the publication number.[11]

Alabama Troops	M374	(49)
Arizona Troops	M375	(1)
Arkansas Troops	M376	(26)
Florida Troops	M225	(9)
Georgia Troops	M226	(67)
Kentucky Troops	M377	(14)
Louisiana Troops	M378	(31)
Maryland Troops	M379	(2)
Mississippi Troops	M232	(45)
Missouri Troops	M380	(16)
North Carolina Troops	M230	(43)
South Carolina Troops	M381	(35)
Tennessee Troops	M231	(48)
Texas Troops	M227	(41)
Virginia Troops	M382	(62)
Confederate Organizations and General and Staff Officers	M818	(26)

M818 deserves an explanatory word. The service records for general officers and staff officers are indexed there, as the title of the collection makes obvious. Also in that place are all of the organizations that were Confederate in origin but not identified with a particular state. That includes some familiar large units such as the 7th Confederate Cavalry Regiment and the 1st Confederate Engineer Regiment. It also includes smaller units raised by the central government that obviously belong in this setting such as the signal corps

11. An invaluable source for further information about the records described in this section is *Military Service Records: A Select Catalog of National Archives Microfilm Publications* (Washington, D.C.: National Archives Trust Fund Board, 1985). This large (330 pages) and detailed guide is available (for $12 in 1999) at the National Archives.

companies and the foreign battalions. Less obvious and often confusing is the unfortunate tendency to consider field artillery battalions as Confederate units, obscuring the clear state identity of the individual batteries that made up those battalions. When the battalion system was perfected in the winter of 1862–63, some proud veteran batteries of Virginia and South Carolina and Mississippi troops, for instance, were brought together in a single battalion, in what soon proved to be a decidedly advantageous tactical grouping. The artillery battalion was not a Virginia unit, of course, nor Carolinian, nor Mississippian. As a result, some records of the men in the multistate battalions wound up filed under the Confederate miscellany.[12] That unhappy anomaly drives historians and researchers to distraction. Caveat emptor.

Manuscript Records of Confederate Soldiers at the National Archives

Almost all surviving official records are at the National Archives and were used to create official Compiled Service Records for individual soldiers. The compilation of the service records was a task of heroic proportions, and it was done with a patience and thoroughness that deserve our respect. Anyone who has a unit identity for a Confederate soldier can easily find his record in the Compiled Service Records. Those records are organized in the same fashion as the indexes enumerated above. Here are the National Archives publications numbers for the service records, with the number of rolls again shown in parentheses:

Alabama Troops	M311	(508)
Arizona Troops	M318	(1)
Arkansas Troops	M317	(256)
Florida Troops	M251	(104)
Georgia Troops	M266	(607)
Kentucky Troops	M319	(136)
Louisiana Troops	M320	(414)
Maryland Troops	M321	(22)
Mississippi Troops	M269	(427)
Missouri Troops	M322	(193)

12. The victims of that anomaly in artillery record keeping are indexed in M818, and the records themselves are in M258, cited below in the text. Those service records in M258 are on five rolls, 47–51. The great majority of the units covered there are from the Army of Northern Virginia—some of them famous units such as the Stuart Horse Artillery and the battalions of Carter M. Braxton, Frank Huger, R. C. M. Page, and William T. Poague.

North Carolina Troops	M270	(580)
South Carolina Troops	M267	(392)
Tennessee Troops	M268	(359)
Texas Troops	M323	(445)
Virginia Troops	M324	(1,075)
General and Staff Officers	M331	(275)
Organizations Raised Directly by the		
Confederate Government	M258	(123)

The typical Compiled Service Records for all of the men in a Confederate regiment run to about ten rolls of microfilm, although some large units take up more than twice that space, and a few regiments of small size with poor records fill up only five or six rolls. Each state's service records are arranged numerically by regiment or alphabetically by company (as with batteries). Cavalry comes first, artillery second, infantry last. The records often include a wealth of information about a soldier, but the format of the records sometimes will be disappointing to a researcher. Muster rolls that were prepared for purposes of paying the men are the essential component of the records. The men who prepared the muster rolls did so for specific administrative purposes, without any eye at all toward the desires of historians a century and more in the future.

The vast majority of the paper included in an average service record is not original material but rather copies laboriously extracted from the originals by War Department copyists years ago. A company muster roll included as many as one hundred men, each of whom has an individual service record. Each man's line of information from that original appears in his record, but obviously only on a copied sheet, since the original contains many men's data and also is of large and unwieldy dimensions.

Each man's service record consists of a jacket or envelope that gives his name, rank at entry into and exit from service, and the unit in which he served. Cross-references at the bottom of the jacket sometimes mention other units to which a soldier belonged, but that system is not complete by any means. Within the jacket are such things as card extracts from pay musters, hospital records, prisoner-of-war registers, parole ledgers, general or special orders from army headquarters, appointment books, and promotion lists. Many service records include no original manuscripts at all—just the card extracts. Some men's records, though, include original items pertaining only to themselves or to themselves and one or more other soldiers. The most common sorts of the latter are requisitions signed by commissioned officers for forage or other supplies, pay vouchers, and copies of special or general orders.[13]

The clerks who compiled the service records (blessings to their memory for a job superbly done!) necessarily reached a point at which they declared the job finished. Years later microfilmers did their work and the completed product went into service. The service records did not include everything available, of course; such a thing would have been impossible to do. When the work on the compilation of the service records was terminated, the remaining filed papers were arranged alphabetically by name. In due course, that file was microfilmed under the title "Unfiled Papers and Slips Belonging in Confederate Compiled Service Records." It bears the publication number M347 and includes 442 rolls. As must be obvious from its size (as many rolls as the regular records for Texas organizations), this is an important source for soldier records. For some reason, very few historians use it or even are aware of its existence, perhaps because it is a little harder to find and use than the regular records. Some Confederates enjoy far more coverage in this addendum than they do in their main service record.

Someone looking for a single Confederate soldier can get a copy of his service record, once the unit is identified, quite inexpensively. Requests to the National Archives, using the form number NATF-80 (10–93), "Orders for Copies of Veterans Records," eventually will get a photocopy of the record for seventeen dollars—up from ten dollars as of early 2000. Do not send money with the form; the Archives will send a bill. The process often takes many weeks, even several months, to unfold.[14]

A researcher who goes to the National Archives to use the Compiled Service Records also should examine several other rich lodes there, among them the following:

M347—"Letters Received by the Confederate Secretary of War" (151 rolls). This collection includes a mass of correspondence from men in the field to the secretary. Most of it is in one of two categories: importuning for advancement of some sort or grumbling about superior officers. Some of this makes for fascinating reading and has important overtones. The collection is

---

13. For a useful article about the nature of Confederate records, see Ralph W. Donnelly, "Confederate Muster Rolls," *Military Affairs* 16 (Fall 1952): 132–35.

14. At this writing, early in 2000, the National Archives is contemplating a system that will contract out response to such inquiries to private vendors. Such a system quite likely will increase the cost to the public—but also improve service dramatically.

indexed, thoroughly but awkwardly, in a microfilm publication numbered M409.

M474—"Letters Received by the Confederate Adjutant and Inspector General" (164 rolls). This collection is almost precisely like the last one, only with a different addressee. Its index is M410. Since the adjutant and inspector general was the Confederate army's paramount bureaucrat, M474 differs from M347 in tenor. The secretary of war's correspondents tended to be a bit more politically inclined; the A&IGO's of more military mien.

M921—"Orders and Circulars Issued by the Army . . . of Northern Virginia" (5 rolls). The general orders are almost exclusively composed of the reports of courts-martial. A large number of Confederates were convicted of a remarkable number and variety of evil deeds. This invaluable collection is not indexed (except for Virginia units, and that in a format not readily available).[15] The army's special orders are of narrower focus than the general orders, dealing as they do primarily with individuals' transfers and promotions. The special orders have never been indexed at all.

Several other collections at the National Archives include tremendous amounts of interesting material on Confederate soldiers. Much of it is virtually unused and seems destined to remain that way. Even historians of prominent reputation, working on supposedly definitive reexaminations of Confederate units or leaders, often do not take the time and effort to go to the National Archives and open the spigot on its cornucopia. Anyone who does so with care will be amply rewarded.

Pensions

A researcher on the trail of a Confederate soldier can hope for no better luck than to find his man—or better yet the man's widow—in a postwar pension file. The pivotal element in achieving certification for a pension was establishing bona fide Confederate service. Applicants for a pension therefore recounted wounds and other war experiences, identified superior officers, and supplied dates connected with their military activities. Most application forms included such useful information as place and date of birth, and they required signatures of comrades who could attest to an applicant's service. The signatures of comrades also are marginally useful for fixing those attesting men in a time and place long after the war.

15. The manuscript index to general orders that pertain to Virginians and Virginia units is in the author's possession, having been produced over the years at Fredericksburg.

Widows' pension applications are even more fertile sources than those of the veterans themselves. Most states' forms required widows to establish not only the military service of their dead husband but also the particulars of his death and the specifics about their marriage.[16] A pension file that covers first a veteran and then later his widow (and they are not uncommon, given the relative life spans of women over men) provides vital statistics from the cradle to the grave.

Finding pension applications is not as easy as finding official service records. There are hundreds of thousands of pension applications neatly arranged at the National Archives—but they have nothing to do with Confederate veterans. The United States government had a pension program for Union veterans, not for Confederates, which hardly is surprising. The Confederate pension files are deposited at state archives across the South. In Virginia, they are at the state archives arranged alphabetically by city or county (and in three groupings by date).[17]

Many Confederates who had served in the Mexican War, and their widows, eventually drew Federal pensions based on that service—Stonewall Jackson's widow, for one. Those applications and related files repose at the National Archives and have been thoroughly indexed.[18]

The U.S. Census

Genealogists have used the censuses of the United States for years, but Civil War historians rarely have taken the trouble to do so. The men who were to fight in the Civil War stand out clearly on the pages of the Eighth Census (1860), their military age and gender identifying them row upon row. The Seventh Census (1850) obviously has some of the same lads at earlier ages. Both are thoroughly covered by head-of-household indexes produced by the

16. Quests for family information often reap more gratifying results from pension files than from official service records. In proving marriage and relationship, widows supplied not only dates of marriage and death of their veteran-husbands but also the places of those events and names of preachers and doctors who officiated.

17. A few Federal benefit programs for Confederate veterans came into effect early in the twentieth century, but by then most potential applicants were beyond benefiting. The three groupings into which Virginia pensions are arranged come from the legislation authorizing the pensions: Act of 1888, Act of 1900, and Act of 1902.

18. Virgil D. White, *Index to Mexican War Pension Files* (Waynesboro, Tenn.: National Historical Publishing Company, 1989).

ardent genealogists of the Mormon church. The census is an essential tool for identifying Confederates.[19]

Meanwhile, the unsealing in 1982 of the Thirteenth Census (1910) opened a new horizon for those in quest of Confederate veterans in any locality. That census was the first to accept the notion that Confederate veterans existed. Earlier censuses had identified the Union veterans among those enumerated, but Confederates did not attain legal recognition by the Federal census taker until 1910. Since the column in which the census taker indicated veteran status ("CA" or "CN" for Confederate army or Confederate navy) is near the right margin of a very wide form, it is possible to pick the old Confederates out with the greatest of ease as the pages wind past. Using that system, it is a relatively simple matter to determine that there were eighty-one Confederate veterans living in King and Queen County, Virginia, in 1910 (as well as six strayed Yankee veterans) and to make a list of them. The breadth of the census inquiry by that date—it included education, literacy, eyesight, and several other things beyond the usual domestic data—makes the 1910 census a worthy tool with which to chase aging Confederates of the sort who frequent the pages of *Confederate Veteran* and other periodicals of that era.[20]

Printed Rosters and Reference Sources

Rosters of individual units have appeared over the years in desultory fashion. Recourse to Charles E. Dornbusch's wonderful four-volume *Military Bibliography of the Civil War* will identify those single-unit rosters.[21] The *Military Bibliography* is one of the half-dozen invaluable sources that any serious stu-

19. An invaluable tool for using the census records is *Federal Population Censuses, 1790–1860* (Washington, D.C.: National Archives Trust Fund Board, 1979). The Eighth Census (1860) is National Archives microfilm publication M653, in 1,438 rolls. The Seventh Census (1850) is M432, of 1,009 rolls.

20. *The 1910 Federal Population Census* (Washington, D.C.: National Archives Trust Fund Board, 1982). The census records are microfilm publication T624, constituting 1,784 rolls.

21. The New York Public Library published the first three volumes of Dornbusch's classic reference work in 1961, 1967, and 1972. Volume 1 covers the Yankees and volume 2 the Confederacy, with biographies of both sides in the back of volume 2. Volume 3 lists campaign and battle studies and a broad array of military literature arranged topically. Volume 4 (Dayton, Ohio: Morningside House, 1987) updates the first three and includes a cumulative index that affords substantial new material about full names and dates of life of authors listed in all four volumes. Charles Dornbusch was dying in 1987, and I produced the Confederate portion of the bibliography's fourth volume, as well as all of its index.

dent of the war must have on hand for ready reference. Existing published statewide Confederate rosters are reviewed below with admittedly subjective commentary.

Virginia. I edit the regimental history series for Virginia and therefore am susceptible to outraged allegations of partiality for suggesting that the Virginia rosters are decidedly the best extant for any former Confederate state. Each unit history is supported by a roster that includes a synopsis of the military service record of each man, based on the Compiled Service Records at the National Archives, the state pension records, the state roster, and other sources. Entries are included for men having no official record but mentioned unofficially in other sources (notably the late nineteenth-century state roster project). Unofficial records are clearly identified. The rosters include extensive efforts by their authors (at least in most cases) to find personal data on the soldiers from local sources such as cemeteries and obituaries and family records. The Virginia series is a model of its type, making Virginians the most readily traceable Confederates.[22]

An invaluable source for Virginia organizations and company commanders is Lee A. Wallace, Jr., *Virginia Military Organizations, 1861–1865*, published in 1964. This wonderful book is among the best Confederate reference books ever produced, by about the best Virginia Confederate historian ever hatched.[23]

North Carolina. The Old North State has benefited not only from the first comprehensive statewide Confederate roster—John W. Moore, *Roster of North Carolina Troops in the War Between the States* (1882)—but also from the first really professional modern attempt to produce a new statewide Confederate roster. The current project, started by Louis Manarin and ably continued by W. T. Jordan, *North Carolina Troops, 1861–1865: A Roster* (Raleigh, 1966–), which reached its fourteenth volume in print in 1998 and is nearing completion, is a magnificent accomplishment. It contains unit histories and

22. As of January 2001, the Virginia series numbers 137 volumes in print. The final handful of books are pending release. They will be followed by a comprehensive index, which will be the single most valuable reference tool extant on Virginia Confederate soldiers. The series publisher is H. E. Howard, Appomattox, Virginia.

23. The 1964 edition was published in Richmond by the Virginia Civil War Commission, in ecru wraps. Stuart E. Brown, Jr., of the Virginia Book Company in Berryville, bought a large remainder stock, added a thorough index (the original had, incredibly, appeared without that necessary amenity), and bound the whole into sky-blue cloth. A second edition, extensively revised and improved by Wallace, appeared in 1986 from H. E. Howard, Inc., of Lynchburg.

the military service records of all the men with official records. The excerpted military records in the new North Carolina set are based almost entirely on the official Compiled Service Records. The Carolina volumes, unfortunately, usually do not contain personal information on its soldiers beyond age and occupation; the project was designed to include other personal information in its research files. When the North Carolina rosters are completed and a comprehensive index appears, which is not too many years away, that state will be very well served indeed. Walter Clark's five-volume set, *Histories of the Several Regiments and Battalions from North Carolina in the Great War, 1861– '65*, contains many references to individual soldiers and is worthy of being consulted. In addition, Louis Manarin's *A Guide to Military Organizations and Installations, North Carolina, 1861–1865* (Raleigh, 1961) is useful for identifying and tracing regiments, battalions, and independent companies. The inclusion of local designations of companies helps identify them with their parent unit.[24]

Louisiana. More than eighty years ago the state of Louisiana issued a comprehensive listing of its Confederate soldiers in four volumes, one thin and the other three very thick: *Records of Louisiana Confederate Soldiers and Louisiana Confederate Commands*. The commissioner of military records for the state was Andrew B. Booth; his name customarily appears as editor of the set. The original printing was on paper that has turned dreadfully brittle over the years, and many copies were damaged by a fire and the attendant smoke and water. A modern (1984) reprint makes this old standard work available again and in much sturdier format. The Louisianans did a creditable job on *Records*, despite some handicaps and the resultant gaps. Their work is the first place to turn for a Louisiana soldier. The rosters include personal biographical material, as opposed to military service data, so infrequently as to be rated inconsequential. A fine reference tool of more recent vintage but much narrower scope is Arthur W. Bergeron, Jr., *Guide to Louisiana Confederate Military Units, 1861– 1865*.[25]

24. Moore's four-volume set was published in Raleigh by Ashe and Gatling. Four of Clark's five volumes were published in Goldsboro by Nash Brothers, the fifth in Raleigh by E. M. Uzzell; all five bear a 1901 imprint. Manarin's slender (eighty pages in three collations) but useful guide was published by the North Carolina Confederate Centennial Commission.

25. The four-volume Booth set was published in New Orleans in 1920 by the Commissioner Louisiana Military Records. The pagination, which is cumulative, reaches 1,195. The 1984 reprint (Spartanburg, S.C.: Reprint Company) combines the slender first volume of the original with the second volume and thus appears in three large volumes. Bergeron's book was published in Baton

Georgia. As the Civil War Centennial approached, the Georgia Confederate Pension and Record Department undertook the task of preparing rosters of Georgia's Confederates. The decision to spend a part of the centennial's substance on something of long-term value, rather than exclusively on reenactments, concerts, and wreath layings, is of lasting credit to the state. Unfortunately, the project ran out of steam after finishing with the infantry units from Georgia, and that state's cavalry and artillery remain without rosters. The infantry rosters are of somewhat uneven quality and cannot be considered definitive. With few exceptions, the entries contain only military information. The six volumes of Georgia rosters, compiled under the direction of Lillian Henderson, bear the title *Rosters of the Confederate Soldiers of Georgia, 1861–1865* (Hapeville: Longino & Porter, 1959–64). A subsequent index to the six volumes increases their usefulness greatly. The rosters were still available from the state of Georgia not long ago for a very modest price. A wonderful Georgia reference book that is so rare as to be unobtainable is James Madison Folsom, *Heroes and Martyrs of Georgia*, published in 1864; fortunately, a reprint edition appeared in 1995.[26]

Alabama. The only faint trace of a published roster for Alabama is the short listing of units and their commanders, down to company level (and including localities of origin) in Willis Brewer, *Alabama, Her History, Resources, War Record, and Public Men* (Montgomery: Barrett & Brown, 1872). A reprint (Spartanburg, S.C.: Reprint Company, 1975) offers the chance to own this useful book, but it is not a roster by any means.

Arkansas. The cupboard is bare of rosters for Arkansas troops. Army of Northern Virginia devotees (may their breed increase) will find a roster of the only Arkansas regiment in that army included with the Texas Brigade (q.v.).

Florida. Frederick L. Robertson did a reasonably good job on an early ros-

---

Rouge by Louisiana State University Press in 1989. Booth reported many useful details about his project and the records from which it was drawn in *Report of A. B. Booth, Commissioner of Military Records, to the Governor* . . . (New Orleans, 1918). In an untitled, three-page pamphlet dated July 12, 1922, and addressed to various Confederate memorial groups, Booth announced completion of his project—and launched a bitter attack on detractors who had sought to take over the commissioner's job for personal gain.

26. The index to Henderson's six volumes was prepared by the Lake Blackshear Regional Library in Americus and published fourteen years after the end of the main project (Spartanburg, S.C.: Reprint Company, 1982). Burke, Boykin and Company of Macon published the prohibitively scarce first edition of *Heroes and Martyrs*. Butternut and Blue of Baltimore published the 1995 reprint. The reprint is augmented by a fine introduction and a thorough new index, both crafted by the nonpareil authority on Confederate Georgia, Keith S. "Bo" Bohannon.

ter of Florida Confederates in *Soldiers of Florida in the Seminole Indian, Civil and Spanish-American Wars* (Live Oak: Democrat Book and Job Print, 1909). Some names are missing, and the entries are often without annotation, but the Robertson roster for more than a century was a good starting point—in fact, the only printed list of Florida soldiers. The absence of an index is a major drawback. A reprint edition, published in Macclenny, came out in 1983. A recent massive work (2,543 pages plus index) on Confederate Floridians certainly will be definitive for many decades to come. David W. Hartman and David Coles, comps., *Biographical Rosters of Florida's Confederate and Union Soldiers, 1861–1865*, 6 vols. (Wilmington, N.C.: Broadfoot, 1995), combines extracts of official service records on every Florida soldier with personal data on many of them.

Kentucky. Fifty years after the war, the adjutant general of the state of Kentucky issued a two-volume work, *Confederate Kentucky Volunteers, War 1861–1865* (Frankfort: State Journal Company, 1915–18). The rosters include very little annotation. A reprint (Utica, Ky.: McDowell Publications, 1980) is made vastly more useful by addition of an index.

Maryland. William W. Goldsborough was a major who commanded Maryland Confederate troops and wrote two books with almost identical names but of markedly different contents. His 1869 book is a narrative of the war experiences of Maryland units and is a justly prominent piece of history. *The Maryland Line in the Confederate Army, 1861–1865* (Baltimore: Press of Guggenheimer, Weil, 1900) is pertinent to this essay because it includes rosters of most Maryland units. The lists of soldiers include no remarks about service, although unit sketches include some lists of casualties. A separately printed index (Annapolis: Hall of Records Commission, 1944) is a necessary adjunct to make *The Maryland Line* a useful research tool. The book and its index were brought together under one cover in a reprint edition (Port Washington, N.Y.: Kennikat Press, 1972) and again in 1983 (Gaithersburg: Butternut Press).[27]

Mississippi. That indefatigable southern historian Dunbar Rowland turned out the basic Mississippi Confederate reference in 1908, but it does not constitute a roster of the state's troops. Rowland contributed a huge article—more than 560 pages—on Mississippi's Confederate units and their officers, down to company level, to *The Official and Statistical Register of the*

27. A useful tool for Maryland soldiers' personal data is Daniel D. Hartzler, *Marylanders in the Confederacy* (Silver Spring, Md.: Family Line Publications, 1986).

State of Mississippi (Nashville, Tenn.: Press of the Brandon Printing Company, 1908). Although Rowland did what he set out to do, and did it well, no roster of enlisted men for the state exists.

An early and very useful Mississippi reference by John C. Rietti, *Military Annals of Mississippi*, is limited in value by its random coverage. Rietti, a veteran of service as sergeant with the 10th Mississippi, included diaries, rosters, company or regimental histories, and casualty lists almost at random. For some Mississippi units, Rietti is priceless; for some he is of little use; on others, he includes not a word.[28]

South Carolina. The fine South Carolina historian Alexander S. Salley compiled three volumes of excellent rosters early in this century under the title *South Carolina Troops in Confederate Service* (Columbia: State Co., 1913–30). Infantry regiments numbered 1 through 5 are covered in those volumes, but the series ends at that point. The state had copies of volumes 1 and 3 for sale for $3 each until the mid-1970s, but the scarcity of the second volume prompts book dealers to ask a price for it equivalent to that of a small automobile. There is, unfortunately, no indication that the seventy-year-old roster project will be revived.

Tennessee. The Civil War Centennial in Tennessee generated a nice two-volume set of unit histories and rosters titled *Tennesseeans in the Civil War* (Nashville: Civil War Centennial Commission, 1964–65). The roster volume (volume 2) consists of a complete listing of Tennesseeans in each army (Yankees separate), showing the unit(s) in which each man served. No details of any sort about the service are included. The set is indispensable for work on Confederate soldiery.

One of the best summaries of the service of a southern state's units is John Berrien Lindsley, *The Military Annals of Tennessee . . . Embracing a Review of Military Operations, with Regimental Histories and Memorial Rolls*. By the end of Lindsley's thick tome, on page 910, the author had achieved all of the gaudy goals established in the labyrinthine title. It is a splendid book but useful almost entirely for western theater purposes, as Tennessee sent only three regiments to full-time service in the Army of Northern Virginia.[29]

28. The first edition of Rietti apparently appeared in Jackson in 1895. A reprint (Spartanburg, S.C.: Reprint Company, 1976), adds a very valuable index that helps unravel Rietti's chaotic arrangements. The first edition was both very limited and fragile (in flimsy, brittle wraps) and accordingly is excessively rare.

29. The first edition was Nashville: J. M. Lindsley, 1886, and was very handsomely printed and bound. A reprint edition in two volumes (Wilmington, N.C.: Broadfoot, 1995) actually is far more useful, since it adds an exhaustive (180 pages) index.

Texas. It is hard to imagine, given their attitude toward their state and their ancestors, that Texans have not yet attempted a roster of Confederate soldiers, but it is plain fact that they have not. The only three Texas units in the Army of Northern Virginia were infantry regiments in Hood's famed brigade. Rosters of those three regiments, plus the 3rd Arkansas and some other stray hangers-on with the brigade, appear in Harold B. Simpson, *Hood's Texas Brigade: A Compendium* (Hillsboro: Hill Junior College Press, 1977). The roster entries are disappointingly terse and include none of the wealth of personal biographical data that is available about the veterans of that storied unit.[30]

Reference Books About Officers

Published sources cover most Confederate officers of field grade or staff rankings to at least some degree. The standard source on field officers must be identified, with unbecoming immodesty, as Robert K. Krick, *Lee's Colonels* (4th ed., Dayton, Ohio: Morningside, 1992). The book provides biographical sketches of the nearly two thousand men who achieved field grade in the Army of Northern Virginia and lists more cursorily almost twice as many others who held field grades elsewhere in the Confederacy.[31]

Confederate chaplains are listed in an appendix (pages 115–34) to Herman Norton, *Rebel Religion* (St. Louis: Bethany Press, 1961). The listing is no more than one-half complete, but it represents a worthy start. A similar appendix (pages 138–57) is in Charles F. Pitts, *Chaplains in Gray* (Nashville, Tenn.: Broadman Press, 1957). An informal manuscript roster of chaplains with service records in M331, National Archives, runs to substantially more than twice the size of either the Norton or Pitts appendexes—and M331 is very far from definitive, because many chaplains' records are filed with their regiments.

Confederate surgeons do not appear in even a rudimentary unified list, but they are the subject of two strong regional compilations and several smaller listings. Medical men of the Army of Tennessee are shown in a very lengthy register in *Southern Historical Society Papers* 22 (1894): 165–280. That listing

30. The roster appears in one of four volumes in a set on the brigade by Simpson, all published by Hill Junior College, 1968–77. Each of them appeared in an array of special and limited editions (full leather, leather with silk endpapers, flannel-covered leather, etc.), in addition to the trade versions in cloth with dust wrappers.

31. A new fifth edition of *Lee's Colonels*, which will update more than one-half of the individuals' entries, is projected for 2001.

is strengthened by careful modern indexing which supplies many fuller names and identities than shown in the original. The two-volume *Index-Guide* (Mill-wood, N.Y.: Kraus International, 1980) to the *SHSP* is, in fact, a very useful tool for all sorts of Confederate research because many of its entries involved research that went far beyond mere clerical recording.

Many of the surgeons of the Army of Northern Virginia are listed, with reference to their area of service, in an appendix (pages 393–420) to Wynd-ham B. Blanton, *Medicine in Virginia in the Nineteenth Century* (Richmond: Garrett & Massie, 1933). The appendix is labeled "Virginia Surgeons in the Civil War," but in fact it includes numbers of non-Virginians who happened to serve in the state and with the largest army employed there. The author of this essay has been marking additional names into a copy of the book for thirty years and now has added substantially more interlineations than there were original entries. Despite the gaps, Blanton's list is a good point of reference.

"South Carolina Physicians in the Confederacy" are enumerated in two separate alphabetical listings on pages 333–47 of Joseph I. Waring, *A History of Medicine in South Carolina, 1825–1900* (Columbia: R. L. Bryan, 1967). Surgeons from the other Carolina are covered in Walter Clark's classic five-volume work on North Carolina military units, cited above, and in a fifty-seven-page pamphlet, *Provisional Record of Confederate Medical Officers, Of-fered by the Confederate Veterans Committee, Medical Society, N.C.* (N.p., n.d. [ca. 1900]).

Staff officers with duties neither clerical nor medical, who far outstripped in number and importance their humanitarian brethren, were listed in a rare and valuable work compiled by Marcus J. Wright and published by the Gov-ernment Printing Office in 1891. Wright Howes identified a companion vol-ume of the same vintage and typeface as being issued in a run of only twenty-five copies, which probably also is true of the staff book. About five thousand names are included in the alphabetical listing, along with dates of appoint-ment and some details of service. The book does not cover regimental staff and central staff functions but rather just those staff officers serving with gen-eral officers in the field. Marcus Wright also compiled lists of staff officers arranged by the general they served, rather than alphabetically. One of those lists—unfortunately an early and incomplete set, transcribed with a painful number of errors—was published in 1982. Robert E. L. Krick of Richmond (and of impeccable ancestry) is preparing a full biographical register of Army of Northern Virginia staff officers, with their brethren from other commands in an appendix.[32]

Wright's office also produced a useful, but unfortunately rare, listing of Confederate artillery officers and units, *Artillery Officers, C.S.A.* [Washington, D.C., 188–]. The enumeration is thorough, extensive (186 pages), and abetted by a thirty-seven-page index.

Confederate Marines

Ralph W. Donnelly's two volumes, *Biographical Sketches of the Commissioned Officers of the Confederate States Marine Corps* (Washington, N.C.: Author, 1973) and *Service Records of Confederate Marines* (Washington, N.C.: Author, 1979), are invaluable reference works. Donnelly, a career historian with the U.S. Marine Corps, employed extensive research in original records to compile individual entries. He added personal information as well as military service. Whenever he found a variant spelling for a name, Donnelly included it in the service record. Each volume contains an excellent index.

United Daughters of the Confederacy Records

Membership in the United Daughters of the Confederacy (UDC) is open to female descendants of Confederates. Application forms require proof of that qualification and ask for full names and precise biographical/genealogical data, running from the applicant back to the soldier whose record qualifies her for membership. That sort of information of course is of considerable use to researchers, especially if they are trying to separate several possible candidates of similar names from one another. Although the UDC existed in the nineteenth century, a well-organized central accumulation of records dates only from the last eighty years, and apparently the records are really thoroughly complete for a shorter spell than that. National UDC headquarters maintains a giant file (more than one million cards) of Confederate names, including reference to applications for UDC membership by descendants of each man. The head-

---

32. *List of Staff Officers of the Confederate States Army* (Washington, D.C.: GPO, 1891); *List of Field Officers, Regiments, and Battalions in the Confederate States Army* [Washington, D.C., 1881]; Joseph H. Crute, Jr., *Confederate Staff Officers* (Powhatan, Va.: Derwent Books, 1982). The R. E. L. Krick staff book has a projected publication date of 2002.

quarters also owns microfilm copies of the National Archives service records for the entire Confederacy.

UDC headquarters records are not available to the general public and doubtless never will be. There is no reason that they should be; the organization exists for other purposes and cannot conceivably provide the staff to answer inquiries. Interested researchers, however, can gain access to some UDC records by working with local chapters of the organization, which are ubiquitous throughout the South. The local organizations sometimes can solicit help with particular problems from national headquarters.

Miscellaneous Sources for Confederate Biography

A plethora of other sources can be useful in pursuing the traces of a Confederate soldier. A few of them are explained below in brief entries that vary from specific to generic and generally include uninhibited subjective analyses.

1. The expanded-biography editions of the thirteen-volume *Confederate Military History* (Atlanta, Ga.: Confederate Publishing Company, 1899) include a great many sketches of Confederates. A reprint edition of the set (the expanded volumes of the original are extremely rare) appeared in 1987, including an extremely useful cumulative index. The set is a very important piece of Confederate literature.[33]

2. Several biographical compendiums focused on surviving Confederate veterans near the turn of the century. Among the larger of these are William E. Mickle, *Well Known Confederate Veterans and Their War Records* (New Orleans: Author, 1907), with a second volume in 1915; Sid S. Johnson, *Texans Who Wore the Gray* ([Tyler?], 1907); and Mamie Yeary, *Reminiscences of the Boys in Gray* (Dallas: Smith & Lamar, 1912). Yeary's fat book (nearly one thousand pages) has been reprinted with an index to both names and units.

3. The thick six-volume reference set *Who Was Who in America* (Chicago: Marquis Who's Who, 1963–72) includes tens of thousands of entries, many of them on nineteenth-century Americans. Although the set generally is overlooked by students of the Civil War, it supplies information on thousands of soldiers, particularly those who went on to moderately distinguished careers in some profession. Most Confederates who have entries in this work are not

---

33. The reprint (Wilmington, N.C.: Broadfoot, 1987) appeared in nineteen volumes, including the exhaustive two-volume index.

the subject of sketches readily available anywhere else. The small-town dignitaries listed extensively in *Confederate Veteran* sometimes turn up here. Sources of similar scope are *Appleton's Cyclopedia of American Biography*, 6 vols. (New York: D. Appleton, 1887–89), and *National Cyclopedia of American Biography*, 63 vols. (New York: J. T. White, 1893–1984). Neither of those sets is aimed at the same lofty biographical targets as *Dictionary of American Biography*, which of course is much too august a source to be of use in seeking Confederates of the lower commissioned grades or from the ranks.

4. Every southern state was covered by at least two statewide history and biography sets between the end of the war and the early part of the twentieth century. These are invaluable for finding Confederate biographical information. Most states had more than two; Virginia enjoys coverage from six sets. It is impossible in this format to list each of the sources, but they will be readily available in the states involved. One series too often overlooked is *Hardesty's Historical and Geographical Encyclopedia*, which appeared in a multitude of slightly varied editions during the 1880s. The main volume was unchanged from region to region, but biographical material was added to make special editions for rather small areas. Most of Virginia was covered two counties at a time. A volume exists, for instance, for Berkeley and Jefferson Counties, West Virginia. Those contemporary sketches of the ordinary folk in a locality in the 1880s include a great many Confederates, of course; in fact, the great majority of the men covered were veterans. Almost no one uses *Hardesty's* to search for Confederates, and everyone should.

5. The *National Union Catalog of Manuscript Collections* incorporates descriptions of manuscript collections from every major institution in the country and a great many minor ones as well. The scope of *NUCMC*, which already stands at more than two dozen tall and wide volumes, grows annually. Any good-sized college library will have a set in its reference room. The very thorough indexes to the volumes are worth searching for an individual or a unit, if there is any likelihood that a man wrote enough letters or other papers to make them worth saving somewhere. Each volume is indexed and cumulative indexes combine to cover several volumes at once.

6. Virtually every antebellum southern college and university eventually published a list of graduates and former students. Most of the published lists include mention of Confederate service, together with personal details such as date of birth and death and civilian occupation. This useful information can be augmented, sometimes to a very large degree, by use of an institution's alumni records and other archives. Inevitably, some schools are much more

able and willing to help than others. A researcher who finds that his subject attended Virginia Military Institute for even a few days can rejoice because the pleasant people and superb records of the Institute will answer about as many questions as can be asked. The news is much less good at the University of Virginia and the Citadel, for instance, where mid-nineteenth-century students are not now of much moment. Medical schools are almost universally strong on records, perhaps because their graduates generally wind up well able to be generous alumni. An astounding number of southerners went to two medical colleges in Philadelphia—the University of Pennsylvania and Jefferson Medical College. No southern schools can match the record of those two for producing Confederate surgeons.

7. Most southern states provided soldiers' homes for their veterans who lived to advanced ages. Some of the homes (and many veterans' camps) issued registers of those veterans who belonged to them, generally including particulars about the unit with which each veteran served. That information, as has been emphasized several times in this essay, is the key that unlocks a soldier's record. The Maryland home is one for which a fine published roster exists. Virginia's home, in Richmond, kept detailed records about inmates. Although those Richmond records never have been published, they have been indexed and are at the Virginia Historical Society. More than five thousand veterans are on the list, which is a not inconsiderable percentage of the state's soldiers. The applications filed by veterans for admission to the home are at the Virginia State Library.

8. A familiar sight in southern cemeteries is the official Confederate gravestone of trim white marble, with a top sloping gently upward from both sides to form a point. Local lore has it that the point is designed to keep Yankees from desecrating the stones by sitting on them, but in fact the stones actually were supplied by the U.S. government. Anyone on the trail of a Confederate buried beneath such a stone should know that the application forms for the stones survive and are packed with interesting details about the Confederates for whom they were requested. The applications are filed at the National Archives Military Field Branch, Suitland, Maryland. Indexes cover various spans of years. The index for 1906–24, however, has been misplaced.

The sources described above do not begin to exhaust the options available to someone in serious quest of the military and personal experiences of a Confederate soldier. Many other invaluable resources—such as county histories, cemetery lists, obituaries, historical society card files, family records, and much

more—are the familiar milieu of genealogists and historians. All of these options combine to make the search for a Confederate soldier an interesting and
challenging venture and one that has a very large chance of success. With few
exceptions, someone who searches for traces of a Confederate and does not
find him simply failed to look hard enough or in the proper places.

Index

197–98; McLaws's admiration for, 92; per-
sonality of, 186–87, 234–35; relationship
with Longstreet, 60–61, 65, 67–85, 94,
114–16
Lee, William H. F. "Rooney," 10
Lee Considered, 233–36
Lee's Colonels, 257
Lee's Lieutenants, 237
Lee's Tarnished Lieutenant, 236–37
Leigh, Benjamin Watkins, 8, 14, 29–30, 37
Lenoir Station, Tenn., 95
Lewellen, J. Richard, 243
Lexington, Va., 179, 198
Lincoln, Abraham, 233
Lindsley, John B., 256
Logan, Thomas M., 230
Lomax, L. L., 198, 205–206, 210–11
Longstreet, James, 54; and Knoxville campaign,
85–116, 237; praised by modern author,
236–37; quarrel with Hill, 158–59; reflec-
tions on his attitude, 57–84
Loudoun Light Horse, 175, 177
Louisiana troops, how to find and use records
of, 243, 245–46, 253–54
Louisiana unit: 1st Infantry, 27
Lynchburg, Va., 121–22, 143, 199
Lynchburg Beauregard Rifles, 4

McCausland, John, 190, 193, 197–98, 212–13
McClellan, George B., 117
McClellan, Henry B., 82
McCrady, Edward, 158, 161
McDowell, Irvin, 237
McGowan, Samuel, 223, 230
McGuire, Hunter Holmes, 7, 22, 32–33, 38–
39, 51, 83, 169
McIntosh, David G., 155, 170
McLaws, Emily Taylor, 88–92
McLaws, Lafayette, 118; admiration for Lee,
92; biographical sketch, 87–93; children of,
89; and Knoxville campaign, 78–80, 85–
116; and Longstreet, 63–64, 67, 70–82,
85–116
McPherson, James B., 27
Magruder, John B., 90, 118

Mahone, William, 78–79, 118, 228
Manarin, Louis, 252–53
Manassas, battle of (1861), 64, 125, 151, 175,
177, 225
Manassas, battle of (1862), 65, 158–62, 166,
168, 215
Marietta, Ga., 224
Marines, Confederate, 259
Marr, John Q., 151
Marshall, Charles, 80
Marshall, Tex., 122
Martin, John F., 108
Martinsburg, Va., 164
Marvel, William, 240
Maryland campaign, 1862, pp. 54, 90, 127,
137, 162–65
Maryland troops, how to find and use records
of, 243, 245–46, 255
Maryland unit: 1st Cavalry, 195
Massachusetts units: 1st Infantry, 26; 20th In-
fantry, 26
Maury, Anne H. H., 218
Maury, Dabney Herndon, 221
Maury, Elizabeth Herndon, 216, 218–22
Maury, Matthew Fontaine, 218, 220–21
Maury, Nannie Belle, 218–20
Maury, Richard L., 219, 221
Maury, William A., 218
Maxcy, Jonathan, 144
Mechanicsville, battle of, 155
Medicine in Virginia in the Nineteenth Century,
258
Mencken, H. L., 28
Mexican War, 88, 145, 169, 250
Mickle, William E., 260
Middleburg, Va., 183
Middleton, J. J., 114
Midway, Tenn., 87
Military Bibliography of the Civil War, 251–52
Mine Run campaign, 176, 179
Mississippi State University, 228
Mississippi troops, how to find and use records
of, 243, 245–46, 255–56
Mississippi units: 10th, 256; 12th Infantry, 126;
13th Infantry, 109, 112; 16th Infantry, 227;